Palgrave Studies in Journalism and the Global South

Series Editors
Bruce Mutsvairo
Utrecht University
Utrecht, The Netherlands

Saba Bebawi
University of Technology Sydney
Ultimo, Australia

Eddy Borges-Rey
Northwestern University Qatar
Ar-Rayyan, UK

This series focuses on cutting-edge developments in journalism in and from the Global South and illuminates how journalism cultures and practices have evolved from the era of colonization to contemporary globalization. Bringing previously underrepresented research from the Global South to the English speaking world, this series will focus on a broad range of topics within journalism including pedagogy, ethics, history of journalism, press freedom, theory, propaganda, gender, cross-border collaboration and methodological issues. Despite the geographical connotations of the term 'Global South' the series will not be defined by geographical boundaries, as Western countries are home to millions of immigrants and the contributions of immigrant journalists will be covered.

Albert Sharra • Ufuoma Akpojivi
Editors

Technologies and Media Production Cultures

A Global South Perspective

Editors
Albert Sharra
Department of Political Studies
University of Witwatersrand
Johannesburg, South Africa

Centre of African Studies
University of Edinburgh
Edinburgh, UK

Ufuoma Akpojivi
Information and
Communication Studies
University of Ghana
Accra, Ghana

ISSN 2662-480X   ISSN 2662-4818 (electronic)
Palgrave Studies in Journalism and the Global South
ISBN 978-3-031-78581-8   ISBN 978-3-031-78582-5 (eBook)
https://doi.org/10.1007/978-3-031-78582-5

© The Editor(s) (if applicable) and The Author(s), under exclusive license to Springer Nature
Switzerland AG 2025

This work is subject to copyright. All rights are solely and exclusively licensed by the
Publisher, whether the whole or part of the material is concerned, specifically the rights of
translation, reprinting, reuse of illustrations, recitation, broadcasting, reproduction on
microfilms or in any other physical way, and transmission or information storage and retrieval,
electronic adaptation, computer software, or by similar or dissimilar methodology now
known or hereafter developed.
The use of general descriptive names, registered names, trademarks, service marks, etc. in this
publication does not imply, even in the absence of a specific statement, that such names are
exempt from the relevant protective laws and regulations and therefore free for general use.
The publisher, the authors and the editors are safe to assume that the advice and information
in this book are believed to be true and accurate at the date of publication. Neither the
publisher nor the authors or the editors give a warranty, expressed or implied, with respect to
the material contained herein or for any errors or omissions that may have been made. The
publisher remains neutral with regard to jurisdictional claims in published maps and
institutional affiliations.

Credit: John Lamb

This Palgrave Macmillan imprint is published by the registered company Springer Nature
Switzerland AG.
The registered company address is: Gewerbestrasse 11, 6330 Cham, Switzerland

If disposing of this product, please recycle the paper.

This book is dedicated to our families, who provided all the support, love, and encouragement during the editing of this book.

Foreword

In an era where digital technologies are rapidly reshaping industries, the media sector has been profoundly transformed. However, much of the scholarship on these changes has historically focused on the Global North, often overlooking the rich contributions from the Global South. Given the rapid transformations in regions like Africa, addressing this gap has never been more critical. *Technologies and Media Production Cultures: A Global South Perspective* is a timely collection that explores how technological advancements intersect with media culture and journalism practices in Africa. It builds on earlier scholarship, such as Atton and Mabweazara (2011) and Mabweazara, Mudhai, and Whittaker (2014), which offered significant insights into these intersections. The rapid technological developments since then necessitate a fresh examination of how African newsrooms are navigating these changes. This volume provides an updated analysis of how digital tools are reshaping Africa's media landscape.

The book explores how technologies—ranging from artificial intelligence (AI) to social media platforms—are transforming the production, dissemination, and consumption of news. A key theme is the unequal access to technology across Africa. The digital divide remains a significant barrier, particularly in economically disadvantaged areas. This edited collection shows how media practitioners in the Global South are not merely adopting imported technologies but actively reshaping them to fit their unique socio-political, economic, and cultural contexts, thereby creating new production cultures that challenge dominant global frameworks. From the integration of AI to the rise of influencers in the attention economy, the book covers a range of recent developments and their impact on news production.

A key strength of the volume is its grounding in empirical cases, offering insights into how digital tools are being used in African media. From AI-driven journalism in Nigeria to the use of social media platforms in Uganda, these case studies highlight how African journalists are not passive recipients of technological change but active agents who selectively adopt technologies to meet their professional and cultural needs.

The contributors examine various case studies from across the continent, illustrating how newsrooms are adapting to the digital era. They offer critical insights into how traditional media are integrating new technologies, emphasizing that the adoption of digital tools is shaped by socioeconomic, political, and cultural factors. The chapters collectively highlight the uneven adoption of technologies across African newsrooms, influenced by digital literacy, economic disparities, and infrastructural challenges. For example, in Nigeria, the introduction of AI poses challenges such as erratic power supplies and limited internet access, despite its potential to enhance journalistic productivity. Additionally, ethical concerns persist, as AI tools like chatbots struggle to meet the critical thinking and ethical standards necessary for investigative reporting.

Another important focus of the book is the tension between global technological trends and local journalistic practices. Mabweazara et al. (2014) have argued that while technologies from the Global North often dominate media innovation, African journalists adapt these tools to suit local contexts, reflecting a hybridity in media practices. This volume expands on that idea by examining how African journalists balance global pressures with localized practices. For example, journalists in Malawi adopt digital strategies not only to modernize but also as a means of survival in competitive and resource-constrained environments (Sharra, 2023).

The book also engages with debates on the pressure to adopt emerging technologies in the Global South, arguing that journalism's future in these regions should be guided by institutional and contextual factors rather than an uncritical embrace of change. Case studies, such as how Facebook's algorithms regulate content in African languages like Shona, illustrate both the potential for audiences to shape these platforms and the limitations of automated systems in non-Western languages.

Contributors also address the impact of digital technologies on news quality. Some note that the drive for speed has diluted editorial rigour in online reporting compared to legacy media. There is a lack of literature on how digital tools are transforming newsroom management in Africa, a gap this book addresses. For example, it examines how Malawi's *Nation Publications Limited* adopted newsroom software, revealing how technology is reshaping both processes and journalistic culture, including challenges of implementing newsroom software. The influence of social media on radio broadcasting is also explored, showing how African radio stations use platforms like Facebook to engage with audiences and create multimedia content. This integration has changed how radio content is produced and consumed, fostering a more interactive audience experience.

At a time when the global media ecosystem is increasingly complex, this book reminds us that the Global South is not a passive recipient of technological innovation but an active agent in shaping the future of media. By focusing on Africa's experiences, we gain valuable insights into the broader implications of media technologies and their transformation of cultures, economies, and societies worldwide.

Technologies and Media Production Cultures: A Global South Perspective is a vital contribution to media studies, offering fresh insights into the challenges and opportunities posed by digital technologies in African journalism. It emphasizes the importance of understanding local contexts when examining media practices. I am confident this volume will inspire scholars and practitioners alike to rethink the global media landscape. It stands as both a significant academic contribution and a call for more inclusive and equitable approaches to understanding the intersections of media and technology in a globalized world. While the future of journalism in Africa is uncertain, this volume shows it is also full of promise.

University of Glasgow, Glasgow, UK   Hayes Mawindi Mabweazara

References

Atton, C., & Mabweazara, H. M. (2011). New Media and Journalism Practice in Africa: An Agenda for Research. *Journalism, 12*(6), 667–673.

Mabweazara, H. M., Mudhai, O. F., & Whittaker, J. (Eds.). (2014). *Online Journalism in Africa: Trends, Practices and Emerging Cultures.* Routledge.

Sharra, A. (2023). "Digital First" as a Coping Measure for Malawi's Print Newspapers. In *New Journalism Ecologies in East and Southern Africa: Innovations, Participatory and Newsmaking Cultures* (pp. 113–132). Springer.

ACKNOWLEDGEMENTS

Editing this book was a rewarding and excellent experience we could never have imagined. So many people contributed to making this book a reality. We would like to sincerely express our gratitude to all contributors for their commitment and sacrifice; without them, this book would not have seen the light of the day. Also, we want to appreciate the anonymous reviewers of our book proposal. Their rigour and invaluable comments were critical and made this book possible. Likewise, we want to thank all anonymous peer reviewers who reviewed the various chapters despite their busy commitments. Our gratitude goes to the Palgrave Macmillan production team for their role in steering the book project right from conceptualisation to production. Lauriane Piette, Editor (Journalism, Media and Communication) and Rubina Infanta Rani, Production Editor, deserve special mention for making the process smooth and enjoyable. Last but not least, we are grateful to our family members and friends for all the support they provided us throughout the entire period of editing this book.

Praise for *Technologies and Media Production Cultures*

"*Technologies and Media Production Cultures: A Global South Perspective* is an innovative, remarkable and authoritative collection on the way in which digital technologies are gradually transforming and shaping African newsroom cultures and journalistic practices. Grounded in empirical studies by eminent and emerging scholars who are experts in the field of media studies, journalism and communication studies, the volume provides compelling insights into the emerging dialectic around the deployment of digital technologies in the production, dissemination and consumption of media content. This is a must-read collection for undergraduate and postgraduate students and researchers in the field of media studies, journalism and communication as well as media professionals, policymakers and anyone keen to know more about how technology is implicated in media production cultures in the Global South."
—Professor Tendai Chari, *University of Venda, South Africa*

"The unstoppable tour de force for journalism globally has been the impact of technology, digitisation and social media. The consequences of the massive changes are impossible to ignore, as they continue to accelerate and change practices in the profession forever. This book, *Technologies and Media Production Cultures: A Global South Perspective*, edited by Albert Sharra and Ufuoma Akpojivi captures the nuances, differences and similarities in how various countries in the global south are navigating their paths to hold onto what will always remain journalism *per se*, while also acknowledging and encapsulating the changes in the practices of the craft. It tackles issues—including the use of technology for good, social media and news production, algorithms and consumption patterns, and changes to language dynamics—that will remain relevant for the next few decades to come."
—Prof. Glenda Daniels, *Associate Professor of Media Studies, University of the Witwatersrand, Johannesburg, South Africa*

CONTENTS

Part I Technologies and Traditional Media   1

**1 Introduction: Media Culture and Practice in the
Digital Age**   3
Albert Sharra and Ufuoma Akpojivi

**2 AI and Effective Journalism in a Technology-Deficient
Environment: Prospects, Challenges and Ethical Concerns**   19
Adebukola Olubunmi Ayoola

**3 Shaping Journalism Futures: A Call for Contextualised
Technology Adoption**   43
Eric Noel Mtemang'ombe and Francis Chikunkhuzeni

**4 Digital First in Malawian Newsrooms: A Comparative
Analysis**   63
Ekari Immaculate Phiri, Mzati Nkolokosa,
Maclan Kanyangw'a, and Albert Sharra

**5 Towards Automation: News-Wrap Implementation at
Malawi's Nation Publications**   85
Albert Sharra and Tisaukirenji Tembo

xvi CONTENTS

6   The Illusion of Change: Unveiling News Production and
    Consumption Dynamics in Zimpapers News Hub   109
    Samuel Anesu Muzhingi and Jennings Joy Chibike

Part II   Journalism and Social Media Platforms   129

7   Traditional Media and New Technologies: Facebook
    Radio Programming in Uganda   131
    Fred Max Adii and Fred Kakooza

8   The Algorithmic Power and Subtitles in African Language
    on Facebook Peripheral News Outlets: Language Policy
    and Practices   151
    Limukani Mathe

9   "Negotiating Liquidity": South African Journalists'
    Perceptions of Their Identities on Social Media   175
    Xolo Luthando Tyhalibongo, Blessing Makwambeni,
    and Trust Matsilele

10 The Attention Economy of Micro-Influencers in Malawi:
    The Case of Stanford Sinyangwe   201
    Nick Mdika Tembo

11 Conclusion: Technologies and Journalism in African
    Newsrooms   221
    Albert Sharra and Ufuoma Akpojivi

Index   227

Notes on Contributors

Fred Max Adii is a Media Manager at Vision Group in charge of digital platforms. He has recently graduated with a Master of Journalism and Communication from Makerere University. Adii has keen interest in new media technologies and their impact on broadcast media.

Ufuoma Akpojivi is the Policy, Research and Learning Lead at Advocates for International Development, United Kingdom, a research associate at the University of South Africa, and a visiting scholar at the University of Ghana. Prior to this, he was an associate professor and Head of the Media Studies Department at the University of the Witwatersrand, South Africa, and a visiting professor at the School of Media and Communication, Pan-Atlantic University, Nigeria. He is a C2-rated researcher of the National Research Foundation (NRF) South Africa and a recipient of numerous teaching and learning awards.

Adebukola Olubunmi Ayoola, PhD is a female Nigerian senior lecturer and Head of the Department of Political Science and International Relations, KolaDaisi University, Ibadan. She holds a PhD in International Relations from Obafemi Awolowo University, Ile-Ife, Nigeria. Before joining academics, she spent about 10 years in the newsroom. She has been a lecturer for 12 years and has taught at Wesley University, Ondo University, Bowen University, Iwo University and KolaDaisi University. Adebukola has contributed to several journals both locally and internationally.

xvii

Jennings Joy Chibikeis a Media and Communication Lecturer at Lupane State University in Zimbabwe. He is also a DPhil candidate at Midlands State University in Zimbabwe. He holds a Master of Science Degree in Journalism and Media Studies. His research interests are in Indigenous language media, identity, political communication and human rights and the media.

Francis Chikunkhuzeni is Lecturer in Journalism and Media Studies at the Malawi University of Business and Applied Sciences (MUBAS). He holds a Doctor of Philosophy degree in Comparative International Communication Policy from Coventry University in the United Kingdom and a Master of Arts degree in Journalism and Media Studies from Rhodes University in South Africa.

Fred Kakooza is a senior lecturer in the Department of Journalism and Communication, Makerere University, Uganda. His areas of specialization include broadcast, digital multimedia journalism, visual communication and photography. He has published in the area of new media and health, safety of journalists, and media and COVID-19 as well as digital journalism in Uganda. He is currently the Principal Investigator for Digital Communications and Public Service Delivery in Uganda funded by Carnegie.

Maclan Kanyangw'a is a lecturer at the Malawi University of Business and Applied Sciences (MUBAS) and a doctoral candidate at the University of Botswana. He teaches and conducts research on the role of social media in shaping aggressive forms of political participation with a focus on hate speech, online trolls and incivility, misinformation and disinformation. Prior to this, he spent two years in the newsroom as a journalist.

Blessing Makwambeni is a senior lecturer and postgraduate co-ordinator in the Department of Media and Communication at the Cape Peninsula University of Technology. He holds a PhD in Communication from the University of Fort Hare and has previously taught journalism and media studies at the National University of Science and Technology in Zimbabwe. Blessing has published extensively in the broad areas of digital politics, audience studies, journalism practice, development communication and strategic communication.

Limukani Mathe is a research fellow in the Research Focus Area of Social Transformation at the North-West University. He is also attached to the School of Communication at North-West University as Lecturer for Journalism and Media Studies. He previously taught journalism and media studies at the University of Johannesburg and the University of Fort Hare. He holds a PhD from the University of Fort Hare.

Trust Matsilele is Senior Lecturer in Journalism and Communication at Birmingham City University and has published over 40 peer-reviewed papers and a solo-authored monograph. He publishes in areas of changing journalism ecologies and the intersection of technology and society.

Eric Noel Mtemang'ombe is a professional journalist working as a senior business news analyst with Nation Publications Limited (NPL). He is reading for a Master of Arts degree in Media Studies at the Malawi University of Business and Applied Sciences (MUBAS). Eric is an enterprising communications specialist with demonstrable experience in media training, having worked with reputable training institutions in Malawi such as MUBAS and the Malawi Institute of Journalism (MIJ). In his teaching career, Eric has taught multimedia news production, desktop publishing, multimedia animation and news writing.

Samuel Anesu Muzhingi is a PhD student at University of Kansas, William Allen White School of Journalism and Mass Communication. He holds a Master of Arts in Communication from Daystar University and a Bachelor of Science Honours Degree in Journalism and Media Studies from the National University of Science and Technology. His research interests focus on the societal impact of emerging technologies.

Mzati Nkolokosa is a journalist, writer and linguist. He has worked with three media houses in Malawi for 17 years. During his newsroom years, he also held an adjunct faculty position in the Department of Literary Studies at the University of Malawi. He is currently studying for a PhD in Linguistics at the University of Essex. His research interests are in media, language and health.

Ekari Immaculate Phiri is an associate lecturer in the Department of Literary Studies, University of Malawi. She is currently teaching Malawian oral literature and conducting research in digital literature. Her research interests are Migration Studies, Gender Studies and Popular culture. She is a holder of a bachelor's degree in Education Language from the University of Malawi where she is in her final year of studying master's degree in Literary and Cultural studies.

Albert Sharra is a Joint-postdoctoral research fellow at the University of Witwatersrand in South Africa and the University of Edinburgh in the United Kingdom. He is also a visiting researcher at CAMRI, University of Westminster. Albert is a multi-award-winning journalist with more than 10 years of newsroom experience. His research is in digital media, culture and society, artificial intelligence, comparative African politics and social movements. He is a Mentor of Digital Media Innovators at the International Press Institute (IPI).

Nick Mdika Tembo is Professor of English in the Department of Literary Studies at the University of Malawi. He is also a research associate in the Department of English at the University of the Free State. His teaching and research interests are in trauma and memory studies, holocaust and genocide studies, childhood studies, African life writing and social media technologies. He has extensively published book chapters and journal articles in these areas.

Tisaukirenji Tembo is a lecturer in the Department of Journalism and Media Studies at the Malawi University of Business and Applied Sciences (MUBAS). She holds a Master of Arts in Journalism and Media Studies from the University of the Witwatersrand, Johannesburg, South Africa. Her research interests include critical media studies, media audiences and participatory studies.

Xolo Luthando Tyhalibongo holds an MA in Public Relations and Communications from Cape Peninsula University of Technology and has more than 15 years of experience in driving public relations and communication activities for agencies, government and educational institutions.

LIST OF FIGURES

Fig. 2.1   Experience of respondents with the use of AI.
(Source: Author)   30

Fig. 2.2   Prospect of AI and efficient journalism delivery.
(Source: Author)   31

Fig. 2.3   Use of AI in low-level technology environment.
(Source: Author)   31

Fig. 2.4   Potential benefit of AI for fact-checking. (Source: Author)   32

Fig. 2.5   Use of AI to communicate in a better way. (Source: Author)   32

Fig. 2.6   Challenges associated with the use of in low-tech
environment. (Source: Author)   33

Fig. 2.7   Responsible use of AI in journalism delivery. (Source: Author)   34

Fig. 2.8   Strategies to avoid bias and discrimination. (Source: Author)   35

Fig. 2.9   How to ensure human relevance. (Source: Author)   35

Fig. 2.10   Ethical concerns with the use of AI. (Source: Author)   36

Fig. 2.11   How to build public trust in the use of AI. (Source: Author)   36

Fig. 3.1   UTAUT model. (Source: Venkatesh et al., 2003)   50

Fig. 5.1   Work flow pathway. (Source: Fieldwork 2023)   97

Fig. 8.1   iHarare.com Facebook post (webcam screenshot). (Source:
iHarare.com)   161

Fig. 8.2   iHarare.com Facebook post (webcam screenshot). (Source:
iHarare.com)   163

Fig. 8.3   iHarare.com Facebook post (webcam screenshot). (Source:
iHarare.com)   164

Fig. 8.4   *Hatirare263* Facebook post (webcam screenshot). (Source:
Hatirare263)   165

Fig. 10.1   Prophet Habakkuk's image to promote what looks like a
phone accessories business. (Source: Author)   214

PART I

Technologies and Traditional Media

CHAPTER 1

Introduction: Media Culture and Practice in the Digital Age

Albert Sharra and Ufuoma Akpojivi

Technologies have revolutionised the media industry by transforming the processes through which media messages are produced, packaged, distributed and consumed. This is largely discernible in news production and distribution where producers are even more dependent on technology and its affordances to create, distribute and monetise media content. The ways these digital news producers adopt technologies and use them in producing, packaging, and distributing media messages are neither uniform nor unilateral due to the political, socio-economic and cultural contexts of the media organisation and nation-states. Voltmer (2008) argues that media organisations in developing countries are under-resourced, and this has

---

A. Sharra (✉)
Department of Political Studies, University of Witwatersrand, Johannesburg, South Africa

Centre of African Studies, University of Edinburgh, Edinburgh, UK

U. Akpojivi
Advocates for International Development, London, UK

Communication Science, University of South Africa, Johannesburg, South Africa
e-mail: Ufuoma.Akpojivi@a4id.org

© The Author(s), under exclusive license to Springer Nature   3
Switzerland AG 2025
A. Sharra, U. Akpojivi (eds.), *Technologies and Media Production Cultures*, Palgrave Studies in Journalism and the Global South,
https://doi.org/10.1007/978-3-031-78582-5_1

impacted their news production process and culture. However, Atton and Mabweazara (2011) argue that across the continent, technologies are being deployed into newsroom practices and shaping culture even if not at the dominant level due to socio-economic, political and cultural reasons. This edited volume builds upon these arguments to examine the deployment of technologies in African media, including the ways they are impacting media culture and practice. We are interested in demonstrating whether and in what ways technologies are affecting media culture and the practice itself. In the next sections, we unpack what these two terms mean and provide a snapshot of how they are captured in the chapters in this book.

TECHNOLOGIES AND MEDIA CULTURE

Before diving into the discussion of technologies, their appropriation and impact in the newsroom, it is salient to deconstruct 'Global South' and how we have approached it within the context of this study. The term 'Global South' has become a buzzword which cuts across scholarship and society (Mignolo, 2011). The term has also evolved and it is imperative to always contextualise it before use. In this book we subscribe to Mignolo's argument that the Global South is not about geographical location as some scholars have advanced to, referring to underdeveloped and emerging economies located in the south of the equator, but "regions of the world at the receiving end of globalisation and suffering the consequences" (2011, p. 184). We do not also view the Global South as a community of passive recipients of globalisation but as "epistemic places where global futures are being forged by delinking from the colonial matrix of power" (Mignolo, 2011, p. 184). While these epistemic places can be anywhere in the world, we are particularly interested in African countries in the Sub-Saharan region. Although the dominance of the Global North in new technology development and adoption is worrisome, recent developments in digital technologies present an opportunity for Africa to avoid coloniality and continue to delink from the colonial matrix of power. In this book we focus on the impact of technologies on media production cultures. Technology has changed newsroom cultures (Atton & Mabweazara, 2011), and such impact can be felt even in the least technologically advanced countries. Aker and Mbiti (2010) argue that there is no African country where the impact of technology is not felt. This means that even in technologically disadvantaged countries, there is an aspect or element of technology that can be found, and this technology is evident in the newsroom. The history of the media from the Global North to the Global South has been rooted in technological advancement. For instance, Johannes Gutenberg's movable-type printing press, which commenced the printing press culture, was innovative at the time of its invention and changed the practice and culture of publication-newspapers and periodicals (Beckwith, 2009). Likewise, the first newspaper in Africa, *Iwe Irohin*, published in Nigeria in 1859 by Rev Henry Townsend (see Olaniyan, 2022), was technologically driven/oriented at that time. Other subsequent technological advancements like radio broadcasting, with the earliest broadcast made in 1923 in South Africa (BBC, 2024), and the first television broadcast in Africa by Western Nigeria Television Service in 1959 in Nigeria (Akpojivi, 2018) were not isolated from technology. These technological inventions have shaped society and (re)revolutionised our understanding of journalism, how it is practised and the culture of journalism and newsrooms. As Akpojivi (2024) argues, the appropriation of technology in journalism and in the newsroom at large has changed newsroom culture, which impacts largely the practice of journalism, and this is the crux of this edited collection.

However, before we examine the broader impact of these emerging technologies in media culture, it is important to conceptualise what is newsroom culture before examining the intersection of technologies within the newsroom culture and its broader impact on journalists, the profession and wider practice. Culture generally refers to the way of life of people. Clark (2014) sees newsroom culture as "the norms, practices, habits and routines of a workplace that create the conditions for excellent or substandard work". These norms and practices outline and govern journalism and how it is practised within a media organisation. The importance of this norm cannot be ignored as outside laying the basis for media production, in this case, sourcing for news, news production and dissemination, whether print or broadcast, it defines the tradition, ethos and identity of that media organisation which might differ across media organisations (see Gripsrud, 2017). When journalistic norms are not followed, it undermines the credibility, professionalism and trust in the media and its production process (Ryfe, 2009), as newsroom culture shapes the routines that fulfil both the functional and symbolic needs of journalism. Consequently, media and journalism culture plays a crucial role in the practices of journalism. Gripsrud (2017) posits that this media culture is not isolated from the socio-political, economic, cultural spheres of society and its spheres, as the media production is largely influenced by these spheres as the primary goal of any media organisation.

TECHNOLOGY AND MEDIA CULTURE: THE INTERTWINED RELATION

Ryfe (2009) argues that journalism has always been faced with the challenge of "adopt or die", and this assertion has become more pronounced over the years following technological innovations. The emergence of technologies such as the radio, television and the internet and the subsequent decline in print circulation, has raised the issue of the death of print media and this debate has lingered on for the past 40+ years (see Wilding et al., 2018). This debate has further been excavated by the emergence of new technologies like Artificial Intelligence (AI), which has not only shaped journalism and how news is processed (content and information) but has disrupted how it is distributed and consumed. Wilding et al. (2018), while describing this disruption, stated there has been "unprecedented loss of revenue, technological disruption on a grand scale, the hamster-wheel impulses of the 24/7 news cycle, questions about journalism's quality and authority" (2018, p. 9). This means that the newsroom has to be responsive to these disruptions. Such responsiveness entails adapting and "being an agent of change", and Ryfe (2009) posited that in newsrooms where journalism culture has been responsive to these technologies, it has impacted and transformed the profession.

This technology has significantly transformed newsroom culture, influencing how news is gathered, produced and disseminated. Therefore, making technology and newsroom culture go hand in hand, as they are intertwined. As Mutsvairo (2019) puts it, change in journalism is largely driven by technological change. This intersection between technology and newsroom culture is evident in various aspects, from the integration of digital tools in the reporting process to the shift in journalistic practices and the evolving roles of media professionals. One of the most significant changes brought about by technology and its appropriation in the newsrooms is the shift from traditional print and broadcast media to digital platforms.

The advent of the internet, social media and generative AI has revolutionised how news is consumed, with audiences increasingly turning to online sources for real-time updates (Newman, 2024). This shift has compelled news organisations to adapt to new technologies, resulting in the adoption of digital-first strategies (see Sharra, 2023). Sharra (2023), while expounding on this from the Malawian perspective, posited that the Malawian press adaptation of the digital-first strategy has enabled them to remain relevant and competitive in this era of concentration and proliferation of the media as they struggle for the limited resources and audience. Deuze (2007) notes that the digitalisation of news production has blurred the lines between traditional and new media, creating a hybrid newsroom culture where journalists are expected to be proficient in various multimedia tools.

Mutsvairo (2019) argues that the integration of digital tools into the newsroom has also transformed the journalism process of reporting. Journalists now have access to a wide range of technologies that facilitate data collection, analysis and visualisation. Tools such as data analytics software, content management systems and social media monitoring platforms have become essential in modern newsrooms, enabling journalists to gather and process information more efficiently. From the Global South perspective, Moyo (2019) argues that journalists in Africa were able to use these different technologies to report on the Panama Papers that detail the illicit financial activities of some African leaders, thus strengthening the democratic process of fostering accountability and transparency. These technologies have also enhanced the ability of journalists to engage with their audiences, allowing for greater interactivity and feedback (Pavlik, 2001).

This engagement and interactivity with the audience is one of the fundamental principles that define journalism and newsroom culture. Gripsrud (2017) argues that the audience is at the heart of journalism and media production. The need to respond and meet the ever-increasing needs of the audience has made the media organisations adopt and appropriate technology in a way that it remains relevant (see Sharra, 2023) and competitive, that is, attract huge audiences to media content following the rising decline in audienceship (see Daniels, 2020). According to Daniels (2020), the media landscape has seen the fragmentation of audiences and decline in readership/viewership, and the resultant loss of revenue due to numerous factors including new technology.

However, to address this salient problem, media culture over the years has focused on the attention economy, an important feature of the modern media landscape enabled by the appropriation of technology within the newsroom culture. The attention economy according to Goldhaber (1997) places focus on the consumption of news as a critical value that will generate or yield revenue for the media organisation, especially in an era of declining readership/viewership and revenues following the fragmentation of the media and the emergence of new technologies. This attention economy highlights the relationship between the media industry and its news consumers-audience—as the audiences are exposed to multiple news sources; therefore, the media organisation has to capitalise on their power to draw attention of the audience to their content (Simon, 1971). According to Simon, while buttressing the above further, attention is a scarce commodity because audiences are exposed to a plethora of information, thus the need for media organisations to capture and maintain the focus of their audiences in this saturated media environment.

With the decline of traditional print media, news organisations have increasingly relied on online platforms to reach audiences. To this end, newsrooms culture has shifted towards creating content that is optimised for social media distribution, with headlines and stories designed to capture immediate attention, and they are able to do this using these new technologies of AI, social media and digital media. Tandoc (2014) argue that media organisations are beginning to leverage social media algorithms to prioritise content and generate high levels of engagement, such as likes, shares and comments. This has incentivised newsrooms to produce content that is likely to go viral, often favouring sensational or emotionally charged stories that can attract clicks. This metrics-driven journalism is another significant factor in the promotion of the attention economy within newsrooms. The availability of real-time analytics allows news organisations to track how audiences interact with their content. Metrics such as page views, click-through rates and time spent on articles have become crucial indicators of success. Consequently, newsroom culture increasingly prioritises these metrics, often at the expense of traditional journalistic values such as depth, accuracy and public service (Napoli, 2011). Journalists are now often expected to produce content that can quickly attract large audiences, leading to a focus on quantity over quality. This has given rise to practices like clickbait—using provocative headlines that may oversell or misrepresent the actual content to drive traffic (Munger, 2020).

The shift towards the attention economy has also influenced content strategies within newsrooms. To capture and retain audience attention, news organisations have adopted strategies that include personalisation, push notifications and continuous updates. Personalised content, delivered through algorithms, ensures that users are constantly presented with news that aligns with their interests, further engaging them in a cycle of continuous consumption (Thorson & Wells, 2016). Push notifications and live updates serve to keep audiences engaged throughout the day, creating a sense of urgency and immediacy that can drive repeat visits to news sites. However, this constant demand for engagement can also lead to information overload, where the sheer volume of content becomes overwhelming, and the quality of news consumption deteriorates.

While the attention economy has driven innovation in how news is produced and distributed, it has also raised concerns about the impact on journalistic integrity and public discourse. The emphasis on capturing attention can lead to the trivialisation of important issues, where news coverage becomes fragmented and sensationalised, focusing on what is likely to generate clicks rather than what is most informative or significant (Hindman, 2018). This shift poses a challenge for news organisations that strive to balance the demands of the attention economy with their responsibility to provide accurate, context-rich journalism that serves the public interest.

Technology and its appropriation within the newsroom in the Global South and Africa specifically have posed broader challenges within the newsroom, which the chapters in this edited volume have expounded upon from the different case studies examined. The intersection of technology and newsroom culture has brought about the pressure to produce news and media content quickly in a 24/7 news cycle, leading to concerns about the erosion of journalistic standards (see Sharra, 2023). The emphasis on speed and the need to cater to the fast-paced digital environment can sometimes result in less rigorous fact-checking and a reliance on sensationalism to attract clicks (Olaniyan, 2022). This shift has raised ethical questions about the role of technology in shaping newsroom practices and the potential impact on the credibility of journalism.

Moreover, the rise of automation and artificial intelligence (AI) in newsrooms has sparked debates about the future of journalism. While AI-driven tools such as automated reporting software can enhance efficiency by generating news stories based on data, there are concerns about the implications for journalistic jobs and the quality of content. As Carlson

(2018) argues, the increasing use of automation in news production may lead to a devaluation of the human element in journalism, potentially undermining the role of journalists as gatekeepers of information. However, it must be noted that technology and AI mean different things to different journalists depending on their context. Munoriyarwa et al. (2021), in their study of the South African newsroom, argued that journalists have varied understandings of AI and other technologies in the newsroom, a finding similar to Nigeria in Akpojivi's (2024) study. The case studies examined in this edited volume attest to this, as the varied understanding is rooted in the digital divide that still exists across the continent. This digital divide has impacted the ability of journalists in the Global South to leverage on the potentials of these technologies to have journalism that is truly inclusive and diverse (Van Dijk, 2019), as not only is audience reach limited, but underserved regions or regions without technologies are underserved or ignored, thereby leading to disparities in content, distribution and accessibility.

This raises the broader question of how scholars can theorise technology and its appropriation within the newsroom of Global South countries. Such a theorisation should go beyond the normative approach of technology and its broader impact but about how media practitioners are using or appropriating these technologies and AI to address the fundamental challenges confronting society, including the newsroom and to strike a balance between embracing innovation and maintaining the core values of journalism. Moyo (2019) argues that techno-progressive theory is crucial within the newsroom of Africa, as it shows the intersection between technology and journalism and how it fosters change and development. The disruption of technology is centred on journalistic agency, context of use and institutional/organisational factors (Sewell 1992 cited in Moyo, 2019).

The Changing Media Practices

There is a symbiotic relationship between media culture and practice in that they shape each other. As the discussion above shows, technologies have altered the traditional ways of doing journalism and this has directly affected media practice. The chapters in this volume demonstrate this in multiple ways using case studies from different countries. They show how the changing nature of the media landscape, from how newsrooms are structured to the processes of doing journalism to meet the audience's needs, affects media practice. Unlike what the existing scholarship shows, media practice in the digital age is more demanding. We are in the age where news consumers are newsmakers and have multiple news sources. News sources are also taking advantage of the timeliness of digital media to bypass the traditional media and connect directly with their audiences (Fisher, 2018). The dilemma is that news consumers "need the information at the same time journalists get it" (Lim, 2014) and this has directly affected how journalists do their job to meet their societal obligations.

Media practice is captured by three key aspects. These are agency, production and engagement (Hobart, 2010; Couldry, 2004). Applying these to the discourse demonstrates how technologies have challenged the traditional way of doing journalism. We use the word "doing" deliberately to capture the gist of the concept of media practice. As Couldry notes, the key question in understanding media practice from a theoretical standpoint is: "what are people doing in relation to media across a whole range of situations and contexts?" (2004, p. 119). Generally, media practice is an array of activities, processes and behaviours employed in the production, distribution and consumption of media material. In other words, as Hobart (2010) succinctly puts it, media practice focuses on how media producers create content, how users engage with media material and how agency shapes the ways media material is consumed, shaped and reshaped. In this edited volume, we treat media practice as something "humans do … a form of action" (Couldry, 2012) in producing media content, and we are interested in how these are changing in the digital age.

To illustrate this in a clear context, it is important to employ a number of examples and scenarios that demonstrate the need for media producers to do things differently. Firstly, think of a journalist covering a political rally that is being live-streamed by the organisers and another attending a press briefing that is not. While the former has a monopoly of the information, the latter needs to employ different strategies to produce a news article worthy of paying for.

The first four years of Donald Trump as President of the Republic of the United States remains one of the historical moments that demonstrated a major shift in doing journalism or precisely journalism practice. Instead of waiting for a press briefing or a press statement landing in the email box, journalists kept their eyes on Trump's X's (Twitter) page, waiting for the White House announcements to produce news. Being the first to access Trump's posts became every journalist's wish but to produce news with value for money from such posts for audiences, most of them with access to the same posts, became a daunting task to doing journalism, and continues to haunt the newsroom today.

Similarly, the news that Osama Bin Laden is dead was "published on X first before mainstream media reported it" (Hu et al., 2012, p. 2571) and created an online discourse dominated by elites and shaped the whole coverage of the news. In South Africa, the decision by *The Daily Vox* newspaper to deploy its reporters to join the #FeesMustFall protesters on Wits University campus in 2015, to report live from the protesting crowds, reduced the mainstream media to playing the catch-up role, signalling the need to change the ways tradition media conducts its journalism (Wits Journalism, 2016).

Paying attention to these cases helps us to understand what is changing from the practice perspective as captured in the different chapters of this volume. The change in the ways important information was communicated from the White House, for instance, affected how journalists accessed the news, and the need to do things differently which, as discussed above, is illustrated by the notion of agency. Not only that, but also to report on information that is already online meant the journalists taking an initiative to enrich the information and serve their audiences. This example shows the relationship between journalism and online platforms, including the culture of sharing. Online platforms now act as both sources of and spaces for publishing news. Cammaerts and Couldry (2016) note that "journalism was traditionally not about sharing in the immediate time, which made a scoop a measure of success".

Another important aspect is the relationship between new media and traditional media. The two now complement each other. During the early days of technology, media studies scholars were quick to highlight that new media are here to destroy traditional media. However, such scholarship ignored the potential of traditional media to monopolise the media space by incorporating new media into the traditional system. Chapters in this edited volume are grouped into two. The first four chapters use case studies of traditional media organisations that have integrated new media in their businesses while the remainder focus on online media only. It is now common for traditional media organisations to have online platforms where they do business as online news media, and sometimes in ways that sustain their traditional media (Sharra, 2023). Atton (2008) notes that media practices in mainstream and new media shape each other. He argues that media practices in new media take the same pattern as traditional media, the "social and political processes such as decision-making processes, the structure of editorial meetings and ideological disputes" (Atton, 2008, 213). Drawing on what Johnson and Bourdieu (1993) calls "habitus", Atton (2008, p. 213) observes that the "habitus of practitioners affects how they participate in social arena of media production", highlighting that the habitus of alternative media might have been developed from the experiences of the mainstream media.

This is an important point to note as we search for answers on how technologies have affected media practice in Africa. Changes happening in media have a long history and media practice has never been static. As Deuze (2007), p. 860) notes, journalism is "liquid" and always changing in every aspect that makes it. Thus, recent technological developments should be seen as only enlarging and accelerating existing media processes. This approach prevents us from facing limitations that come with studying journalism using fixed definitions, newsroom-centric approaches or human and techno-centrism. Similarly, it allows us to "acknowledge both the rapidly changing set of formal and technological aspects and the complex set of interactions between new technological possibilities and established media forms" (Atton & Mabweazara, 2011, p. 669). Treating media practice in new media as an extension of the traditional system allows us to conceptualise media practice as normative or routine practices that produce journalism and are always impacted by changes in technologies (Mutsvairo, 2019).

Thus, as we reflect on media practice, the theorisation should be person-focused looking at what media personnel are doing in the process of producing news. How are they creating the content? What systems are they using and how? How different are those approaches to traditional approaches of doing journalism in traditional media? This is what most of the chapters in this edited volume focus on as summarised below.

Summary of the Chapters

After the introductory chapter by Albert Sharra and Ufuoma Akpojivi, Adebukola Olubunmi Ayoola opens up the Technologies and Traditional Media thematic section in Chap. 2 by examining the integration of Artificial Intelligence (AI) into journalism, particularly in technology-deficient environments like Nigeria. It explores the potential benefits, challenges, and ethical concerns associated with AI-driven journalism. She argues that while AI can enhance efficiency and productivity, issues like bias, misinformation, and the risk of job displacement are highlighted. The chapter concludes that AI should complement, not replace, human journalists, emphasising the need for ethical guidelines, training and a balanced approach to integrating AI into the journalism industry. Chapter 3 by Eric Noel Mtemang'ombe and Francis Chikunkhuzeni examines how the integration of Artificial Intelligence and Machine Learning into journalism practice has created both optimism and apprehension. They critique the techno-optimistic view that these technologies will radically transform journalism, arguing instead that technology adoption in journalism is a gradual, complex process influenced by institutional and contextual factors. The study focuses on the Malawian online journalism context, and they use this case study to illustrate the low adoption rate of hypermedia features and the factors that influence this adoption, including performance expectancy, social influence, and facilitating conditions. The chapter concludes that while emerging technologies offer potential, their impact on journalism will likely be incremental rather than revolutionary.

Ekari Phiri, Mzati Nkolokosa, Maclan Kanyang'wa and Albert Sharra in Chap. 4, examine the adoption of technologies in different newsrooms in Malawi and how the technologies are influencing media practices. The chapter focuses on a digital-first, a concept adopted by traditional media organisations to incorporate online platforms in their newsrooms. Using case studies of Malawi's oldest media organisations and an online news outlet, the chapter argues that digital-first is helping traditional media to remain relevant and compete effectively with new media. In Chap. 5, Albert Sharra and Tisaukirenji Tembo examine the implementation and impact of News-Wrap, a newsroom automation software, at Malawi's Nation Publications Limited (NPL). They explore how the software aimed to enhance efficiency and reduce costs in news production faced challenges such as inadequate technology infrastructure, leading to its suspension. The study highlights the importance of considering local contexts and engaging stakeholders when introducing new technologies in developing newsrooms.

Samuel Muzhingi and Jennings Chibike open up the second thematic section titled "Journalism and Social Media Platforms" in Chap. 6, by examining how Zimpapers News Hub, a digital news platform in Zimbabwe, has not significantly altered traditional news production and consumption patterns. They argued that despite technological advancements, journalists continue to adhere to conventional practices, and users' reading habits remain similar to those in the pre-digital era. The study emphasises the persistence of established media routines, challenging the notion that digital platforms have revolutionised journalism in Zimbabwe. In Chap. 7, Fred Max Adii and Fred Kakooza explore how digital platforms like Facebook have transformed traditional radio programming in Uganda, focusing on 94.8 XFM. They discuss how these platforms enhance audience engagement, facilitate multimedia content production and create new revenue streams while promoting citizen journalism and real-time interaction with listeners. Limukani Mathe and Gilbert Motsaathebe, in Chap. 8, investigate how peripheral news outlets in Zimbabwe, such as iHarare.com and Hatirare263, navigate and manipulate Facebook's English-dominant algorithm to promote indigenous Shona language content. They highlight the challenges of language regulation on Western social media platforms and advocate for a more Afrocentric approach to internet governance to support multilingualism and local languages in journalism.

Chapter 9, by Xolo Luthando Tyhalibongo, Blessing Makwambeni and Trust Matsilele, explores how South African journalists navigate and perceive their identities on social media. The study reveals the tension that journalists experience between their professional and online personas. The chapter highlights the lack of comprehensive mechanisms by media institutions to support journalists in managing these fluid identities effectively. Conclusively, Chap. 10 by Nick Mdika Tembo examines the role of micro-influencers in Malawi's attention economy, focusing on how individuals like Stanford Sinyangwe leverage social media to shape societal discourse. Also, the chapter examines the intersection of traditional journalism and social media, highlighting the potential of micro-influencers to complement mainstream media by engaging niche audiences and creating innovative content.

CONCLUSION

The chapter concludes by emphasising the intricate relationship between technology and newsroom culture in shaping modern journalism. As digital tools increasingly permeate African newsrooms, they are redefining traditional practices and influencing how media content is produced, distributed and consumed. While these advancements offer significant opportunities for innovation and audience engagement, they also pose challenges, particularly in maintaining journalistic standards and addressing the digital divide. The need for a balanced approach that leverages technological benefits while preserving core journalistic values is critical for fostering a more inclusive and accountable media landscape in Africa. This is what this edited volume has demonstrated, and we hope we have broached a conversation on this very important issue.

REFERENCES

Aker, J., & Mbiti, I. (2010). Mobile Phones and Economic Development in Africa. *Journal of Economic Perspective, 24*(3), 207–232.

Akpojivi, U. (2018). *Media Reforms and Democratisation in Emerging Democracies of Sub-Saharan Africa*. Palgrave.

Akpojivi, U. (2024). Journalism 2.0, News Practice and Culture in Nigeria: A Critical Examination of Nigerian Television Authority and Nigeria Info FM. In B. Mutsvairo (Ed.), *The Routledge Companion to Journalism in the Global South* (pp. 198–208). Routledge.

Atton, C. (2008). Alternative Media Theory and Journalism Practice. https:// direct.mit.edu/books/edited-volume/chapter-pdf/2221468/978026 2268974_cai.pdf.

Atton, C., & Mabweazara, H. (2011). New Media and Journalism Practice in Africa: An Agenda for Research. *Journalism, 12*(6), 667–673.

BBC. (2024). Retrieved August 18, 2024, from https://www.bbc.co.uk/world-service/specials/1624_story_of_africa/page17.shtml#:~:text=The%20first%20 radio%20broadcasts%20in,1933%2C%20and%20Senegal%20in%201939.

Beckwith, C. (2009). *Empires of the Silk Road: A History of Central Eurasia from the Bronze Age to the Present*. Princeton University Press.

Cammaerts, B., & Couldry, N. (2016). Digital Journalism as Practice. In *The SAGE Handbook of Digital Journalism* (pp. 326–340). Sage.

Carlson, M. (2018). Automating judgment? Algorithmic judgment, news knowledge, and journalistic professionalism. *New media & society, 20*(5), 1755–1772.

Chris, A., & Mabweazara, H. (2011). New Media and Journalism Practice in Africa: An Agenda for Research. *Journalism, 12*(6), 667–673.

Clark, P. (2014). What Defines a Healthy Newsroom Culture? Online. Retrieved June 3, 2024, from https://www.poynter.org/reporting-editing/2014/ what-defines-a-healthy-newsroom-culture/

Couldry, N. (2012). *Media, Society, World: Social Theory and Digital Media Practice*. Polity. https://books.google.com/books?hl=en&lr=&id=AcHvP9tr bkAC&oi=fnd&pg=PR5&dq=Couldry,+Nick.+%E2%80%9CMedia+Cultures:

+A+World+Unfolding.%E2%80%9D+Media,+Society,+World:+Social+Theory +and+Digital+Media+Practice.+Cambridge:+Polity,+2013.+156%E2%80%937 9.+Print.&ots=MzUvWEMHKE&sig=lect_opGj5Gy5PQutZALkoXZvoE.

Couldry, N. (2004). Theorising Media as Practice. *Social Semiotics, 14*(2), 115–132. https://doi.org/10.1080/1035033042000238295

Daniels, G. (2020). *Power and Loss in South African Journalism: News in the Age of Social Media*. Wits University Press.

Deuze, M. (2007). *Media Work*. Polity.

Fisher, C. (2018). What is meant by 'trust'in news media?. *Trust in media and journalism: Empirical perspectives on ethics, norms, impacts and populism in Europe*, 19–38.

Goldhaber, M. H. (1997). The Attention Economy and the Net. *First Monday, 2*(4). https://doi.org/10.5210/fm.v2i4.519

Gripsrud, J. (2017). *Understanding Media Culture*. Bloomsbury.

Hindman, M. (2018). *The Internet trap: How the digital economy builds monopolies and undermines democracy*. Princeton University Press.

Hobart, M. (2010). *What Do We Mean by "Media Practices"?* (Theorising Media and Practice). Berghahn Books. http://franklinevans.com/cooper/1993_bourdieu_fieldofculturalproduction.pdf.

Hu, M., Liu, S., Wei, F., Wu, Y., Stasko, J., & Ma, K.-L. (2012). Breaking News on Twitter. In *Proceedings of the SIGCHI Conference on Human Factors in Computing Systems* (pp. 2751–2754). ACM. https://doi.org/10.1145/2207676.2208672

Johnson, R., & Bourdieu, P. (1993). *The Field of Cultural Production: Essays on Art and Literature*. Polity.

Lim, J. (2014). *Redefinition of online scoops: Online journalists' personal and institutional responses to online scoops*. First Monday.

Mignolo, W. (2011). The Global South and World Dis/order. *Journal of Anthropological Research, 67*(2), 165–188. https://doi.org/10.3998/jar.0521004.0067.202

Moyo, L. (2019). Data Journalism and the Panama Papers: New Horizons for Investigative Journalism in Africa. In B. Mutsvairo, S. Bebawi, & E. Borges-Rey (Eds.), *Data Journalism in the Global South*. Palgrave.

Munger, K. (2020). All the news that's fit to click: The economics of clickbait media. *Political Communication, 37*(3), 376–397.

Munoriyarwa, A., Chiumbu, S., & Motsaathebe, G. (2021). Artificial Intelligence Practices in Everyday News Production: The Case of South Africa's Mainstream Newsrooms. *Journalism Practice, 17*(7), 1374–1392.

Mutsvairo, B. (2019). A New Dawn for the 'Developing' World? Probing Data Journalism in Non-Western Societies. In B. Mutsvairo, S. Bebawi, & E. Borges-Rey (Eds.), *Data Journalism in the Global South*. Palgrave.

Napoli, P. M. (2011). *Audience evolution: New technologies and the transformation of media audiences*. Columbia University Press.

Newman, N. (2024). Journalism, Media and Technology Trends and Predictions 2024. Online. Retrieved August 18, 2024, from https://reutersinstitute.politics.ox.ac.uk/journalism-media-and-technology-trends-and-predictions-2024.

Olaniyan, A. (2022). *From Iwe Irohin to* Saharareporters.com*: Hardcoding Citizen Journalism in Nigeria*. PhD Thesis, University of the Witwatersrand, South Africa.

Pavlik, J. V. (2001). *Journalism and New Media*. Columbia University Press.

Ryfe, D. M. (2009). Broader and Deeper: A Study of Newsroom Culture in a Time of Change. *Journalism, 10*(2), 197–216.

Sewell, W. H. (1992). A theory of structure: Duality agency and transformation. *American Journal of Sociology, 98*, 1–9.

Sharra, A. (2023). 'Digital First' as a Coping Measure for Malawi's Print Newspapers. In T. Matsilele, S. Mpofu, & D. Moyo (Eds.), *New Journalism Ecologies in East and Southern Africa*. Palgrave Macmillan.

Simon, H. A. (1971). Designing organisations for an information-rich world. In M. Greenberger (Ed.), *Computers, Communications, and the Public Interest* (pp. 37–72). Johns Hopkins University Press.

Tandoc Jr, E. C. (2014). Journalism is twerking? How web analytics is changing the process of gatekeeping. *New media & society, 16*(4), 559–575.

Thorson, K., & Wells, C. (2016). Curated flows: A framework for mapping media exposure in the digital age. *Communication theory, 26*(3), 309–328.

Van Dijk, J. (2019). *The Digital Divide*. Polity Press.

Voltmer, K. (2008). Comparing media systems in new democracies: East meets South meets West. *Central European Journal of Communication, 1*, 23–40.

Wilding, D., Fray, P., Molitorisz, S., & McKewon, E. (2018). *The Impact of Digital Platforms on News and Journalistic Content*. University of Technology Sydney.

Wits Journalism. (2016). *State of the Newsroom: South Africa Inside/Outside*. Johannesburg.

CHAPTER 2

AI and Effective Journalism in a Technology-Deficient Environment: Prospects, Challenges and Ethical Concerns

Adebukola Olubunmi Ayoola

INTRODUCTION

The advancement in technology and development of Artificial Intelligence (AI) is no doubt a breakthrough in science and a positive development in this present world. Looking at it from the perspective of how the use of AI has improved the quality and quantity of human activities and output, it is indeed a welcome development to our world. However, there are numerous ongoing debates about the prospect of AI performance at workplace and the possible effect it might have across board. This has brought fear to so many who believe that the introduction of AI to workplace might result in loss of jobs across sectors. Introduction of AI to the journalism profession is also a controversial topic with particular focus on its deliverability and efficiency based on peculiarity of the profession and its ethical

A. O. Ayoola (✉)
Department of Political Science and International Relations, KolaDaisi University, Ibadan, Nigeria
e-mail: adebukola.ayoola@koladaisiuniversity.edu.ng

© The Author(s), under exclusive license to Springer Nature Switzerland AG 2025
A. Sharra, U. Akpojivi (eds.), *Technologies and Media Production Cultures*, Palgrave Studies in Journalism and the Global South,
https://doi.org/10.1007/978-3-031-78582-5_2

19

consideration which emphasizes truth, fairness and objectivity in content delivery. Another issue of concern is the environmental factors associated with technological advancement level, especially in a Third World Country in Africa. There are those who believe in its effectiveness and ability to do better than human beings, and therefore it should be made to replace human beings. This is seen as a strategy to reduce cost and maximize profit which might translate to job loss (Lewis et al., 2019; Kothani & Cruikshank, 2022; Guzman, 2023). Others like Dawson (2010), Broussard et al. (2019) and Aitamurto et al. (2019) considered such actions as a misplaced and miscalculated attempt due to possible inaccuracies in its algorithms. They believe that AI can only complement human beings at workplace and is not a substitute for effective journalism and efficient delivery. The adoption of AI in newsrooms and the research on its impact are predominantly focused on Western countries. Few African countries have started incorporating AI but mostly in government sectors and agencies like health, education and finance but little information exists about the use of AI technology in newsrooms across Africa. Therefore, this study examines the prospects, challenges and ethical concerns of AI based journalism in a technology-deficient environment with a particular focus on Nigeria.

NIGERIAN MEDIA LANDSCAPE AND AI ADOPTION

Media adoption of AI in Africa is said to be at 20% due to factors such as a low share of skilled talents and slow download speeds (UNCTAD, 2023). The 20% is largely concentrated in social media networks like TikTok, Twitter (X-handle) and LinkedIn. The Nigerian media landscape was formerly dominated by print, radio and television but now is being disrupted by digital platforms. According to the Nigeria Broadcasting Commission (NBC), there are currently 740 broadcast stations in Nigeria comprising both television and radio stations (Oguntola, 2023; Aluko-Olokun, 2023). The NBC also emphasized the need for all these stations to embrace digital broadcasting. The country embarked on transitioning from analogue to digital broadcasting in 2004 with a deadline set for 2015 for all broadcast stations in the country to have gone digital. The country's transition to becoming fully digitalized has been hindered by several challenges ranging from technological, financial, human capital and knowledge deficit, among others (Olajide & Olanrewaju, 2022).

The print media in Nigeria is put at about 100, both national and local, titles (Adeyemo, 2024). The broadcast and print media comprise public and privately owned organizations which assumed the responsibility to serve the teeming Nigerian populace. The people entrust in the credibility and integrity of the media, on their needs to be informed about events within and outside their immediate and distant environment. The media also owe the people the responsibility of serving them nothing but the truth based on equity and fairness. With advancement in media technology, there has been a shift from the traditional media, that is, television, radio and newspaper, to social media or online platforms as sources of news. This has forced many of the traditional media in Nigeria to also employ online platforms as additional channel to reach their target audience of whom more than 90% rely mostly on online sources for their news consumption (Adeyemo, 2024). According to Adeyemo, sources such as Facebook, YouTube, Instagram, Telegram and TikTok have become most accessed channels for news and other contents in the country.

As a result of the trends and reality, popular traditional media in Nigeria, that is, *Nigeria Television Authority, Channels Television, Africa Independent Television, Arise TV News, News Agency of Nigeria, The Guardian Newspaper, The Nation, The Punch, ThisDay* and *Vanguard Newspaper*, among others, are employing the online channels by maintaining social medial handles to keep up with the trend. And their transition to online platform was a welcome development. Many of these media channels leverage on the online platforms to also boost their patronage as well as get monetized for economic gain. All these media channels have in one way or the other leverage on the opportunity provided by AI to enhance content delivery and maximize their consumer base but not without a cost. While the traditional media try to maintain balance in keeping to the ethical principle guiding journalism, such could not be guaranteed with the regular social media platforms especially with series of content manipulations and fake news saga being experienced daily by their audience. On the other hand, government in its effort to provide censorship, embarked on antisocial media laws and other forms of surveillance to clampdown on the authors of online fake news (Kperogi, 2022). These actions of government were also regarded as biased and a deliberate attempt to gag the online journalists and activists.

Overall, Nigeria media both traditional and online are exposed to the use of AI and have at one time or the other explored with the technology. However, there are a lot of misuses occasioned by ignorance,

22 A. O. AYOOLA

unaffordability or deliberate intention to misinform the audience. These social media handlers most of the time get away with these acts due to several factors ranging from the porosity of these platform, lack of technology to track them, lack of required capital and expertise to address the issues (Olajide & Olanrewaju, 2022). The challenge before us, therefore, is the possibility of a responsible use of AI in Nigeria in spite of its level of technological know-how and still keeping to the ethical guidelines and principles of the journalism profession.

AI AND JOURNALISM

A lot has been said about the introduction and use of Artificial Intelligence in workplace generally and journalism. Several testimonies have been reported on how AI is transforming many industries, including journalism. AI-powered tools can help journalists automate tasks, gather data and analyze information more efficiently and effectively. However, the use of AI in journalism raises several challenges, particularly in technology-deficient environment.

According to Jaakkola (2023), Whittaker (2019), Guzman (2023) and Khaled Diab (2023), AI has the potential to improve journalism in many ways. This includes media content analysis and production like mining, comment moderation, news writing, story discovery, its ability to automate routine tasks like fact-checking, transcribing interview and generating summaries which provide the journalist the space to focus on other tasks. In addition, AI can also help in identifying and verifying newsworthy information by data gathering from different sources, from social media to government websites and scholarly databases and help stay ahead of others in breaking new stories (Lewis et al., 2019; Diab, 2023; Guzman, 2019, 2023). These can help journalists to identify trends and patterns that would be difficult to find. AI has also the capacity to help journalists create new audiences and engage in new ways, that is, AI can be used to create personalized news feeds and generate chatbots that can answer readers' questions and translate languages. Carlson (2015) Lopez et al. (2021), Parrat-Fernandez et al. (2021), Hadi Rashedi (2020) and Aitamurto et al. (2019) posit that AI has the potential that can also be beneficial in a technology-deficient environment like in the developing countries, as it can be used to gather and analyze data from remote areas where there is no access to internet or other resources, produce content in languages that are not widely spoken or written and translate content into other languages for the benefits of reaching a wider audience. Kothani and Cruikshank (2022) also agree that there are lots of opportunities to adapt to the use of AI in Africa. With all these prospects, there is the tendency for media corporations to downsize workforce by replacing them with chatbots and ChatGPT, which may result in newsroom becoming almost worker-less factories as machines churn out endless copy at superhuman speed.

As beautiful and enticing as the prospect of AI use in journalism appeared, several challenges were identified by scholar and experts especially in technology-deficient environment as presented in literature. Some of the challenges include lack of access to the technology, cost of procurement, inadequate training and bias (Lopez et al., 2021; Guzman, 2023; Aitamurto et al., 2019; and Lewis et al., 2019). As explained by these authors, not all journalists have access to the latest AI-powered tools, thereby creating a digital divide between journalists in developed world and developing countries. Another concern is the issue of cost as AI-powered tools are expensive to develop and maintain, making it inaccessible and unaffordable to smaller news organization. Many journalists do not have the required skills or training to use AI-powered tools effectively, thereby leading to errors and inaccuracies in reporting (Dawson, 2010; Carlson, 2018; Broussard et al., 2019; Whittaker, 2019). A major challenge raised is the issue of bias as AI algorithms can be biased, reflecting the biases of data which they are trained on, translating to biased reporting which are inaccurate or misleading, representing the interests of powerful groups and individuals. It also has the potential to be used for manipulating public opinion, that is, creating fake news articles or to spread disinformation (Khaled Diad, 2023; Carlson, 2018; Aitamurto et al., 2019). They emphasize that this could undermine trust in journalism, making it difficult for people to get accurate information about the world around them. Last, but most importantly, is the fear and threat of job displacement for journalists as many would be relieved of their jobs since AI tools has the capacity to do more than man within a shorter period (Lopez, 2021; de-Lima-Santos & Ceron, 2022; Broussard et al., 2019; Lewis et al., 2019; Guzman, 2019, 2023).

Ethical issues have always come to the front burner and become a cause of concern associated with the use of AI in journalism. These include transparency, accountability and threat to privacy. Sharing similar view, Micheal and Aaron (2019), Patching and Hirst (2021), Aitamurto et al. (2019), Carlson (2018), Hadi Rashedi (2020), Carlson (2015) and Lewis et al. (2019) all expressed concern about the potentials for AI to be used to spread misinformation and propaganda which negates the ethics of journalism. Ethical concerns include challenge of how to avoid bias, how to design hybrid human-AI workflows that reflect domain values, how future generations of media practitioners could be educated to use AI-driven media tools responsibly. Journalists must be held accountable for the information they publish, even if it is generated using AI tools. It is also important to be transparent about how AI is being used in journalism by disclosing which AI tools are used, how they work and what data they are trained on, the lack of transparency and accountability in AI system raises ethical concern. The issue of privacy is another major concern stressed: the threat to privacy posed by the collection and use of personal data by AI algorithms. It is important to use AI tools in a way that respects people's privacy. On the other hand, Parrat-Fernandez et al. (2021), Calvo Rubio and Ufarte Ruiz (2021), Aitamurto et al. (2019), Lewis et al. (2019), Lopez et al. (2021) and Hadi Rashedi (2020) expressed optimism in addressing the ethical concerns as they suggest ways to maximize the benefits and minimize risks associated with using AI in journalism. These include deep learning approach to detect fake news by investing in training and education for journalists on the responsible use of AI, developing ethical guidelines for the use of AI in journalism by ensuring transparency and accountability in the AI systems, and working to ensure that everyone has equal access to the benefits of AI regardless of their location or socioeconomic status. In addition is the use of forensic techniques to uncover manipulated content. With these, they believe ethical issues could be minimized as the introduction of AI in journalism is a positive development which they insist should be embraced.

Based on the above views and submission, the introduction of AI use in journalism is no doubt a positive development but adequate measures must be put in place in many essential areas to reduce risks associated with AI and maximize its potentials especially in a technology-deficient environment to avoid damages.

Theoretical Framework

The responsibility of the journalist as the fourth estate of the realm, or the middleman between the government and the governed compels on him the duty to serve the public nothing but the truth. This is regardless of the situation, condition or environment within which he has to operate. The truth is sacrosanct as his credibility and integrity will be judged or determined by his accuracy. This work therefore relies on the Gatekeeping Theory of Mass Communication as the basis of analysis. According to Shoemaker and Vos (2009), and Davie (2020), gatekeeping is the process of selecting and filtering or sieving media contents to determine which among the numerous available news items will best serve or meet the information needs of the public. A process of culling and crafting uncountable pieces of information to a limited number of messages that will eventually reach the people daily. It deals with the most suitable and beneficial information diet to the target public. This is because, some news contents are sometimes considered as unfit for public or a category of audience. Such contents could be regarded as obscene, indecent or injurious to the consuming audience. The selection or filtering must be carried out by the editor and others along the production process as watchdogs of the society to determine which content will make it through the information gate to the final consumers. The gatekeeping theory of mass communication is aimed at sanitizing the information environment and protecting the sanity of the entire public.

Journalism is the act of gathering news, processing it based on laid down ethics and disseminating the news to the target public for the purpose of keeping them informed about what goes on within and around them. According to the American Press Institute, "journalism is the activity of gathering, assessing, creating, and presenting news and information. It is also the product of these activities". John Merrill (2011) sees journalism as the activity of journalists and the institution of journalism. David Ryfe (2019) defines journalism as "a process of gathering, analyzing, and disseminating news, information and commentaries. It is a form of communication that aims to inform citizens about the world around them". The purpose is specifically to affirm the norms, values and beliefs of the communities. American journalist and comics creator Joe Sacco (2012) says that journalism is all about the production and distribution of reports on current events based on facts and supported with proof or evidence. In all, journalism is about gathering the news, analyzing it and disseminating such to the people with the purpose of bridging the information gap between the people and their immediate and distant environment. And to achieve these, he is bound by his professional ethics to perform his gatekeeping role as the watchdog of the society to save the target public from being exposed to contents that may be injurious to them as emphasized by Shoemaker and Vos (2009).

Artificial Intelligence: AI definition is stemmed from the Turing's test by the famous British mathematician, Alan Turing who invented the theoretical Turing machine (Turing 1947 in Copeland, 2024). The Turing test is a simple technique of placing something behind a curtain and making it speak with humans, while its ability to sound like human being confers the status of AI on it. He introduced the concept of AI referred to as "Intelligent Machinery" with the idea of training a network of artificial neurons to perform specific tasks. This he called "Connectionism" (Turing 1948 in Copeland, 2024). This attempt was reportedly used during World War II for deciphering of the German codes (Copeland, 2024). Over the decades, the definition of AI has grown beyond the Turning's suggestion that an Intellect is a person with knowledge gained through the years or a thing that knows nothing, but it can learn. Taking it a step further, AI is described as "a step device living in a kind of world. At each step, it receives information (from the world) and influences (at the world) by the information it works out" (Dimiter, 2020). He went further that AI is such a program which in an arbitrary world will cope not worse than a human being. By interpretation in a layman's word. AI is a program that can perform the task and function of human being in an arbitrary world. According to Dimiter, AI is a world and a device that lives in it with one vital thing missing, the meaning of life. In other words, it is a machine capable of performing human functions and even consolidating on those functions but lacked one essential component—life itself. And according to the Oxford language definition, "AI is the theory and development of computer systems, able to perform tasks normally requiring human intelligence, such as visual perception, speech recognition, decision-making, and translation between languages".

Professional Ethics: The principles, codes of conduct regulating the practice of a profession. Professional ethics is more like the legal frameworks guiding the operations within any profession without which one may be prohibited from participating in some of these professions. Professional ethics is also seen as the personal and corporative rules that govern behavior within the context of a particular profession (Heidi Von Weltzien Hoivik, 2002). The journalism ethics enjoins professionals to seek and report the truth at all times. This also includes fact-checking, not intentionally distorting information, identifying sources, avoiding stereotypes and supporting the open exchange of opinions. It also demands that journalists must strive to minimizing harm, act independently and be accountable for all error and avoid conflict of interest and corruption (Crichton et al., 2010). This presupposes that a journalist in performing his gatekeeping role must be seen to be fair and balance to all parties involved in the news story. He is expected to be objective by always reporting the truth without fear or favor. Patching and Hirst (2021) looked at the ethical problems associated with journalism profession as responsible for major series of crises that had shaken the global journalism to its foundation in the last decades. These include the coronavirus pandemic and the Black Lives Matter movement among others, and their reportage which most times did not conform to ethical practices. The situation might be worse with the use of AI and its attendant cases of inaccuracy, manipulation of fact, generation of fake algorithms, bias and discrimination. Allowing the AI to take the lead in the newsroom without human attendant raises many ethical concerns in the gatekeeping role of the media.

METHODOLOGY

This study employed both primary and secondary sources of data. Primary data was sourced through questionnaire method. The choice of questionnaire was based on the ability to reach large number of respondents simultaneously within a short time and it was administered electronically. Questionnaire was structured to elicit responses from the respondents based on their individual experiences in relation to the subject matter. And the questions were open-ended to allow for further details as may be necessary. The target was 75 respondents were administered questionnaire but only 62 returned their questionnaire. Questionnaires were purposively sent to practicing journalists and researchers across all cadres in selected print and electronic media, television, radio and newspaper organizations in Lagos, Oyo, Osun, Ondo and Ekiti states in south/west Nigeria with a sample size of three media organization from each state. The respondents comprise news reporters, program officers, presenters, newscasters, social media handle managers, editors and executives, while the researchers are academia whose cadre ranges from assistant lecturers to senior lecturers, associate and full professors of mass communication and media studies from selected universities (public and private) across the five states. The academia was included to have a balanced view. In all, 50 of the respondents were media practitioners while 12 were academia. Secondary data

28 A. O. AYOOLA

was sourced through books, journals, and other relevant internet materials. Data was analyzed based on descriptive method. It employed the use of figure, that is, pie charts, bar charts and diagrams to present data and show the percentage and degree of agreement and disagreement in the various responses.

ANALYSIS OF DATA AND DISCUSSION

The targeted respondents that were administered questionnaires were 75 in total but only 62 of them attended to it, and returned the instrument. Overall, 77.4% of the responses showed low exposure to the use of AI among media practitioners and researchers while those exposed to it have reported cases of fake algorithms and inaccuracy of data across board. There were deliberate manipulations of data, misrepresentation of data as well as bias and discrimination because of poor expertise, lack of requisite knowledge/technical know-how and unaffordability of required technology and software. Ethical concerns raised by the respondents are issues of transparency and accountability (44.4%), bias and discrimination (24.1%), as well as respect of privacy (20.1%). The respondents emphasized the challenges created using AI in respect of the aforementioned ethical issues. According to them, the environment is not always transparent, data processed by AI application are most of the time inaccurate, there are also elements of bias and discrimination occasioned by manipulations, and it does not respect individual person's privacy. While they agree on the high prospect of AI-powered journalism in Nigeria due to its ability to enhance efficiency and productivity, they believe that these challenges could be managed or eliminated through the following: training and skill acquisition for journalists, investment in AI technology and enforcement of ethical guidelines. These, they believe, will make journalists remain relevant and equipped on the responsible use of AI. It was also established that many of the challenges raised were caused by the absence of or low level of human participation in cause data processing. The responses of 62 respondents from respective questions generated based on the subject matter are represented in the charts below.

This above figure shows that 77.4% of respondents are beginners in their level of experience with using AI, 14.5% are at intermediate level, 6.8% has no experience and only 1.3% operating at an advanced level. This means that while over 90% of the respondents are exposed to the use of AI, only 1.3% are operating at advance level of expertise.

2   AI AND EFFECTIVE JOURNALISM IN A TECHNOLOGY-DEFICIENT...   29

This represents the degree of agreement on AI ability to improve efficiency and accuracy of journalism. The different colors represent the different categories of respondents. Color 1 stands for journalists, 2 and 3 represent other media practitioners in the line of production while 4 and 5 represent lecturers and researchers respectively. This shows that journalists and researchers strongly agreed on the prospect of AI to enhance efficient and accurate journalism delivery. Other media practitioners (e.g., programs, engineering, photography and others) also agree on this belief.

All the respondents agree that AI can help journalists in many ways achieve their task to discover news stories and sources in an environment with low level of technology. The chart, however, shows that this view is highly expressed by the category of respondents who are journalists. They, however, advocated for acquisition of technology and skills for efficient delivery.

The above figure shows the responses of respondents on the potential benefits of AI-powered journalism: 49.2% agree that it can increase accuracy, thereby reducing time spent on production process; 33.9% agree on its ability to reduce workload as it helps with processing big data and saves them the stress of doing that manually; 13.6% agree on its ability to help improve transparency while 1.6% also agree on its ability to save time and resources for journalist as well as help the public identify trustworthy sources and avoid false information; 1.6% express no belief.

The figure above shows that only 59 out of the 62 respondents answered the question on how AI can be used to help journalists communicate better; 32.2% of them say it can help with the use of simple languages to communicate to the audience; 35.6% say it can help with visualizing data; 28.8% say it can help provide interactive content; 1.6% agree with total views of 96.6% earlier expressed that AI can aid journalists in simplifying and communicating complex information effectively to the public by using Natural Language Processing (NLP) algorithm in generating content.

The above figure shows that 57 respondents responded to the challenges associated with the use of AI in journalism in a technology-deficient environment: 43.9% say limited access to technology, 26.3% say lack of expertise, 24.6 say bias and discrimination while the remaining 5.2 say nothing.

This figure shows that only 30 respondents attempted this question. Some of their responses include enlightenment campaign, training and skill acquisition, setting rules and regulation, enforcement and no idea.

This figure shows responses from only 54 respondents and suggestions in percentages.

This figure shows 54 respondents and responses in percentage

The above figure shows responses from 54 respondent and issues raised in percentages

This figure shows responses from 53 respondents and their suggestions on how to build public trust in percentages

The discussion is divided into four sub-headings based on the analysis of responses presented in the above figures. These are Prospect of AI Use in Journalism in Nigeria, Challenges Associated with Use of AI in Nigeria, Ethical Concerns and Ways to Address Them and Conclusion on Future of AI-Journalism in Nigeria.

Prospect of Using AI in Journalism Industries in Nigeria

Based on responses from Figs. 2.2, 2.3, 2.4 and 2.5, respondents agreed in a "Yes" or "No" answer that AI has the potentials to positively impact journalism in Nigeria in spite of the low level of technology, low power supply and high cost of internet but Fig. 2.1 showed that 77.4% of the total respondents are beginners when it comes to level of exposure to and the use of AI while 14.5% are at the intermediate level. It should also be noted that all the respondents are media practitioners, media researchers

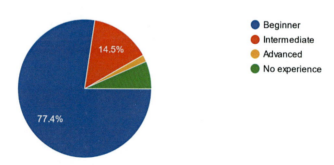

Fig. 2.1 Experience of respondents with the use of AI. (Source: Author)

To what extent do you agree or disagree with the following statement: AI can improve the efficiency and accuracy of journalism in a technology deficient environment?

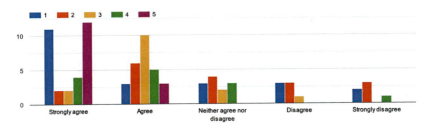

Fig. 2.2 Prospect of AI and efficient journalism delivery. (Source: Author)

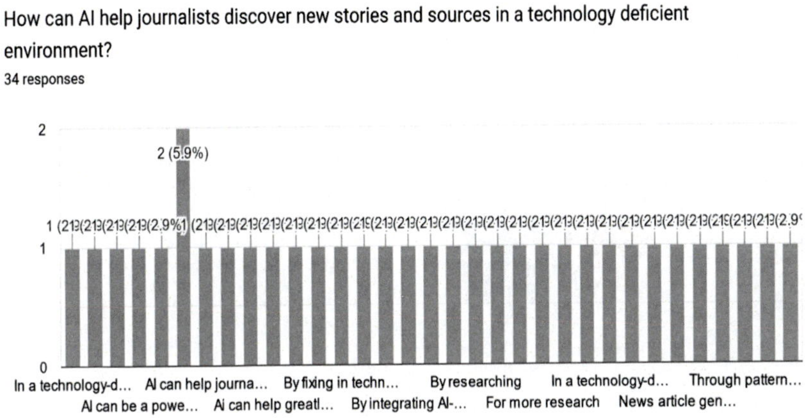

How can AI help journalists discover new stories and sources in a technology deficient environment?
34 responses

Fig. 2.3 Use of AI in low-level technology environment. (Source: Author)

and lecturers in the media discipline. Some of the prospects of AI mentioned in those charts include its ability to help journalists communicate complex information by using simple language, provide interactive content, visualizing data, verify information and fact-check claims through increased accuracy, reduced workload, saves time and resources and lots more. These corroborated Aitamurto et al.'s (2019) submission on the ability of AI to improve effectiveness and efficient delivery in journalism in a technology-deficient environment and in many other ways as posited by

What are the potential benefits of using AI to verify information and fact-check claims in a technology deficient environment?
59 responses

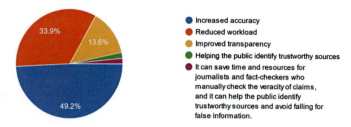

Fig. 2.4 Potential benefit of AI for fact-checking. (Source: Author)

How can AI be used to help journalists communicate complex information to the public in a way that is clear and engaging, even in a technology deficient environment?
59 responses

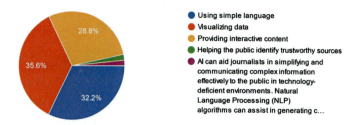

Fig. 2.5 Use of AI to communicate in a better way. (Source: Author)

the likes of Jaakkola (2023), Whittaker (2019), Guzman (2023) and Diab (2023). However, these prospects can be explored when the practitioners are aware of them and are skilled in the use of AI. With the recorded low level of experience in the use of AI as attested to by 77.4% of the respondents, it confirms that journalists and media practitioners in Nigeria are yet to fully take advantage of and integrate AI into the production process. The low level of experience may not be unconnected with other factors occasioned by the environment.

What are the potential challenges of using AI in journalism in a technology deficient environment?
57 responses

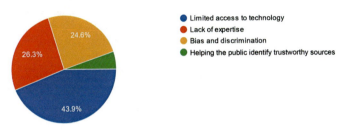

Fig. 2.6 Challenges associated with the use of in low-tech environment. (Source: Author)

CHALLENGES ASSOCIATED WITH AI JOURNALISM IN NIGERIA

Aside the low level of exposure and experience recorded from respondents presented in Fig. 2.1, there are other numerous challenges mentioned in the responses which inhibits or limits journalist from exploring this innovation. Some of the issues mentioned as shown in Fig. 2.6 had 57 responses; 43% of them agreed that limited access to technology is the greatest challenge to the use of AI in journalism in Nigeria, 27% said lack of expertise on the part of journalists and other media practitioners while 24.6% said bias and discrimination. From the responses, accessing the AI technology is a major challenge to media practitioners and journalists in Nigeria because it is capital intensive and as such unaffordable to many of them. The issue of expertise is a two-faced challenge of skill and finance. Accessing the required training costs money and time. Journalists in low-income countries of Africa and Nigeria prioritize livelihood and survival over other venture that may further plunge their meager income. This confirms the views expressed by Lopez et al. (2021), Guzman (2023), Aitamurto et al. (2019) and Lewis et al. (2019) separately that inadequate training, lack of access to technology and cost of procurement are the basic challenges that can be encountered by journalists and media practitioners in their bid to use AI in carrying out their duties especially in a low income and technology-deficient environment. Therefore, many do not really see the necessity or importance of additional skill at all costs. Bias and discrimination have to do with lack of accuracy of AI models in most instances. According to some of the respondents who have tried using AI to generate news story and produce media contents at different times said all data generated by AI models are highly inaccurate with unverifiable sources. A major deficiency on part of the technology. A situation described as dangerous and put the integrity of their organization on the line. These negative experiences have discouraged many others from exploring the technology, but these experiences may not be unconnected with the submissions of Dawson (2010), Broussard et al. (2019) and Whittaker (2019) that many journalists lacked the required skills in AI-powered tools, thereby recording errors and inaccuracies in their reporting. Nevertheless, the respondents believe some of these challenges are surmountable. As shown in Fig. 2.8, 54 respondents gave suggestions on how to address bias and discrimination; 46.3% of them recommend training of AI models on unbiased data, 37.7% suggest use of diverse data sets while 13% emphasize subjecting AI models to regular audit. These suggestions are in line with the submissions of Diad (2023), Carlson (2018) and Aitamurto et al. (2019). To achieve these recommendations, a lot of funding and expertise are required which are beyond the reach of average media organization and practitioners in Nigeria.

Ethical Concerns of AI-Powered Journalism in a Technology-Deficient Environment

Figures 2.7, 2.10 and 2.11 all addressed ethical issues related to use of AI in journalism in a technology-deficient environment. As shown in Fig. 2.10, 54 respondents mentioned ethical issues as it applied to their

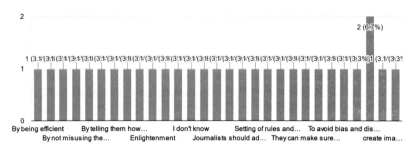

Fig. 2.7 Responsible use of AI in journalism delivery. (Source: Author)

What are some strategies for avoiding bias and discrimination in the use of AI in journalism?
54 responses

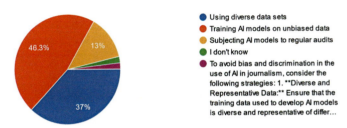

Fig. 2.8 Strategies to avoid bias and discrimination. (Source: Author)

How can journalists ensure that AI does not displace human journalists in a technology deficient environment?
55 responses

Fig. 2.9 How to ensure human relevance. (Source: Author)

various experiences. Three major concerns were raised in the following distribution: 44.4% of the 54 respondents mentioned issue of transparency and accountability, 24.15% said bias and discrimination while 20.4% said privacy. These three major concerns were part of the main challenges associated with the use of AI-powered tools in journalism as seen in Fig. 2.6 corroborating the views of Dawson (2010), Broussard et al. (2019) and Whittaker (2019), who further noted lack of skill on part of journalists as responsible for the bias, discriminations, inaccuracies and errors leading to ethical questions. Fig. 2.7 shows a wide range of responses given by 30 respondents on how journalists can use AI in a responsible and ethical manner in a technology-deficient environment; the responses were further recaptured in Fig. 2.11 as how journalist can build public trust using AI,

What are some of the ethical concerns surrounding the use of AI in journalism in a technology deficient environment?
54 responses

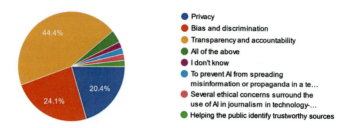

Fig. 2.10 Ethical concerns with the use of AI. (Source: Author)

How can journalists build public trust in the use of AI in journalism in a technology deficient environment?
53 responses

Fig. 2.11 How to build public trust in the use of AI. (Source: Author)

and 53 responses presented in the following distributions: 35.8% emphasized on the need to educate the public about AI. That is, journalists can make the public to accept AI-powered journalism through aggressive sensitization and enlightenment campaign on the benefits so that they become receptive to it. Besides, 32.1% said journalists must be transparent about the process of how AI is being used, and the public should be carried along in the stage by stage of how AI tools are involved in the content being served to them. This is a way to build public trust and gain forgiveness in case of any unforeseen error. Furthermore, 30.2% of the respondents said the public should be incorporated in the development of AI-powered journalism tools and platforms to imbibe in them that a sense of belonging as part of the process from the very beginning and thereby also taking part of the responsibility for any eventual error(s). Transparency on the part of the professionals goes a long way to earn public trust which might be unattainable when the process is shrouded in secrecy.

Future of AI-Powered Journalism in Nigeria

From the responses presented in the charts, the prospect for AI-powered journalism in Nigeria is high due to its ability to enhance efficiency and productivity as mentioned in Figs. 2.2, 2.3, 2.4 and 2.5. However, a lot has to be done in the area of sensitization to create awareness on the need to explore the numerous opportunities available with the use of AI-tools by journalists and media practitioners in the country. This is a way to fill the gap of low level of experience recorded in Fig. 2.1. In addition, journalists and media practitioners still have a lot do around training and skill acquisition in the use of AI, invest in AI related technology and make it accessible and affordable for all. It is also imperative to invest in training AI models on unbiased data, using of diverse data sets and subject AI models to regular audit to address the challenges associated with AI-powered tools such as inaccuracies and errors of bias and discriminations as presented in Figs. 2.6 and 2.8.

One important issue is the fear and concern that AI-powered journalism will lead to job loss in the media sector in future. As revealed in Fig. 2.9, AI cannot displace human beings, even though it can enhance performance and do more within a shorter period than humans. It must also be acknowledged that the technology depends on human beings to operate or be programmed for the system to work perfectly. As such, AI tools will serve a complementary purpose to human beings for improved performance and effective journalism delivery in a country like Nigeria. Having established this fact, we must focus on human-centered journalism by empowering journalists to acquire relevant skills and expertise in AI while using AI tools to augment. Embracing AI in journalism is inevitable and should be encouraged in Nigeria.

Conclusion

The prospect of AI-powered journalism in Nigeria is very high despite the low level of technical know-how. These prospects also have attendant challenges which could mar the entire production processes if not addressed.

Another major concern is the issue of job loss. That is, the chances of AI replacing humans at workplace especially in our media organizations. Replacing humans with AI for effective journalism delivery is considered a major risk as test cases resulted in fake algorithm, inaccuracies, bias and discrimination in data processed. For effective service delivery of AI-powered journalism, the role of humans remains sacrosanct to provide the lead and direction in the set courses of action to be able to achieve the desired result. Therefore, journalists and other professionals in the media sector must continue to engage in training and retraining exercises to acquire necessary expertise and update their knowledge from time to time to remain relevant in the discharge of their duties. Introduction of hybrid human-AI newsroom will be a better idea to eliminate the shortcomings associated with the use of AI. Government should also take the lead by providing supports and intervention in the procurement of technology and software packages needed for effective use of AI in service delivery. Regulations should be put in place and enforced to ensure responsible use of AI in journalism to protect the sanity of the target public, while offenders should be made to face the law and serve as deterrence to others.

References

Adeyemo, T. (2024). The Nigeria Media Landscape and Digital News Report. Reuters Institute for the Study of Journalism, University of Oxford. June. https://reutersinstitute.politics.ox.ac.uk/digital-news-report/2024/nigeria

Aitamurto, T., Ananny, M., Anderson, C. W., Birnbaum, L., Diakopoulos, N., Hanson, M., Hullman, J., & Ritchie, N. (2019). HCI for Accurate, Impartial and Transparent Journalism: Challenges and Solutions. In *Paper Presented at the 19th CHI Conference on Human Factors in Computing Systems*. https://dl.acm.org/citation.cfm?id=329907

Aluko-Olokun, A. (2023). With 740 Functional Broadcast Stations in Nigeria, Industry Craves for Reforms. Nigeria Democratic Report. February. https://www.ndr.org.ng/with-740-functional-broadcast-stations-in-nigeria-industry-craves-for-reforms/

American Press Institute. americanpressinstitute.org

Broussard, M., Diakopoulos, N., Guzman, A. L., Abebe, R., Dupagne, M., & Chuan, H. (2019, July). Artificial Intelligence and Journalism. *Journalism & Mass Communication Quaterly, 96* (3). https://doi.org/10.1177/1077699019859901

Calvo Rubio, L. M., & Ufarte Ruiz, M. J. (2021). Artificial Intelligence and Journalism: System Review of Scientific Production in Web of Science and Scopus (2088–2019). *Communication & Society, 34*(2), 159–176. https://doi.org/10.15581/003.34.2.159-176. www.communication-society.com

Carlson, M. (2015). The Robotic Reporter. Digital. *Journalism, 3*(3), 416–431. https://doi.org/10.1080/21670811.2014.976412

Carlson, M. (2018). The Information Politics of Journalism in a Post-Truth Age. *Journalism Studies, 19*(13), 1879–1888. https://doi.org/10.1080/1461670x.2018.1494513

Copeland, B. J. (2024, January 4). Connectionism. *Encyclopedia Britannica*. Retrieved March 19, 2024, from https://www.britannica.com/technology/connectionism-artificial-intelligence

Crichton, D., Christel, B., Shidham, A., Valderrama, A., & Karmel, J. (2010). Journalism in the Digital Age. A Project for CS181. Stanford University, California. November. https://cs.stanford.edu/people/erobert/cs181/project

Davie, G. (2020, July). Gatekeeping Theory of Mass Communication. Mass Communication Theory: Theoretical Overviews. https://masscommtheory.com/theory-overview/gatekeeping-theory/

Dawson, R. (2010, April 15). The Rise of Robotic Journalists. Ross Dawson. https://cutt.ly/jtiCpbX

de-Lima-Santos, M.-F., & Ceron, W. (2022). Artificial Intelligence in News Media: Current Perceptions and Future Outlook. *Journal and Media, 3*(1), 13–26. https://doi.org/10.3390/journalmedia3010002

Dimiter, D. (2020, November). AI – What is this. A Definition of Artificial Intelligence. *PC Magazine*. Bulgaria. www.dobrev.com

Google's English Dictionary. Oxford Languages. https://languages.oup.com/google-dictionar-en/

Guzman, A. L. (2019, November). Prioritizing the Audience's View of Automation in Journalism. *Digital Journalism, 7*(11), 1–6. https://doi.org/10.1080/21670811.2019.1681902

Guzman, A. L. (2023). Talking about "Talking with Machines": Interview as Method within HMC. In *The SAGE Handbook of Human-Machine Communication*. SAGE Publishing. https://doi.org/10.4135/9781529782783.n3. https://www.researchgate.net/publication/371938940_Talking_about_Talking_with_Machines_Interview_as_Method_within_HMC

Jaakkola, M. (2023). Reporting on Artificial Intelligence: A Handbook for Journalism Educators. UNESCO. Unesdoc.unesco.org. https://unesco.org/ark:/48223/pf0000384551

40 A. O. AYOOLA

Khaled Diab. (2023). What future for journalism in the age of AI. https://www.aljazeera.com/author/khaled_diab_201412288346311720/

Kothani, A., & Cruikshank, S. A. (2022). Artificial Intelligence and Journalism: An Agenda for Journalism Research in Africa. *African Journal Studies, 43*(1), 17–33. https://doi.org/10.1080/23743670.2021.1999840

Kperogi, F. (2022, July). *Digital Dissidence and Social Media Censorship in Africa.* Routledge. https://doi.org/10.4324/9781003276326

Lewis, S. C., Guzman, A. L., & Schmidt, T. R. (2019, April). Automation, Journalism, and Human-Machine Communication: Rethinking Roles and Relationships of Humans and Machines in News. *Digital Journalism, 7*(2), 1–19. https://doi.org/10.1080/21670811.2019.1577147

Lopez, M. T., Fieiras-Ceide, C., & Martin, V.-A. (2021, January). Impact of Artificial Intelligence on Journalism: Transformations in the Company, Products, Contents and Professional Profile. *Communication y Sociedad. Universadad de Navrra, 34*(1), 177–193. https://doi.org/10.15581/003

Merrill, J. C. (2011). Journalism and Democracy. In W. Lowrey & P. J. Gade (Eds.), *Changing the News: The Forces Shaping Journalism in Uncertain Times.* Routledge.

Micheal, K., & Aaron, R. (2019). *The Ethical Algorithm.* Oxford University Press.

Oguntola, T. (2023). National Broadcasting Commission Approves 67 New Broadcast Stations, Fines 17, Sanctions 302. Leadership.ng. https://leadership.ng/nbc-approves-67-new-broadcast-stations-fines-17-sanctions-302/#:~:text=The%20directors%20general%2C%20Ntional%20Broad casting,functional%20broadcast%20stion%20in%20Nigeria

Olajide, I. F., & Olanrewaju, M. M. (2022). Challenges of Digital Broadcasting in Nigeria. *Global Journal of Education, Humanities & Management Sciences, 4*(2) https://www.gojehms.com/index.php/GOJEHMS/article/view/152/0

Parrat-Fernandez, S., Mayoral-Sanchez, J., & Mera-Fernandez, M. (2021). The Application of Artificial Intelligence to Journalism: An Analysis of Academic Production. *Profesional de la informacion, 30*(3), e300317. https://doi.org/10.3145/epi.2021.may.17

Patching, R., & Hirst, M. (2021, August). Journalism Ethics at the Crossroads: Democracy, Fake News, and the News Crisis. https://doi.org/10.4324/9780429242892

Rashedi, H. (2020). *Exploring the Future of Modern Journalism with Artificial Intelligence.* MEDCOM.

Ryfe, D. (2019). The Ontology of Journalism. Sage Journals. https://journals.sagepub.com

Sacco, J. (2012). Journalism. Jonathan Cape. Bibtex, books.googl.com.ng

Shoemaker, P. J., & Vos, T. P. (2009). *Gatekeeping Theory.* Routledge. ISBN 978-0-41-598139-2

UNCTAD. (2023). Trade: Unlocking sustainable strategies for people, planet and prosperity. https://unctad.org/publication/annual-report-2023

Von Weltzien Hoivik, H. (2002). Professional Ethics- A Managerial Opportunity in Emerging Organisations. *Academia.* https://www.academia.edu/18432291/Professional-Ethics-a-Managerial-Opportunity-in-Emerging-Organisation

Whittaker, J. (2019). *Tech Giants, Artificial Intelligence and the Future of Journalism* (Routledge Research in Journalism). Taylor & Francis Group. https://www.routledge.com

CHAPTER 3

Shaping Journalism Futures: A Call for Contextualised Technology Adoption

Eric Noel Mtemang'ombe and Francis Chikunkhuzeni

INTRODUCTION

Quandt and Singer declared that the internet had heralded a new form of journalism that would involve journalists producing content across different platforms. In this novel form of journalism, a cohort of technical-savvy journalists imbued with the competence to produce content for different media platforms would produce content that "is both distinct from other forms of digital content and integrated with those forms to a far greater extent that is either the past or present" (Quandt & Singer, 2009, p. 141). The prediction typifies the optimism that previous researchers (Deuze, 2004; Domingo et al., 2007) had made that the internet as a convergent media platform would create unique opportunities for journalists to incorporate the unique features of the online medium such as hyperlinks and multimedia to create more compelling, user-friendly, and interactive

---

E. N. Mtemang'ombe (✉) • F. Chikunkhuzeni
Department of Journalism and Media Studies, Malawi University of Business and Applied Sciences, Blantyre, Malawi
e-mail: ericnoeljr@gmail.com; fchikunkhuzeni@mubas.ac.mw

© The Author(s), under exclusive license to Springer Nature Switzerland AG 2025
A. Sharra, U. Akpojivi (eds.), *Technologies and Media Production Cultures*, Palgrave Studies in Journalism and the Global South,
https://Doi.org/10.1007/978-3-031-78582-5_3

content. These predictions largely assumed that digitalisation of journalism would inevitably transform journalism.

However, contemporary research (Cui & Liu, 2017; Doudaki & Spyridou, 2015; Jacobson, 2010; Steensen, 2011) shows that journalists have not embraced or adopted the use of technology in the way envisioned by the early media theorists. Evidence suggests that across different cultures and professional environments digitalisation in the media is a gradual process that is influenced by several factors.

Nonetheless, a similar scholarship hype about the revolution in journalism has resurfaced with the advancement of Artificial Intelligence and Machine Learning and the potential applications to journalism practice. This chapter advances an argument that while change or continuity assumes both temporal and spatial dimensions, journalism futures should be informed by institutional and contextual factors that determine the adaptation of emerging technologies. This argument is based on a case study aimed at analysing journalists' computer self-efficacy and organisational factors that influence the adoption of the multimedia and hypertext features of the internet in Malawi. To achieve this, the study analysed the extent to which online journalists in Malawi use the hypermedia features afforded by the internet; how the journalists' levels of multimedia production skills influence their use and adoption; and how organisational factors influence application to news products.

The first section of the chapter provides an introduction to studies of technology adoption to highlight the factors that have been advanced to predict, determine, or influence technology adoption. The second presents a model for conceptualising digitalisation and journalism.

The third section explains how the Unified Theory of Use and Acceptance of Technology (UTAUT) as a theoretical framework provides a testable model for analysing the relationship between digitalisation and technological adoption among journalists. The chapter then reports on the findings of the case study of Malawian online journalism to illustrate how institutional and contextual factors are essential in predicting the adoption of technologies in media practice.

Digitalisation and Technology Adoption

The nexus between innovation and adoption has been theorised since the nineteenth century where some of the notable include Modernisation, Diffusion of Innovation, Reasoned Action, Technology Acceptance,

Behavioural and Social Communication, and Motivational and Social Cognition theories. In online journalism (Deuze, 2004; Domingo et al., 2007) postulated that digitalisation would herald a total transformation of journalism practice. But digitalisation in this context, through the development of the internet as a convergent media platform, occurred but the radical transformation to journalism practice that the early media theorists predicted has been contested.

Early media theorists hypothesised that the use of hypermedia would improve user comprehension and information retention (Palacios & Noci, 2009; Larrondo Ureta & Diaz Noci, 2014) as well as give the journalist opportunities to find innovative ways of improving storytelling (Steensen, 2011). They also hypothesised that the use of hyperlinks would help online journalists transition from their traditional role of information providers and gatekeepers to the more dynamic roles of information managers (Quandt & Singer, 2009; Stroobant, 2019; Cui & Liu, 2017).

As a way of measuring the adoption of technology in journalism practice, a cybermedia typology was advanced by García-Orosa et al. (2005) and Palacios and Noci (2009). They proposed that the adoption of the internet as a convergent media platform could be measured by the extent to which journalists utilise its four main features of hypertextuality, hypermediality, interactivity, and immediacy or instantaneity (Palacios & Noci, 2009; Quandt & Singer, 2009). In this theorisation, journalists would be considered to be avid users of the internet and their adoption of the new media technology complete, if they incorporated multiple media elements (audio, infographics, text, video, slideshows, and animations) in their news narratives (Deuze, 2004; Quandt & Singer, 2009) and used hyperlinks to break linearity in the reading patterns (Cui & Liu, 2017; Ryfe et al., 2016; Stroobant, 2019).

However, research (Doudaki & Spyridou, 2015; Jacobson, 2010; Steensen, 2011) suggests that these early theorisations of journalism and digitalisation were idealistic. In their study of Spanish online publications *elconfidencial.com*, *eldiario.es*, *elpais.com*, and *elmundo.es*, Palau-Sampio and Sánchez-García (2020) found that there was high usage of hypertext, but noted that multimedia elements were only used as "a mere extension of the written word, and not as the main narrative format". Hypertextuality was included in 90.3% of the news pieces in the media analysed in this work and 86.8% of the stories reviewed used one form of multimedia (Palau-Sampio & Sánchez-García, 2020). However, they noted that the use of "[hypermedia] resources are primarily automatic and repetitive, more as a response to fashions or trends in audio-visual consumption rather than a prior reflection on how to use them in a complementary and enriching way".

Jacobson (2010, pp. 69–70) also found that *The New York Times* rarely uses links for "non-sequential writing", with database narratives only appearing in the "most dilute form of the packages in this study" and could be applied, if at all, "only to the database of multimedia packages as a whole". Incidentally, in their study of the websites of Colombian newspapers *El Tiempo* and *El Espectador*, Fondevila-Gascón and Segura (2012) found that none of the newspapers analysed included links to related or in-depth content. However, 35% of the newspapers included links to other content in the informative section where the news was found (Fondevila-Gascón & Segura, 2012). The findings supported Quandt's (2008) observation that the copy-and-paste principle is largely acceptable and most of the content published on many of the news sites, especially the smaller ones, was "shovelware" (Doudaki & Spyridou, 2015, p. 6). They also found that when a video is embedded in a story, it is either produced by a media partner of the media house or accessed from freely accessible sources such as YouTube. In both cases, "the videos are not re-edited for the online edition's needs but rather inserted as a mere indication of multimedia content", rendering the "material redundant since it is not conducive to further production of meaning by providing new information or adding different aspects of the story" (Doudaki & Spyridou, 2015, p. 8). The analysis also revealed that most of the links analysed in the story tend to be common when "generated through automated procedures offered via the architecture of the news platform [for instance, links to the latest news or links to news of the same category]" (Doudaki & Spyridou, 2015, pp. 9–10). However, the frequency of links dropped dramatically when journalists took extra time and effort to develop the links.

The sporadic use of the technological affordances—hyperlinks and multimedia—offered by news websites has prompted media scholars (Doudaki & Spyridou, 2015; Duffy & Ang, 2019; Jacobson, 2010) to conclude that the internet has not radically revolutionised journalism. The transformative effect of digital technologies on news presentation on online media is overstated. Research seems to discredit the notion that the development of online journalism can only be measured by its degree of adaptability to the unique features of the internet: hypertextuality, hypermediality, interactivity, and frequency of updating as espoused by García-Orosa et al. (2005) and Palacios and Noci (2009).

While online journalism's growing popularity cannot be contested, its "heralded innovative and transformative power to regenerate and redefine journalism has been embraced with less unanimity in contemporary media scholarship" (Doudaki & Spyridou, 2015, p. 2). Doudaki and Spyridou (2015) noted that normative theorists put technology at the core of their discourse; hence, they would either predict revolution or detect failure, comparing what technology could offer and what journalists were failing to achieve. Currently, the emergence of new technologies, such as Artificial Intelligence and Machine Learning, has re-ignited a form of media scholarship hype that predicts that these emerging technologies will have a transformative effect on journalism practice.

DIGITALISATION AND JOURNALISM: A NEW APPROACH TO AN OLD PROBLEM

The failure of the early techno-optimistic conceptualisations of digital journalism, including online journalism, to accurately explain and predict the transformative effect of the internet on journalism practice necessitates the development of a new framework to explain how journalism is evolving to adapt to emerging technologies such as the internet while accounting for the determinants that influence the adoption of emerging technologies (Duffy & Ang, 2019; Robinson et al., 2019; Zelizer, 2019). Two approaches emerge. Robinson et al. (2019) argue for an approach that studies the way mobile technology, social media, and other digital platforms are reconstituting the media ecology to create new forms of "networked news", while Duffy and Ang (2019) favour an approach that explores how "digitisation finds an incarnation in journalism" instead of being overly concerned with how digitisation impacts journalism. Studying digital journalism as an amalgamation of two concepts—digital and journalism—allows for a more comprehensive study of the phenomena that accurately presents technology as an integral part of the practice of journalism (Zelizer, 2019) without obscuring that they are fundamentally separate.

Zelizer (2019, p. 344) argues that defining journalism in conjunction with its technology ends up confusing the early techno-optimistic conceptualisations (Deuze, 2004; Domingo et al., 2007) with the current iteration of scholarly research that presupposes a limited influence of technology on journalism practice (Doudaki & Spyridou, 2015; Jacobson, 2010; Steensen, 2011). Zelizer (2019) argues:

> This is problematic for three reasons: it obscures the fact that technology is always incrementally changing journalism; it blinds us to the detrimental effects of technological change; and it fosters forgetting of what stays stable in journalism across changing technological modalities. (Zelizer, 2019, p. 344)

She opines that "applauding journalism's technological dimensions can distract attention from existing deficits" as this "simplifies one's grasp of technology and magnifies its celebration in unjustified ways" (Zelizer, 2019, p. 345).

Duffy and Ang (2019) also propose a definition of digital journalism that begins with digital and ends with journalism. In this conceptualisation, "digital journalism is not journalism that is transformed by being digital; it is digitisation as it is embodied in journalism" (Duffy & Ang, 2019, p. 378).

Duffy and Ang (2019) argue that a starting point for defining digitalisation should focus on "the way many domains of social life are restructured around digital communication and media infrastructures". Such an approach would help address the limitations of the "newsroom-first" method adopted by the early media theorists which posited that "digitisation brings opportunities to journalism that have not yet been realised" (Duffy & Ang, 2019).

Duffy and Ang (2019, p. 382) argue:

> Rather than being concerned with how digitisation impacts journalism, the question becomes how digitisation finds an incarnation in journalism. This involves losing the normative accretions surrounding journalism and starting from the principles of digitisation as articulated through the news media.

The conceptualisations presented by Duffy and Ang (2019) and Zelizer (2019) have different starting points for focusing the study of digital journalism, but both propose a model that studies how the development of digital technologies is influencing journalism practice.

Furthermore, Orben (2020, p. 1149) favours an approach that focuses on the "technological affordances which allow for insights to be translated between different types of technologies by examining the activities that they allow users to perform". She notes:

> Such an approach is promising because technologies are ever-evolving, and it is therefore not very useful to study separate technologies as separate entities or redesign theories for each new development.

The convergent point is their collective focus on digitalisation as it is incorporated into journalism. This viewpoint seeks to mitigate the limitations of the conceptualisations of early media theorists which presupposed that digitalisation will transform, that is, "change the state of journalism into another, the altering of sets of norms, and the introduction of new routines" (Robinson et al., 2019), by replacing it with a model that explores how digitalisation is incorporated in journalism and extends journalism practice (Duffy & Ang, 2019). It is, therefore, preferred to adopt an approach that is open to accounts for the interaction between digital technologies and the practice of journalism and how the two shape and influence each other.

UNIFIED THEORY OF ACCEPTANCE AND USE OF TECHNOLOGY

In a bid to explore how digitalisation relates to journalism practice, several theories have been applied, including the Theory of Reasoned Action (TRA) Technology Acceptance Model (TAM), Innovations Diffusion Theory (IDT), Model of PC Utilisation (MPCU), Motivational Model (MM), and Social Cognitive Theory (SCT). After considering the strengths and limitations of these theories, a unified theoretical model was developed to take into account intrinsic and extrinsic factors that interact to shape behaviour change towards the adoption of technology. The Unified Theory of Acceptance and Use of Technology (UTAUT) developed by Venkatesh et al. (2003) provides an eclectic theoretical framework that is built on the consolidation of constructs from several models used in international research. It resonates with journalism scholarship that takes factors related to the capacity of journalists and external agency to explain the adoption of technology by journalists in digital environments (Fig. 3.1).

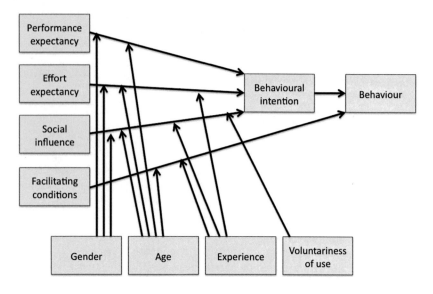

Fig. 3.1 UTAUT model. (Source: Venkatesh et al., 2003)

Background to the Theory

The Unified Theory of Acceptance and Use of Technology (Venkatesh et al., 2003) is a theoretical model that synthesised different postulates of previous technology acceptance models to create an integrated theory that could offer a framework for a holistic analysis of technology acceptance. The UTAUT combines elements from the Theory of Reasoned Action, the Technology Acceptance Model, the Motivational Model, the Theory of Planned Behaviour, the Model of PC Utilisation, the Innovation Diffusion Theory, and the Social Cognitive Theory. Venkatesh et al. (2003, p. 467) note that:

> Thus, UTAUT is a definitive model that synthesizes what is known and provides a foundation to guide future research in [technology adoption studies]. By encompassing the combined explanatory power of the individual models and key moderating influences, UTAUT advances cumulative theory while retaining a parsimonious structure.

The theory was developed to mitigate against the weaknesses of the other models, which could not adequately explain all the factors that influence professionals to adopt technology in their work settings. Venkatesh et al. (2003) observed that the previous models were "quite successful in predicting technology usage behaviour", but there was a requirement to consider a complex range of "potential moderating influences" to glean a more comprehensive picture of the "dynamic nature of individual perceptions about technology". Venkatesh et al. (2003, p. 470) wrote:

> Despite the ability of the existing models to predict intention and usage, current theoretical perspectives on individual acceptance are notably weak in providing prescriptive guidance to designers.

The theory presents four constructs: performance expectancy, effort expectancy, social influence, and facilitating conditions as predictors and/or drivers of technology usage.

The Constructs of the UTAUT

Performance Expectancy

Performance expectancy is defined as "the degree to which an individual believes that using the system will help him or her to attain gains in job performance" (Venkatesh et al., 2003, p. 447). Performance expectancy measures the end-user's improvement through the use of the system, the enhancement of productivity, the positive impacts on performance, and the technology's use for companies and employees (Angulo, 2015).

Venkatesh et al. (2003, p. 447) observed that the performance expectancy construct within the individual acceptance models "is the strongest predictor of intention and remains significant at all points of measurement in both voluntary and mandatory settings". The authors also theorised that performance expectancy would be moderated by age and gender.

Effort Expectancy

Effort expectancy is defined as the "degree of ease associated with the use of the system" (Venkatesh et al., 2003, p. 450). The theorists posited that effort-oriented constructs "are expected to be more salient in the early

52   E. N. MTEMANG'OMBE AND F. CHIKUNKHUZENI

stages of new behaviour when process issues represent hurdles to be overcome, and later become overshadowed by instrumentality concerns" (Venkatesh et al., 2003, p. 450). Angulo (2015) notes that effort expectancy measures the end-users' perceived ease of use, ability to interact with the system without inducing stress, and the importance of using the system.

Social Influence

Venkatesh et al. (2003, p. 451) defined social influence as "the degree to which an individual perceives important peers believe he or she should use the new system". In this conceptualisation, the theory postulates that the "individual's behaviour is influenced by how they believe others will view them as a result of having used the technology" (Venkatesh et al., 2003, p. 451). Social influence measures the end-users' capacity to use the technology's usefulness to coworkers, their use by coworkers, and the perceived level of encouragement from managers to use the technology (Angulo, 2015).

Venkatesh et al. (2003, p. 451) observed that the constructs under social influence constructs "contains the explicit or implicit notion that the individual's behaviour is influenced by how they believe others will view them as a result of having used the technology". The underlying assumption is that people will use the technology if they believe that the usage will improve how they are perceived by their viewers (Angulo, 2015). Nonetheless, Venkatesh et al. (Venkatesh et al., 2003, p. 452) note that "social influence constructs are not significant in voluntary contexts, but they become significant when use is mandated".

Facilitating Conditions

Facilitating conditions are defined as "the degree to which an individual believes that an organisational and technical infrastructure exists to support the use of the system" (Venkatesh et al., 2003, p. 453). The facilitating conditions measure the end-user's knowledge to use the system, the availability of the system and the technology's potential to seamlessly fit with the organisation's corporate culture (Angulo, 2015).

Venkatesh et al. (2003, p. 453) operationalised the constructs that were adopted into the facilitating conditions to "include aspects of the technological and/or organisation barriers that are designed to remove barriers to use". Venkatesh and Davis (2000) demonstrated that issues related to the support infrastructure are largely captured within the effort expectancy construct which taps the ease with which that tool can be applied. Note that this presupposed that support infrastructure is a core concept within the facilitating conditions construct.

In summary, the model postulates that journalists are more likely to adopt and use technology if they believe that it will improve their performance, it will be easy for them to learn the skills that would be required to use the technology and if there will be an extrinsic reward either in the form of approval from supervisors or more professional recognition from their peer. If the institution the journalists work for provides the technology and technical support to complement the intention to use the technology, then journalists will use the technology.

Hence, it is a theoretical model that allows for a holistic and comprehensive analysis of the relationship between digitalisation and journalistic transformation in a way that the cybermedia typology could not. The analytical framework under the UTAUT allows researchers to factor in the journalists' agency and the institutional factors that shape their professional norms and their role conceptualisations within their work environments.

Methods

The study that informed this chapter used quantitative methods. Content analysis and survey research were used to investigate the extent of technology adoption and the factors that determine technology adoption, respectively. Content analysis data was analysed using a combination of frequencies and binomial tests. To analyse the factors that determine or predict technology adoption, the study used a combination of correlation, bivariate regression and multiple linear regression.

Malawi has recognised ten dedicated news websites: Platform for Investigative Journalism (PIJ), *Malawi Voice, Maravi Post, Nyasa Times, Africa Brief, Kulinji, Nation Online, Times Online,* Malawi Broadcasting Corporation (MBC) Online and Malawi Institute of Journalism (MIJ) Online, and Zodiak Online. These are registered with the Media Institute of Southern Africa-Malawi Chapter (MISA-Malawi) and the Media Council of Malawi, and their websites are dedicated to the presentation of news.

FINDINGS

An analysis of sampled online stories established that there is low usage of the hypermedia features on Malawian news sites. The study also established that performance expectancy, social influence, and facilitating conditions are significant predictors of behavioural intentions. However, when regressed collectively, social influence becomes insignificant. Likewise, facilitating conditions are a significant predictor of actual usage, while behavioural intentions are not.

The study found that the rate of technology adoption (hypermedia features) is very low. The analysis showed that out of the 426 stories analysed, 3.5% used links, 1.6% used infographics, and 0.7% used video. None of the stories analysed used animations, slideshows, and audio. On average, only 2.46% of the stories analysed had a hypermedia element (link, audio, video, slideshow, infographics, and animations). This means that there is low adoption of hypermedia when presenting news on online news platforms. Therefore, the study concluded that the rate of technology adoption by Malawian journalists is very low despite the presence of the technology and push from most major media institutions to establish a digital presence. The evidence is consistent with the findings from other studies (Cui & Liu, 2017; Hargittai et al., 2019; Jacobson, 2010; Palau-Sampio & Sánchez-García, 2020; Steensen, 2011) that digitalisation does not have an inevitable and immediate transformative impact on journalism practice. It is an evolutionary process that is gradual and does not manifest itself in the way envisioned by the techno-optimists.

Nonetheless, it was important to ascertain the factors that influence the journalists' adoption of the technology or lack of it. The second phase of the study, survey research involving 67 journalists selected from 13 media institutions found that performance expectancy (B = 0.347, p = 0.006), social influence (B = 0.301, p = 0.013) and facilitating conditions (B = 0.324, p = 0.008) have a positive and significant effect on the formation of behavioural intention.

In terms of the factors that predict and influence technology adoption, the study found that independently, performance expectancy (B = 0.347, p = 0.006) and social influence (B = 0.301, p = 0.013) have a significant influence on behavioural intention. However, when analysed collectively, only performance expectancy (B = 0.337, p = 035) has a significant predictive value on behavioural intention. The analysis further found the variable Facilitating Conditions has a significant predictive value on actual usage.

The predictive value was significant when performance expectancy was regressed independently (B = 0.345, p = 0.006) and when it was regressed alongside the behavioural intention (B = 0.319, p = 0.16). The second set of findings shows that journalists are more likely to adopt digital technologies if they believe that using the technology will improve their performance, there will be an intrinsic reward from their professional peers and there is the technology and technical support to facilitate the transition to a more digital form of journalism.

DISCUSSION

The study confirmed that the use of hypermedia features in Malawi's media was significantly low. The findings reaffirmed the findings of previous research (Doudaki & Spyridou, 2015; Jacobson, 2010; Quandt & Singer, 2009; Steensen, 2011; Stroobant, 2019) which found that the use of hyperlinks and multimedia was lower than theorised by the early media theorists (Deuze, 2004; Domingo et al., 2007).

These findings suggest that the current wave of optimism that followed the development of generative Artificial Intelligence and Machine Learning might not have a transformative effect as the new wave of media scholarship seems to suggest.

ARTIFICIAL INTELLIGENCE AND MACHINE LEARNING IN THE NEWSROOM

The generative text features of Artificial Intelligence and the adaptability offered by Machine Learning have created a new wave of optimism and panic surrounding the evolution of journalism. The techno-optimists see an opportunity that AI could be used to research news topics, write copy, and help edit news content (Cantor, 2023). On the other hand, dystopian theorists believe that AI's potential for auto-generative text and capacity to produce deep fakes could lead to the proliferation of fake news and harmful content (Orben, 2020; Walsh, 2020).

Unfortunately, the development of AI and Machine Learning, despite their vast potential to enhance journalism practice, has been met with apprehension from both professional journalists and other social actors within the journalism value chain. Walsh (2020, p. 848) noted the "use of artificial intelligence and bots to mimic human users and perform simple, structurally repetitive, tasks—to spread 'computational propaganda' ". He wrote:

> As social machines and artificial voices, bots automate and accelerate diffusion and engagement, creating, liking, sharing, and following content at rates vastly surpassing human capabilities. (Walsh, 2020, p. 848)

The potential of AI and Machine Learning to shape contemporary communication is immense. Nonetheless, it would be academic folly to assume that the changes it induces in the foreseeable future will be as immense and direct as postulated by the techno-optimists or the dystopian theorists. The findings of this study, like prior literature on digitalisation and technology adoption, suggest that the effect will be gradual and possibly limited.

FACTORS THAT AFFECT TECHNOLOGY ADOPTION

The early theorisations of media convergence and the new conceptualisations of AI and Machine Learning do not account for the influence of professional inertia in contemporary newsrooms. Previous research (Doudaki & Spyridou, 2015; Lischka et al., 2022) showed that the journalists' level of technical skill in interactive multimedia production (Hargittai et al., 2019) and access to technology influences the level of adoption of hypermedia in modern journalism practice, and, by extension, their advertised transformative effects on journalism. This calls for further exploration of the factors that limit the adoption of hypermedia technologies.

Access to Technology and Level of Skill

The study found that Facilitating Conditions (FC) have a significant and positive influence on technology adoption. This reaffirms the findings of previous studies which showed that access to technology and the technical competencies of the personnel determine the adoption and use of technology in any profession, including in journalism practice (Hargittai et al., 2019; Jamil, 2022). Jamil (2022) proposes a multifaceted approach to studying and analysing the way the digital divide can influence how journalists use and adopt and incorporate technologies in their work. Drawing on the work of Mabweazara (2015), she argues that there are two levels to the digital divide; the first refers to the journalists' access to technology, while the second level explores how the skills use the internet and the unique opportunities it offers to transform journalism or lack of, prevents a smooth transition to digital journalism practice (Jamil, 2022).

In his study of Pakistani new media, Jamil (2022) found that access to the internet and the web by journalists, especially within their newsrooms, has become a ubiquitous necessity for the survival of journalism as a profession (Jamil, 2022). She observed that newsrooms without access to the technology required to develop multimedia content have historically struggled to use hypermedia technologies in their news stories.

Digital skills are also considered "equally critical for professional survival in an increasingly e-permeated society" (Njuguna, 2020). The differences in academic background, prior employment, and living situation further impact technology adoption and use (Hargittai et al., 2019; Kroon & Eriksson, 2019).

In his research on online journalism, employment and the transformation of job skills, Cetinkaya (2017) argues that:

> Despite the fact that the journalism profession remains essentially the same, the changes in terms of the platform and the fact that they are now predominantly technology-driven make it necessary for employees to acquire new skills. (cited in Çatal, 2017, p. 7464)

Journalists proficient in the production of news for legacy media (newspapers, radio, and television) have to learn have to learn new skills to produce content for a platform that they have no technical knowledge or experience. For example, a journalist with specialisation and extensive experience in developing news for print media—newspapers and magazines—will have to learn video editing, graphic design, and audio production to produce video and audio for online media (Çatal, 2017; Steensen, 2011).

Previous research (Hargittai et al., 2019; Jamil, 2022) shows that when there is a knowledge gap, journalists will not develop content for media platforms that they are not comfortable with.

Professional Inertia

The fact that the study found there was a positive and significant influence between social influence and behavioural intentions further supports the study's hypothesis that organisational factors influence journalists' adoption of technology. Specifically, the study theorised that journalists' familiarity with the traditional media and its news production techniques could undermine their capacity to use the features of the new/online media. Jacobson (2010, p. 74) observed that the low adoption of hypermedia features and the prevalence of shovelware strategies might be influenced by the notion that journalists first produce content for their parent media and share it on online media. Journalists prefer producing content for the platform they are most familiar with. In this context, the content of the online platforms would reflect the content produced by the original platform such as the newspaper.

Doudaki and Spyridou (2015, p. 13) also noted that the "copy and paste" or shovelware format adopted by most online media organisations might be "an attempt to promote cost-effective employment schemes used to limit labour costs, and allow for the reproduction of hard and prestigious news from the legacy newspapers on their websites". The inertia, or resistance to adapting digital technologies, has manifested even when media institutions recruit "editorial technologists" to facilitate the transition to a more robust use of hypermedia (Lischka et al., 2022).

Kosterich (2020) notes that "structural and cultural struggles persist even in newsrooms where editorial technologists have accumulated cultural capital" (cited in (Lischka et al., 2022). The editorial technologists intend to use their "computational skills and related agency to shape journalistic practices, co-create new editorial guidelines and, most importantly, to re-negotiate how journalistic values such as impartiality" are usually frustrated, particularly when journalistic doxa, defined as deeply internalised self-evident understandings of how things ought to be and how they ought to be done, are inherited from the larger professional group of "old school" journalists in editorial offices (Lischka et al., 2022).

The group of tech-savvy journalists surveyed in the research (Lischka et al., 2022) reported that:

> Traditional and "old school" journalists don't necessarily see us [tech-savvy editorial technologists] the same way, aren't listening to the ideas, and the rest of the newsroom doesn't always know about technologists' work in a project. The journalists have instant credibility whereas a developer doesn't have kind of that built-in credibility. (Lischka et al., 2022)

The evidence (Lischka et al., 2022; Kosterich, 2020; Stalph, 2020) suggests that professional inertia can undermine the adoption of online technologies even when the media institution has the technology and a core group of tech-savvy journalists and information technology specialists at its disposal to use multimedia and hyperlinks effectively.

This suggests that journalists are more likely to adopt and use technology in their news stories if their organisations invest in the technology and hire competent personnel to provide technical support in the use of the technology. When technology and technical support are absent, journalists will not use the technology even if they have an intention to use the technology.

This is partly consistent with the postulates of the UTAUT and findings from previous studies (Ahmad, 2014; Venkatesh et al., 2016; Venkatesh et al., 2003).

However, it diverges from Venkatesh et al.'s (2003) original conceptualisation which suggested that journalists' access to technology would not be a strong and significant predictor of technology adoption when the journalist's perception of the technology's capacity to improve their performance and perceived ease to learn the system is present.

Using the data available in the analysis there isn't sufficient evidence to make a definitive conclusion on the relationship between the three variables.

CONCLUSION

In conclusion, journalism scholarship should not presuppose that the emergence of new technologies will radically transform journalism practice. As Orben (Orben, 2020, p. 1149) observed: "Although people are very proficient at developing technological changes, it is a lot more difficult to determine whether these changes might influence our complex social system". Those changes will take place in a system with a complex set of organisational and institutional factors, professional cultures, and work environments. The scholarship on digitalisation and technology adoption should focus on the factors that determine technology adoption to predict how journalists may integrate said technologies into their work. Only then will the field advance and produce research that builds on the lessons from past research and advances the field of journalism and digitalisation.

REFERENCES

Ahmad, M. I. (2014, December). Unified Theory of Acceptance and Use of Technology: A Decade of Validation and Development. https://www.researchgate.net/publication/270282896_Unified_Theory_of_Acceptance_and_Use_of_Technology_UTAUT_A_Decade_of_Validation_and_Development

Angulo, N. (2015). Smart Working Environments, Possible Future Scenarios, and Technology Adoption Implications. https://doi.org/10.13140/RG.2.1.2520.2088.

Cantor, M. (2023, May 8). Nearly 50 News Websites Are 'AI-Generated', a Study Says. Would I Be Able to Tell? (blog). *The Guardian*. https://www.theguardian.com/technology/2023/may/08/ai-generated-news-websites-study.

Çetinkaya, A. (2017). Basın işletmelerinde çevrimiçi gazetecilik ile istihdam ve işgücü becerilerinin dönüşümü, *Akademia, 5*(1), 380–398.

Çatal, Ö. (2017). New Technologies Challenging the Practice of Journalism and The Impact of Education: Case of Northern Cyprus. *EURASIA Journal of Mathematics, Science and Technology Education, 13*(11), 10.12973/ejmste/79975.

Cui, X., & Liu, Y. (2017). How Does Online News Curate Linked Sources? A Content Analysis of Three Online News Media. *Journalism, 18*(7), 852–870. https://doi.org/10.1177/1464884916663621

Deuze, M. (2004). What Is Multimedia Journalism? *Journalism Studies, 5*(2), 139–152. https://doi.org/10.1080/1461670042000211131

Domingo, D., Aguado, M., Cabrera, Mª. A, Edo, C., Masip, P., Meso, K.... Avilés, J. A. G. (2007). Four Dimensions of Journalistic Convergence: A Preliminary Approach to Current Media Trends in Spain. In *8th International Symposium on Online Journalism*.

Doudaki, V., & Spyridou, L.-P. (2015). News Content Online: Patterns and Norms under Convergence Dynamics. *Journalism, 16*(2), 257–277. https://doi.org/10.1177/1464884913517657

Duffy, A., & Ang, P. H. (2019). Digital Journalism: Defined, Refined, or Re-Defined. *Digital Journalism, 7*(3), 378–385. https://doi.org/10.1080/21670811.2019.1568899

Fondevila-Gascón, J.-F., & Segura, H. (2012). Hypertextuality in Digital Journalism in Colombia. *Hipertext Net Revista Académica Sobre Documentación Digital y Comunicación Interactiva*, June, 9.

García-Orosa, B., García, X., & López, M. T. (2005). El Perfil Del Periodista de Interneten Galicia. *Mediatika: Cuadernos de Medios de Comunicación*. ISSN 1137-4462, Nº. 11, 2005, Pags. 159–169, January.

Hargittai, E., Piper, A. M., & Morris, M. R. (2019). From Internet Access to Internet Skills: Digital Inequality among Older Adults. *Universal Access in the Information Society, 18*(4), 881–890. https://doi.org/10.1007/s10209-018-0617-5

Jacobson, S. (2010). Emerging Models of Multimedia Journalism: A Content Analysis of Multimedia Packages Published on Nytimes.Com. *Atlantic Journal of Communication, 18*(2), 63–78. https://doi.org/10.1080/1545687090 3554882

Jamil, S. (2022, January). Evolving Newsrooms and the Second Level of Digital Divide: Implications for Journalistic Practice in Pakistan. *Journalism Practice,* 1–18. https://doi.org/10.1080/17512786.2022.2026244

Kosterich, A. 2020. Managing News Nerds: Strategizing about Institutional Change in the News Industry. *Journal of Media Business Studies, 17*(1): 51–68

Kroon, Å., & Eriksson, G. (2019). The Impact of the Digital Transformation on Sports Journalism Talk Online. *Journalism Practice, 13*(7), 834–852. https://doi.org/10.1080/17512786.2019.1577695

Larrondo Ureta, J., & Diaz Noci, J. (2014). Hypertextual Structures of Online News: A Comparative Research on Quality Media. In *Shaping the News Online: A quality Research on International Quality Media* (pp. 249–300). Labcom. www.livroslabcom.ubi.pt

Lischka, J. A., Schaetz, N., & Oltersdorf, A. L. (2022). Editorial Technologists as Engineers of Journalism's Future: Exploring the Professional Community of Computational Journalism. *Digital Journalism,* January, 1–19. https://doi.org/10.1080/21670811.2021.1995456.

Mabweazara, H. (2015). Mainstreaming African Digital Cultures, practices and emerging forms of citizen engagement. *African Journalism Studies, 36,* 1–11. https://doi.org/10.1080/23743670.2015.1119486

Orben, A. (2020). The Sisyphean Cycle of Technology Panics. *Perspectives on Psychological Science, 15*(5), 1143–1157. https://doi.org/10.1177/1745691620919372

Palacios, M., & Noci, J. D. (2009). *Online Journalism, Research Methods a Multidisciplinary Approach in Comparative Perspective.* Bilbao: Universidad del Pa??s Vasco=Euskal Herriko Unibertsitatea.

Palau-Sampio, D., & Sánchez-García, P. (2020). Digital Resources in the Current Journalistic Narrative: Uses and Limitations of Hypertext, Multimedia and Interactivity. *Communication & Society, 33*(2), 1–16. https://doi.org/1 0.15581/003.33.2.1-16

Quandt, T. (2008). (No) News on the World Wide Web? A Comparative Content Analysis of Online News in Europe and the United States. *Journalism Studies 9*(5), 717–738.

Quandt, T., & Singer, J. B. (2009). Convergence and Cross-Platform Production. In K. Wahl-Jorgensen & T. Hanitzsch (Eds.), *The Handbook of Journalism Studies* (International Communication Association (ICA) Handbook Series) (pp. 130–144). Routledge.

Robinson, S., Lewis, S. C., & Carlson, M. (2019). Locating the 'Digital' in Digital Journalism Studies: Transformations in Research. *Digital Journalism, 7*(3), 368–377. https://doi.org/10.1080/21670811.2018.1557537

Ryfe, D., Mensing, D., & Kelley, R. (2016). What Is the Meaning of a News Link? *Digital Journalism*, *4*(1), 41–54. https://doi.org/10.1080/2167081 1.2015.1093269

Njuguna, J. (2020). Training Factors as Predictors of Students' Self-Efficacy Beliefs for Online Journalism Practice. *IAFOR Journal of Education*, *8*(2), 141–157. https://doi.org/10.22492/ije.8.2.08

Stalph, F. 2020. Evolving Data Teams: Tensions between Organisational Structure and Professional Subculture. *Big Data & Society*, *7*(1), 205395172091996.

Steensen, S. (2011). Online Journalism and the Promises of New Technology: A Critical Review and Look Ahead. *Journalism Studies*, *12*(3), 311–327. https://doi.org/10.1080/1461670X.2010.501151

Stroobant, J. (2019). Finding the News and Mapping the Links: A Case Study of Hypertextuality in Dutch-Language Health News Websites. *Information, Communication & Society*, *22*(14), 2138–2155. https://doi.org/10.108 0/1369118X.2018.1477971

Venkatesh, V., Thong, J., & Xu, X. (2016). Unified Theory of Acceptance and Use of Technology: A Synthesis and the Road Ahead. *Journal of the Association for Information Systems*, *17*(5), 328–376. https://doi.org/10.17705/1jais.00428

Venkatesh, V., & Davis, F. D. (2000). A Theoretical Extension of the Technology Acceptance Model: Four Longitudinal Field Studies. *Management Science*, *46*(2), 186–204. https://doi.org/10.1287/mnsc.46.2.186.11926

Venkatesh, V., Morris, M. G., Davis, G. B., & Davis, F. D. (2003). User Acceptance of Information Technology: Toward a Unified View. *MIS Quarterly*, *27*(3), 425. https://doi.org/10.2307/30036540

Walsh, J. P. (2020). Social Media and Moral Panics: Assessing the Effects of Technological Change on Societal Reaction. *International Journal of Cultural Studies*, *23*(6), 840–859. https://doi.org/10.1177/1367877920912257

Zelizer, B. (2019). Why Journalism is About More Than Digital Technology. *Digital Journalism*, *7*(3), 343–350. https://doi.org/10.1080/2167081 1.2019.1571932

CHAPTER 4

Digital First in Malawian Newsrooms: A Comparative Analysis

Ekari Immaculate Phiri, Mzati Nkolokosa, Maclan Kanyangw'a, and Albert Sharra

INTRODUCTION

Although technologies are celebrated for transforming the media industry, their impact on the industry has generated increased interests among researchers. In Africa, print media has been flagged as the most hit with many scholars signalling a "no future" for print media (Roper, 2021). On the other hand, there is growing literature that shows how the print media

---

E. I. Phiri (✉)
Department of Literary Studies, University of Malawi, Zomba, Malawi
e-mail: ephiri@unima.ac.mw

M. Nkolokosa
Department of Language and Linguistics, University of Essex, Essex, UK

M. Kanyangw'a
Department of Journalism and Media Studies, Malawi University of Business and Applied Sciences, Blantyre, Malawi
e-mail: mkanyangwa@mubas.ac.mw

© The Author(s), under exclusive license to Springer Nature Switzerland AG 2025
A. Sharra, U. Akpojivi (eds.), *Technologies and Media Production Cultures*, Palgrave Studies in Journalism and the Global South, https://doi.org/10.1007/978-3-031-78582-5_4

63

in Africa is navigating the ongoing technological revolution. By moving online, print media have not only reinvigorated their relevance but also presented themselves with an opportunity to continue dominating the news production business through what Prenger and Deuze (2017) call "dual-management process", a system that addresses both online and traditional needs of journalism (see Kalombe & Phiri, 2019; Nkomo et al., 2017; Olusola et al., 2017; Sharra, 2023,). Studies show print media are utilising online platforms to sustain their print editions through a strategy which some scholars like Robotham and Pignard-Cheynel (2024) call "Digital First" to mean online first.

Although this has the potential to shift the rhetoric on the future of print media, there is still need for more research that takes a holistic approach that captures both print and broadcast media. There is already growing literature on this but is mainly from the Global North. This study focuses on Malawi, one of the countries with the lowest internet penetration in the world. Our aim is to contribute to the discourse on how journalists and traditional media (radio, television, and print) organisations in developing economies are navigating the digital revolution to remain in the business through digital first. We do this by investigating how four media organisations in Malawi employ digital-first strategy. We argue that the digital revolution has not erased the old ways of doing journalism in Malawi, but has, instead, extended journalism into new territories and amplified previous ways of work (Deuze, 2017, p. 10).

DIGITISATION OF TRADITIONAL MEDIA

Even old media were at one time new, and every new medium will become old at some point in its existence (Stöber, 2004, p. 484). Consequently, the history of journalism has been, and continues to be, shaped by new technologies. Or, put differently, the success of journalism "has always been influenced if not determined by technological advances from manual typesetting to desktop publishing, from bulky cameras to handheld devices, from analogue recording to digital editing, from single-medium to multimedia" (Deuze, 2017, p. 10). In Malawi, the digitisation of the media has been gradual but progressive and can be traced from the period

---

A. Sharra
Department of Political Studies, University of Witwatersrand, Johannesburg, South Africa

Centre of African Studies, University of Edinburgh, Edinburgh, UK

of colonialism. Through the Colonial Office, Britain engaged the British Broadcasting Corporation (BBC) to set up radio broadcasting transmitters sites in East and Central Africa in the 1940s (Armour, 1984). This was complemented with the deployment of the BBC team to work in Africa and also train local staff. As radio boomed in the region, print media also emerged taking different shapes like leaflets, newsletters, and newspapers. The history of both print and radio shows that technology has been central to the development of the media. Thus, journalists have been working under "a general predicament of change" (Hardt, 1995, p. 4) throughout the centuries. Malawi's first newspaper, *Daily Times (formerly Nyasaland Times)*, was founded in 1895 by the Central African Planter. The newspaper was later purchased by the country's first president, Hastings Kamuzu Banda in 1972 (Chitsulo & Mang'anda, 2011) and now operates under the name Times Group. Times Group has *Times Radio, Television, Online*, and three print newspapers: *Daily Times, Malawi News*, and *Sunday Times*. Times Group was founded as a private media and remains so. The nineteenth century witnessed remarkable changes in newspaper production from the forces of the Industrial Revolution which helped mechanised printers to produce more copies, transform layout and design, and revolutionised methods of gathering news (Musson, 1958, pp. 411–412). In Malawi, the period running from 1993 saw the print media market being flooded with new newspapers and magazines. However, as Chitsulo and Mang'anda (2011) note, most of them did not last due to funding issues.

On the other hand, developments in radio transformed from regional broadcasting airing on Short-Wave Modulation (SW) to national and community radios on Amplitude Modulation(AM) and Frequency Modulation (FM). This shift saw countries like Malawi establishing their own national broadcasting corporation: the Malawi Broadcasting Corporation (MBC) in 1964 with the support of the BBC. From a radio operating on AM, MBC now has *Radio 1, Radio 2 FM, MBC Television 1, MBC Television 2*, and *MBC Online*. As we shall demonstrate later, except for Platform for Investigative Journalism (PIJ) which is less than five years old, all the sampled case studies started as traditional media organisations and added online platform. We are interested in this transition, particularly adding online to complement traditional media as well as appreciate how new media organisations like PIJ created to serve online audiences are navigating the digital revolution.

Generally, technology has been a major determinant of the media industry, both as a threat and an enabler of the growth of journalism. Indeed, at every stage in history, new technologies extend and amplify previous ways of doing business (Deuze, 2017, p. 10). Media scholars are interested in the implication of the digital evolution on the media industry. Some researchers have investigated the changing working conditions of journalists in the course of navigating the internet revolution. For example, Deuze (2017) studied the influences of changing labour conditions, professional cultures, and the appropriation of technologies on the nature of work in journalism. In South Africa, the impact of internet has resulted in budget cuts and overworked staff, with less time to do good quality stories, follow-ups, or scoops (Findlay et al., 2017, p. 10). In a different study, Bhavsar (2018) found that a shift in media consumption habits of viewers has opened new doors of opportunities for creative content producers and advertisers, but has challenged traditional means of television viewing and marketing.

DEFINING AND CHARACTERISING DIGITAL FIRST

Digital first has been proposed to explain the changing work of journalists in the wake of the technological advancement of the twenty-first century. One of the most recent studies on digital first in Europe was by Robotham and Pignard-Cheynel (2024). The two researchers analysed production systems of three French-language Swiss newspapers that label their production systems digital first. In interviews with 17 of news-workers, a full range of properties attributed to digital first from the data reflected five dimensions: temporality, content format, workflow, production mindset, and business strategy. It is not possible to discuss the five dimensions in detail in this chapter. However, each dimension will be explained briefly to understand Robotham and Pignard-Cheynel's (2024, pp. 4–11) definition of digital first in print media houses that have adopted both print and digital as business strategies. Temporality refers to newspaper print content republished online. This was the practice in Malawi when print media were adopting technological advancements in news production (Sharra, 2023). According to Robotham and Pignard-Cheynel (2024), workflow refers to stories being written according to digital publication standards, before being repurposed for print, while strategy is about new business models being developed by print media houses in the wake of the digital revolution. Production mindset means that journalists should focus on both digital and print formats of their story. For digital content, format refers to hyperlinks, social media embeds, videos, interactive maps, or infographics. In addition to the five dimensions that define digital first,

Robotham and Pignard-Cheynel (2024, p. 14) suggest that digital first implies putting digital news production as a priority over print news production.

Although their paper focuses on newspapers only, the framework is applicable to broadcast media. In this study, we recognise "any" media organisation that "offers stories across a range of temporalities, dissolving the deadline-driven 24-hour news cycle and placing the online reader and revenue at the centre as engaging with digital first" (Robotham & Pignard-Cheynel, 2024, p. 1717). The most important element of the concept which makes it applicable to broadcast media is that it says with digital-first strategy "news stories should exploit digital potentialities such as hyper-textuality, multimedia, social media embeds etc. while also accounting for its constraints" (2024, p. 1717).

In the broadcast media, digital first is seen in adoption of a combination of 24-hour news-cycle and slow news to publish news as they happen (Lim, 2014). Examples include CNN, BBC, and Aljazeera. It is now normal for broadcast media to broadcast 24/7 and to have the words "Breaking News" at the lower corner of the television for the whole day. It has also become critical for all media organisations to have online pages for posting news as they break while preparing material for the traditional platforms. Thus, while digital first can mean many things, its use in media studies should be understood as online first. In Malawi, almost all traditional media organisations have online platforms where they break the news first while preparing detailed news material for their traditional platform (Sharra, 2023). What is, however, unclear is how different news organisations in Malawi employ digital-first strategy in their day-to-day business, a gap this chapter aims to close using a case study of four news media organisations.

Digital First in Malawi

One of the most important studies in Malawi reports that digital first acts as a coping mechanism for print newspapers (Sharra, 2023). The study concludes that digital first in Malawi was inspired by the quest to be the first at breaking news online while working on detailed piece for the print. The goal was to beat competition brought by social media citizen journalists. According to Sharra (2023, p. 120), digital first follows a two-way approach: first, post briefs of developing stories on social media pages while developing a detailed print version of the story for the following day;

68 E. I. PHIRI ET AL.

and second keep exclusive stories for print first, followed by online platforms. The study demonstrates that the approach was working for Nation Publications Limited (NPL) and Times Group as they were able to compete with social media in breaking news and still publish traditional scoops.

Compared to media houses in the West, we observe that the BBC, for example, was quicker to adopt digital first than media houses in Malawi. In his analysis of digital first at the BBC, Klontzas (2006, p. 3), reports that as early as the mid-1990s, the Director General of the broadcaster, John Birt, recognised the potential of internet as an integral part of the BBC's public service provision as the "third arm" of broadcasting, to complement radio and television. Further, the 1999 *Davies Report* on "The Future Funding of the BBC" (as cited in Klontzas, 2006, p. 3) affirmed the value adding potential of BBC Online to extend the broadcaster's reach and enhance its existing services through further convergence between broadcasting and the Internet. Since then, bbc.co.uk has grown to become one of the top five UK sites in terms of unique users. As observed in the broadcaster's report, "Everywhere our digital services seemed to grow in depth and quality. Audiences no longer regard them as marginal or experimental but as part of the core offering, they expect from the BBC week in, week out" (BBC, 2004/2005).

Consequently, there is more literature on digital first from Europe and the United States than from Africa. We are, therefore, guided by Mabweazara's (2010, p. 22) suggestion that media researchers in Africa should not stick to the Western theories, but should consider the African newsroom context: the socio-economic factors, including rates of internet access, because these have an impact on how media houses and journalists navigate the internet revolution. Inspired by the decolonial scholarship, this chapter investigates what the media and journalists in Malawi are doing to navigate the digital revolution, not how best they are doing what the Western media are doing. The chapter builds up on some of the work that demonstrates African media landscape is changing in the digital age (see Mutsvairo, 2018; Atton & Mabweazara, 2011; Moyo, 2013).

DIFFUSION OF INNOVATIONS THEORY

We adopted Everret Rogers' Diffusion of Innovations Theory to comprehend how the media industry and individual journalists in Malawi are adjusting to the changes brought by the digital revolution. The theory is based on the premise that "getting a new idea adopted, even when it has obvious advantage, is difficult" such that "many innovations require a lengthy period of many years from the time when they become available to when they are widely adopted" (Rogers, 2003, p. 1). Diffusion is defined as the process in which an innovation is communicated through channels over time among members of a social system (Rogers, 2003, p. 5). Messages in diffusion are concerned with new ideas upon which people should adopt new ways of life. According to Rogers (2003, p. 6), diffusion is a special type of communication in that the messages are concerned with new ideas; the newness of the idea in the message content gives diffusion its special character: "The newness means that some degree of uncertainty is involved in diffusion". Rogers considers the uncertainty as the degree to which several alternatives are perceived with respect to the occurrence of an event and the relative probability of these alternatives. Uncertainty implies lack of predictability, of structure and of information. Rogers further describes diffusion as a kind of social change, defined as the process by which alteration occurs in the structure and function of a social system and when ideas are adopted or rejected, certain consequences follow, some social change occurs. It has been observed that most innovations diffuse at a disproportionately slow rate (Rogers, 2003, p. 6 & 10). This view is supported by the slow adoption of digital first in the media in Malawi as will be observed in the findings section. However, the slowness ought to be considered together with factors such as internet penetration rates and low income levels of media content producers and consumers.

The diffusion process has four elements, namely, innovation, communication channels, time, and a social system. Further, the speed of diffusion or the rate of adoption is determined by characteristics of the innovation or application, especially relative advantage, compatibility, complexity, trialability, and observability. Relative advantage refers to "the degree to which an innovation is perceived as being better than the idea that it supersedes" while "compatibility is the degree to which an innovation is perceived as consistent with existing values, past experience, and needs of potential adopters" (Rogers, 2003, p. 15). Some innovations are simple and easy to implement, while others are difficult or complex to implement. It is believed that users are likely to adopt an innovation after they have had a chance to experiment with it or after what is known as trialability. Finally, being able to observe the experiences of another organisation or individual has a positive effect for the diffusion of an innovation, thus observability (Rogers, 2003, p. 16).

We see the media environment in Malawi as a social system, where actors look up to and learn from one another in the adoption of digital first. We also observe that the culture of employees crossing from one media organisation to another facilitates transfer of knowledge. For instance, most print journalists in Malawi have only two options if they want to remain in print. Thus, NPL or Times, and as Sharra (2023) demonstrates, the development of digital-first strategies at the two organisations follows a similar script and timeframe. Nonetheless, we argue that each media organisation has its own ways of responding to changes in a distinctive way. Thus, there is need for more studies that focus on case studies for us to understand how different media organisations are navigating the digital revolution. This chapter is unique in that it combines print, broadcast, and online news organisations in Malawi to understand how different media organisations employ digital first.

METHODS

The goal of the study is to investigate how media houses in Malawi have responded to changing behaviour of media content consumers caused by the digital revolution over the years. We employed the qualitative research because, according to Leavy (2014, p. 1), it "includes attention to the everyday, to the mundane and ordinary, as much as the extraordinary". In addition, qualitative research is an engaged way of building knowledge about the social world and human experience (Domegan & Fleming, 2007, p. 24).

Our study population comprised of journalists and media managers. As pointed out earlier, one of the four elements in the diffusion of innovations is "time", along with the innovation, communication channels, and a social system. Consequently, our selection of media houses was purposive. We selected media houses that have been in existence for over 20 years during which digital-first approach has been employed in response to the changes in audience behaviour as a result of the internet revolution. The selected media houses are the MBC and its two radio stations, two television stations, and online platform; NPL's three newspapers, *The Nation*, *Weekend Nation* and *Nation on Sunday* and *Nation Online*; and Times Group's *Daily Times*, *Malawi News*, and *Sunday Times*, its radio and television stations, Times360 Online. In addition, we selected the PIJ, an online publication established in 2019 and run by two journalists, to better understand how individual journalists are responding to internet revolution changes in the media landscape.

We used multiple data collection tools, namely, individual interviews, observations, and document and digital platform reviews. We interviewed a former online editor with more than 20 years of experience and a current online editor. One determinant in the rate of adoption of an innovation is observability which implies that being able to observe the experiences of another organisation or individuals also has a positive effect for the diffusion of an innovation (Rogers, 2003, p. 16). The former online editor provided insights which others after him have been able to employ in the management of digital first. In addition, we also interviewed two engineers who have been in the broadcasting industry for nearly 30 years and have been active participants in the navigation of the internet revolution. The inclusion of engineers in our study was inspired by Rogers's contention that complexity—that is, the degree of ease or difficulty associated with an innovation for potential adopters—also influences the uptake of technology. Engineers offer technical support to journalists in their digital-first quest.

Interviews helped us to get in-depth information about strategies implemented and challenges being faced by the media in Malawi regarding the internet revolution. An in-depth interview can be highly structured, semi-structured, or unstructured. Eppich et al. (2019, p. 85) suggest that a well-crafted semi-structured interview guide includes predetermined questions while allowing flexibility to explore emergent topics based on the research question. One advantage of in-depth interviews is that the researcher pursues a respondent's interpretation of a subject, in addition to respondents being given considerable liberty in their responses and in discussing areas not raised by the researcher (Powell & Single, 1996, p. 499). The in-depth interviews in this study were particularly useful in gaining knowledge from key actors in the digital-first drive in Malawi. In addition, the interviews were chosen to triangulate our observations on digital platforms of the media houses.

We adopted Thematic Analysis (TA) to synthesise the data. Thematic Analysis is a method of systematically identifying, organising, and offering insights into patterns of meanings (themes) across a data set (Clarke & Braun, 2017, p. 297). In addition, it has been observed that through focusing on meanings across a data set, TA allows researchers to see and make sense of collective or shared meanings and experiences and can be used to analyse large and small data sets, from case study research with 1 or 2 participants to as big as 60 participants (Clarke & Braun, 2017, p. 298). The development of themes followed inductive logic, with each question guiding the categorisation of issues in the data into a theme.

FINDINGS AND DISCUSSION

This chapter sought to answer the following question: How are media organisations in Malawi navigating the internet revolution? Specifically, what digital-first dimensions do media organisations in Malawi employ to remain relevant in the digital age?

NAVIGATING THE INTERNET REVOLUTION

In our analysis of online publications and digital platforms of print, radio and television, we observe that the media have, over the years, employed the five dimensions of temporality, content format, workflow, production mindset, and business strategy described by Robotham and Pignard-Cheynel (2024) in proportion to internet penetration rates and the socio-economic context of Malawi. The process has been gradual but progressive and in line with the development of the digital public sphere. Malawi's digital public sphere of consumers of news media is very small and this is largely because less than 20% of the population have access to the internet (Kainja, 2019; Malawi National Statistical Office, 2019). We also noted that the group of people who consume online media content is the same for the traditional. This was so evident with print media. We learnt about this when we analysed the subscription rates of e-papers for both NPL and Times Group. The data shows the drop in print sales tallies with the increase in e-paper subscriptions for both publications, of course with new consumers, especially those in diaspora. We noted that the media organisations publish for a small elite group, largely working class and students with exceptions of weekly papers as they have an extended target audience like the *Weekend Nation, Nation on Sunday,* and *Malawi News* and *Sunday Times* published by NPL and Times Group respectively. The same was noted with broadcast media. We relied on assessing their programmes and timing. For instance, lunch hour listening, drive time, and news bulletins showed they target the elites. Other groups of people are targeted with specific programmes like MBC's Tikwere (an education programme) aired during the school time and Zokonda Amai (a popular women's forum programme) aired in the morning hours between 8am and 9am. Depending on the group of audience and their access to media, different media organisations employ different strategies, including time and language. For this reason, we noted that the deployment of technologies is largely to provide alternative sources of media content for those who have access.

It is also important to highlight that the way traditional media is responding to digital technologies is a replication of the competition that has been there between print and broadcast media. We found that print media responded to digital revolution by starting Sunday newspapers to compete with electronic media which was the only source of news on Sundays. Both Times and NPL started business with a weekly newspaper, and to compete effectively, they introduced daily papers and, later on, Sunday papers. The recent developments in digital technologies have seen both print and broadcast media adopting online platforms as spaces for complementing tradition platforms. As of 2024, the topmost online news platforms were run by traditional media organisations. We relied on Media Institute of Southern Africa (MISA)-Malawi annual media awards to draw this conclusion. This is the main competition for journalist and media organisations in Malawi. NPL and Zodiak Broadcasting Station have been dominating the MISA Malawi Online Media House of the Year Award which PIJ has recently dominated.

PIJ, a long-form narrative journalism website that has specialised in investigative journalism, is among the first new media organisation to have dominated the MISA Malawi Online Media House of the Year Award. Its inclusion in this study was helpful to appreciate its approaches to issues of temporality, content format, workflow, production mindset, and business strategy.

We also noted that all the sampled media organisations follow the 24-hour and slow news cycles well discussed by Lim (2014) in which they publish briefs to remain on top of the developing news story while preparing a detailed one for both traditional and online platforms. We are interested in this digital-first strategy, and in the following sections, we will demonstrate how NPL, Times Group, MBC, and PIJ employ the strategy in that order.

DIGITAL FIRST AT NPL

The oldest digital-first attempt at NPL, according to Robotham and Pignard-Cheynel's (2024) dimensions, is Nation Online (https://mwnation.com/). The website started as a platform for publishing online news stories appearing in the three newspapers *The Nation, Weekend Nation,* and *Nation on Sunday*. In 1998, NPL launched its first online edition, *Nation Online*, which was redeveloped in 2002 and updated in 2006, according to the information on the website. Gracian Tukula, NPL's first online editor, said:

> We were basically uploading the stories from the print publication later in the day because there was resistance within the organisation that an online publication, which was not bringing any money, would sabotage sales of the print publication which was sustaining the company. (G. Tukula, personal interview, November 18, 2024)

However, business models have changed over the years. NPL is able to generate income from its digital-first approach. One important product from NPL is e-Nation, a digital version of newspapers distributed in PDF format to the subscribed. Our findings show that subscription to e-Nation has been growing over the last five years and it grew substantially during the Covid-19 pandemic. We attribute the growth to Malawi Government's remote work policy. It was during this period that government ministries, departments, agencies, and the private sector transitioned from hardcopy subscription to e-newspaper subscription. However, even after Covid-19 was declared over, some institutions have maintained subscription to e-Nation. The advantage is that e-copies are cheaper than hard copies. At the time of writing this chapter, March 2024, e-copies were at MK1000 per day, half the price of hard copy newspapers. The e-Nation subscription was at 3000+.

Besides Nation Online, NPL has accounts on Facebook, X, Instagram, and YouTube. As of March 2024, Facebook was the most followed with more than 503,000 followers, X (Twitter) had more than 224,000 while Instagram had 17,000 and YouTube and LinkedIn 2000 followers each. Our investigation shows that NPL's YouTube account is used to promote news stories in video format and to connect with advertisers and newspaper subscribers. In-depth news reports are promoted on YouTube to motivate potential readers to buy NPL newspapers or to subscribe to e-Nation. For example, on Saturday, 2 September 2023, NPL posted a video promoting a story that appeared in *Nation on Sunday* the following day. NPL also uses the YouTube account to do business with its clients, both news readers and advertisers. Further, NPL has advertising and newspaper subscription information, including payment for newspaper subscription and adverts, on the YouTube account. Overall, the X account is for breaking news in text, photographs, and videos. In addition, the X account is used to promote front pages of the three newspapers under NPL brand.

The Instagram page is used to break news in text, photograph, and video, and to promote front and back pages of NPL newspapers. The Facebook page, especially, is used to post breaking news in text, audio, and video. In addition to news, NPL uses its Facebook to engage with advertisers. The Facebook page has a link to two WhatsApp numbers: one Telekom Networks Malawi (TNM) and another Airtel Malawi. The two numbers are for booking adverts. Perhaps the most striking finding is that while in the past advertisers had to transact at NPL offices in person, nowadays adverts are booked and paid for on digital platforms. NPL accepts payments via mobile money services which include Airtel Money, TNM Mpamba, and bank transfers. Payments for newspaper subscription are also made on the same digital platforms.

The promotion of stories online is a business strategy in line with Robotham and Pignard-Cheynel's (2024) description of digital first, especially strategy, which is about developing business models in response to the digital revolution. As Sellina Kainja, Online Editor for NPL, said in a personal interview,

> The digital revolution has changed the way news is gathered, displayed and consumed. In the case of gathering, we are now talking of mobile journalism where smartphones can do almost everything that traditional equipment such as TV cameras, and photographers used to do but also able to publish quickly and instantly. In terms of news consumption, readers can access news via digital platforms such as social media and websites which have also eased the reach. We can easily and quickly reach our audience via these digital platforms. Feedback is instant which is almost impossible with traditional media. (S.Kainja, personal interview, June 3, 2024)

Digital First at Times Group

Times Group is Malawi's oldest media house. It traces its history to *The Nyasaland Times*, which was first published in 1895, by R.S. Hynde at the Blantyre Mission Press. The editors of the paper said that they were "devoted to the planting interests of the community—the interest, we venture to state, on which the commercial prosperity of BCA [British

Central Africa] depends" (Woods, 1989, p. 363). From a periodical in 1895, Times Group now has three newspapers: *The Daily Times, Malawi News*, and *The Sunday Times*. In addition, Times Group also operates *Times Radio* and *Times TV* and online platforms.

The website https://times.mw/ carries stories, especially current news, after being published in print. Our observation shows that some stories, especially feature stories, are not posted on the website. A possible explanation for keeping away some stories from the website could be protection of the print newspaper. The website is accessed for free, and it seems plausible for Times Group to limit the number of stories that can be accessed for free. The activities on Times website are similar to those of Nation Online that it would be redundant to capture them here. However, it has to be reported that consistent with its practice of being first, Times Group was the first to introduce e-newspaper in PDF format. It is nearly five years since both media houses introduced e-newspapers and the period suggests that the model is a viable strategy particularly when read from the growing number of e-paper subscriptions.

Times Group also runs Times 360 on X, Facebook, YouTube, and Instagram. As of March 2024, X had 145,000 followers, 989,000 followers on Facebook, 7800 followers on Instagram, and 86,000 subscribers on YouTube. A key finding that distinguishes Times Group from NPL is in the use of YouTube. Journalists at Times Group post select television programmes from Times TV on YouTube. While NPL employs YouTube to promote forthcoming stories in print, Times uses YouTube to post television programmes that have already aired, thus offering viewers the convenience of watching programmes at any time. This finding demonstrates that even television stations are employing digital first to manage viewers' changing behaviours. Television viewers are no longer tied to station programme schedules as was the case in the past. In addition, researchers on Times TV content would no longer have to grapple with issues of access through formal administrative channels. The content is available on YouTube. It is a policy requirement that all journalists at Times Group should file stories for radio, newspapers, television, and online. Consequently, some newspaper stories in Malawi News, for example, end with an editor's note for readers to "watch a full interview on Times TV at 8 tonight". Similarly, news anchors on Times Radio and Times TV end reports with a promotion line that a detailed story would be in the paper the following day.

What stands out for both Times Group and NPL is that newspapers have turned readers into listeners and viewers, courtesy of digital first. Print media are competing with radio and television, especially on breaking news and live reporting. Important events are streamlined live on print media's Facebook pages. Further, sports and arts journalists, for example, are able to post updates of games and live music shows, and the increased number of viewers and comments at such times is a significant demonstration that in the digital information age, journalism is still valued as a trustworthy source of information.

Digital First at MBC

MBC was established by the MBC Act of 1964 with functions and powers to broadcast as a public media. The MBC Act implied that no other radio station could be allowed in Malawi. The first important digital-first finding of this study is that MBC introduced a second channel in 1997, resulting in MBC Radio 1 and MBC Radio 2 FM. The FM qualification is key to understanding MBC's response to technological revolution. It has been reported that radio was intended to have listeners experience high-quality sound and overall reliability of technology (Kuyucu, 2019, p. 115) and MBC Radio 2 brought the experience of high-quality sound and interactive programmes. MBC Radio 2 FM had such programmes as "Your Kind of Music" which, for the first time in broadcasting history in Malawi, allowed listeners to call and choose a song that was played instantly. Such an experience was impossible on MBC Radio 1 for over 30 years.

The second interesting finding is that MBC and TVM were merged in 2011. The merger was a key step in the navigation of the internet revolution. While Malawi had a radio station in 1964, President Banda was against television broadcasting, citing moral reasons. He was of the view that television would degrade morals of Malawians. For the record, the Malawi Censorship Board, established by the Censorship Act of 1966, had a long list of banned books, films, and other forms of entertainment that were deemed lower than Malawi moral standards (Kerr & Mapanje, 2002, p. 79). The first television station, Malawi Television Limited (TVM), was officially launched on April 1, 1999, two years after the death of Dr Banda and five years after he lost power in an election in 1994. The two institutions MBC and TVM were merged on 1 July 2011 and became known as MBC.

What stands out in the merger is that technology was a key enabler of the whole process. Radio journalists at Chichiri and television journalists at Kwacha were able to share notes and content through both official and private channels, using technological advancements. Nine years after the merger, the radio newsroom and the television newsroom were merged. Since 2020, all journalists in MBC's News and Current Affairs Department operate from one newsroom at Kwacha. The radio and television air similar bulletins, unlike in the past when they carried somewhat different bulletins. It is apparent that the greatest finding from the new newsroom is that radio news and radio current affairs programmes are aired from a studio at Kwacha using digital technology that links Kwacha studios and the radio studio at Chichiri studios.

The third finding is on MBC's use of social media platforms. For decades, journalism students learned that radio and television had the advantage of immediacy over print. In addition, radio and television had the advantage of sound while television added the advantage of visuals. However, internet has turned the advantages upside down. Print is enjoying use of sound and visuals on digital platforms and so radio and television have to utilise social media platforms to remain relevant in an information age. One way MBC is achieving relevance is by use of social media platforms, Instagram being the first. On its Instagram account, MBC promotes scheduled programmes, including live sports matches. Since 2022, MBC journalists also post news reports in digital audio, text, and video on Instagram. On its Facebook page, MBC carries news in text and pictures. In addition, MBC does live streaming of MBC Radio 1, and MBC Radio 2 and MBC Television on Facebook since 2019 and on MBC website since 2018. On YouTube, MBC posts important parts of the news items with occasional live streaming when need arises. MBC is also on X, where journalists post stories in text and pictures since 2022. It has to be reported that MBC created X and Instagram accounts in 2017; however, the two accounts became active only from 2022. As of March 2024, MBC's X page had 26,000 followers, 616,000 followers on Facebook, 1200 followers on Instagram, while YouTube had 1000 subscribers.

It is important to note that radio and television live streaming enables people from any part of the world to listen and watch as long as there is internet connection. The ability to stream live on internet can be wholly attributed to the digital revolution and is part of the digital-first strategy of MBC.

Digital First at PIJ

PIJ is an example of an innovation by individual journalists outside the mainstream media. It helps us to understand how individual journalists are navigating the internet revolution in Malawi. This is important because technology adoption usually happens at newsroom level, and it is difficult to appreciate how individual journalists embrace the technologies. One of the observations was that some individual journalists are innovating with technologies and establishing their own online media platforms. In Malawi, this has been an important development over the years. The PIJ sampled for the study is a product of such innovations. PIJ was founded by veteran journalist Gregory Gondwe in 2019. Gondwe identified a gap in investigative journalism in Malawi and the opportunity provided by the internet revolution to establish PIJ.

The publication, available on https://www.investigativeplatform-mw.org, describes itself as "steadfast" in its "mission to guarantee a robust and uncompromised future for investigative journalism in Malawi and beyond" with the "aim to mould journalism graduates into serious, credible investigative journalists who can effectively hold power to account through impactful stories". Information on the PIJ website shows that the publication is "dedicated to leading and setting the highest standards in investigative journalism reporting" with a focus on "promoting accountability and transparency, primarily by exposing corruption and other wrongdoings". At the core of PIJ's mission is "promoting and upholding the public's right to know" achieved through "comprehensive training and mentoring programmes designed for media practitioners in Malawi". To achieve the goals, PIJ collaborates with investigative journalists and organisations within and beyond Malawi.

As observed by Longhi and Winques (2015, p. 106) longform is a term that has always been used to define the longer and more in-depth treatment of a topic. However, the digital revolution has perfected longform journalism, the art of displaying a topic in an immersive and innovative way (Planer & Godulla, 2021, p. 566) in "text, photographs, looping videos, dynamic maps and data visualisation into a unified whole" (Hiippala, 2017, p. 420) that offer a new experience as the one PIJ is providing to its readers.

Additionally, one major self-evident advantage enjoyed by PIJ stems from the very nature of being online: the opportunity to create discussion, to be shared, to become viral (see Lassila-Merisalo, 2014, p. 2). Longform, investigative stories published on PIJ website are shared and go viral on WhatsApp groups both in Malawi and in diaspora. However, despite being an online publication, PIJ has few followers on social media. For example, as of March 2024, it has 43,000 followers on Facebook, 11,000 followers on Twitter, and 113 followers on Instagram. It is also not available on some platforms like YouTube. These platforms are used to promote stories under preparation. Unlike the other three, we noted that PIJ promotes its work in WhatsApp groups, and this may be the reason it has few followers on its official social media pages.

PIJ was born out of two opportunities. One, the opportunity to publish online which is cheaper than in print, and cheaper than starting a radio station in Malawi. Two, PIJ was established out of Gondwe's talent to fill a gap left by a dying investigative journalism in Malawi. As stated on the PIJ website,

> The early promise of a media capable of holding duty-bearers accountable has been eroded. Investigative journalism, in particular, has suffered, increasingly influenced and compromised by political and corporate powers. This decline is evident in the quality of journalism being practised. There is a noticeable lack of depth and rigour in reporting, pointing to a need for enhanced skills in investigative journalism techniques, story processing, and packaging.

It stands out that in response to these challenges, Gondwe sought to achieve his aims with a digital only publication, taking advantage of the internet revolution, thus becoming part of a global trend in which new independent (and generally small-scale and online-only) journalism companies have been formed around the world since the early years of the twenty-first century (Wagemans et al., 2016).

Discussion and Conclusion

The aim of the study was to investigate the extent to which media houses and journalists in Malawi are navigating the communication revolution and meeting the dimensions of digital first. We relied on Robotham and Pignard-Cheynel's (2024) digital-first matrix and the concept of diffusion of innovations theory to illustrate this. *NPL* and *Times Group* meet all the five dimensions of digital first, PIJ meets all except temporality while MBC meets three, namely, workflow, production mindset, and business strategy.

The four case studies discussed above show that different newsrooms approach digital first differently. However, what anchors the initiatives is the quest to be the first online and also utilising online platforms to enhance traditional media. For instance, it is clear that *Times*' and *NPL*'s digital-first approaches have gone beyond news and the newsroom as Sharra (2023) reports in his study. Departments such as advertising and circulation have also adopted digital first. Overall, this study has shown that digital first is both a news approach and a business approach at *Times* and *NPL*. Twenty years ago, clients of *Times* and *NPL* had to visit the offices of the media houses to transact with circulation and advertising staff. All that has changed, largely because Times and NPL have adopted the digital-first approach in their way of doing business. A final analysis of MBC shows that the broadcaster employs its website to engage with potential clients. For example, there is a rate card on MBC's website. However, the broadcaster is not as aggressive in doing online advertising as NPL and Times Group.

We are aware that as we deploy theories and frameworks developed in the West to critically interrogate the appropriation of new technologies by journalists in Africa, we should not lose sight of the localised experiences of journalists in Africa (Mabweazara, 2010, p. 22). For example, while NPL and Times Group have introduced subscription to digital versions of newspapers, there are no paywalls on which readers access news by subscription in Malawi. Even PIJ, which carries exclusive longform investigative stories, is available online for free. The absence of paywalls in Malawi is not surprising when we consider the unavailability of online payment platforms.

In addition, even where the technology is available, paywalls are generating small amounts of revenue. One study determined that paywalls are not a viable business model (Myllylahti, 2014, p. 189). Yet the media in Malawi needs to innovate and make money from selling content. As Kainja (personal interview) observes, the future of digital first is in innovations, that is, paid for content or sponsored content, in partnerships, for instance, investigative stories can be sponsored by the World Bank within the bank's area of interest such as money laundering.

References

Armour, C. (1984). The BBC and the Development of Broadcasting in British Colonial Africa 1946–1956. *African Affairs, 83*(332), 359–402.

Atton, C., & Mabweazara, H. (2011). New Media and Journalism Practice in Africa: An Agenda for Research. *Journalism, 12*(6), 667–673. https://doi.org/10.1177/1464884911405467

BBC. (2004/2005). *BBC Annual Report and Accounts*.

Bhavsar, R. (2018). The Burgeoning Digital Media Consumption: A Challenge for Traditional Television and Advertising Industries-An Analysis. *Amity Journal of Media & Communications Studies (AJMCS)*, 8(1), 17–23.

Chitsulo, E., & Mang'anda, G. (2011). Origins, Development and Management of the Newspaper Industry in Malawi. In *Journalism in Malawi: History, Progress, and Prospects*. UNESCO.

Clarke, V., & Braun, V. (2017). Thematic Analysis. *The Journal of Positive Psychology*, 12(3), 297–298. https://doi.org/10.1080/17439760.2016.1262613

Deuze, M. (2017). Understanding Journalism as Newswork: How it Changes, and How it Remains the Same. *Westminster Papers in Communication and Culture*, 5(2), 4–24.

Domegan, C., & Fleming, D. (2007). *Marketing Research in Ireland: Theory and Practice*. Gill & Macmillan.

Eppich, W. J., Gormley, G. J., & Teunissen, P. W. (2019). In-depth Interviews. In *Healthcare Simulation Research: A Practical Guide* (pp. 85–91). Springer.

Findlay, S., Bird, W., & Smith, T. (2017). "The More Things Change, the More They Stay the Same": The Impacts of Social Media and Digital Technology on Journalism Quality in South African Newsrooms. In *Global Investigative Journalism Conference 2017*.

Hardt, H. (1995). Without the Rank and File: Journalism History, Media Workers and Problems of Representation. In H. Hardt & B. Brennen (Eds.), *Newsworkers: Towards a History of the Rank and File Minneapolis*. University of Minnesota Press.

Hiippala, T. (2017). The Multimodality of Digital Longform Journalism. *Digital journalism*, 5(4), 420–442.

Kainja, J. (2019). Digital Rights: How Accessible Is the Internet in Malawi? *Misa Malawi* (blog). https://malawi.misa.org/2019/02/15/digital-rights-how-accessible-is-the-internet-in-malawi/.

Kalombe, C., & Phiri, J. (2019). Impact of Online Media on Print Media in Developing Countries. *Open Journal of Business and Management*, 7(4), 1983–1998.

Kerr, D., & Mapanje, J. (2002). Academic Freedom and the University of Malawi. *African Studies Review*, 45(2), 73–91.

Klontzas, M. (2006). Digitalisation and the BBC: The Net Effect. In. N. Leandros (ed.), *The Impact of Internet on the Mass Media in Europe: COST A20 International Conference, Delphi (Greece)*, 26–29 April. Bury St Edmunds: Abramis.

Kuyucu, M. M. (2019). Internet Radio Broadcasting: History Differences and Advantages in Media Industry. *Social Science I* (pp. 115–131). Akademisyen Kitabevi A.Ş.

Lassila-Merisalo, M. (2014). Story First—Publishing Narrative Long-form Journalism in Digital Environments. *Journal of Magazine Media*, 15(2), 1–15.

Leavy, P. (2014). *The Oxford Handbook of Qualitative Research*. Oxford University Press.

Lim, J. (2014). Redefinition of Online Scoops: Online Journalists' Personal and Institutional Responses to Online Scoops. *First Monday*.

Longhi, R. R., & Winques, K. (2015). The Place of Longform in Online Journalism: Quality Versus Quantity and a Few Considerations Regarding Consumption. *Brazilian Journalism Research, 11*, 104–121.

Mabweazara, H. (2010). 'New' Technologies and Journalism Practice in Africa: Towards a Critical Sociological Approach. In N. Hyde-Clarke (Ed.), *The Citizen in Communication: Re-visiting Traditional, New and Community Media Practices in South Africa* (pp. 11–30). Juta & Co.

Malawi National Statistical Office. (2019). The 2019 National Household Survey on Access and Usage of ICT Services in Malawi. Zomba. http://www.nsoma-lawi.mw/index.php?option=com_content&view=article&id=232:national-household-survey-on-access-and-usage-of-ict-services-in-malawi-2019&catid=3:reports.

Moyo, L. (2013). The Digital Turn in Radio: A Critique of Institutional and Organizational Modeling of New Radio Practices and Cultures. *Telematics and Informatics, 30*(3), 214–222.

Musson, A. E. (1958). Newspaper Printing in the Industrial Revolution. *The Economic History Review, 10*(3), 411–426.

Mutsvairo, B. (2018). Mapping Social Media Trajectories in Zimbabwe. In *The Routledge Companion to Media and Activism* (pp. 289–297). Routledge.

Myllylahti, M. (2014). Newspaper Paywalls—the Hype and the Reality: A Study of How Paid News Content Impacts on Media Corporation Revenues. *Digital Journalism, 2*(2), 179–194.

Nkomo, N. Z., Kandiro, A., & Bigirimana, S. (2017). The Viability of the Print Newspaper in the Digital Era in Zimbabwe: A Digital Strategy Perspective. *European Journal of Business and Innovation Research, 5*(2), 39–61.

Olusola, A., Ibrahim, S., & Priscilla, G. (2017). An Era of Journalism Transition in South Africa: Traditional Media Versus Online Media. *Journal of Social Sciences, 51*(1–3), 1–5.

Planer, R., & Godulla, A. (2021). Longform Journalism in the USA and Germany: Patterns in Award-winning Digital Storytelling Productions. *Journalism Practice, 15*(4), 566–582.

Powell, R. A., & Single, H. M. (1996). Focus Groups. *International Journal for Quality in Health Care, 8*(5), 499–504.

Prenger, M., & Deuze, M. (2017). A History of Innovation and Entrepreneurialism in Journalism. In J. Pablo (Ed.), *Remaking the News: Essays on the Future of Journalism Scholarship in the Digital Age* (pp. 235–250). MIT Press.

Robotham, A. T., & Pignard-Cheynel, N. (2024). You Said Digital First! A Five-Dimensional Definition According to Journalists from Three Swiss Newspapers. *Journalism Practice, 18*(7), 1702–1721. https://doi.org/10.1080/1751278 6.2022.2104745

Rogers, E. M. (2003). *Diffusion of Innovations* (5th ed.). Free Press.

Roper, C. (2021). South Africa. *Reuters Institute* (blog). https://reutersinstitute. politics.ox.ac.uk/digital-news-report/2021/south-africa.

Sharra, A. (2023). 'Digital First' as a Coping Measure for Malawi's Print Newspapers. In *New Journalism Ecologies in East and Southern Africa: Innovations, Participatory and Newsmaking Cultures* (pp. 113–132). Springer.

Stöber, R. (2004). What Media Evolution Is: A Theoretical Approach to the History of New Media. *European Journal of Communication, 19*(4), 483–505.

Wagemans, A., Witschge, T., & Deuze, M. (2016). Ideology as Resource in Entrepreneurial Journalism: The French Online News Startup Mediapart. *Journalism Practice, 10*(2), 160–177.

Woods, T. (1989). The Myth of the Capitalist Class: Unofficial Sources and Political Economy in Colonial Malawi, 1895–1924. *History in Africa, 16*, 363–374.

CHAPTER 5

Towards Automation: News-Wrap Implementation at Malawi's Nation Publications

Albert Sharra and Tisaukirenji Tembo

INTRODUCTION

In November 2023, we visited the Nation Publications Limited (NPL) headquarters at Ginnery Corner in Blantyre in Malawi to conduct interviews for the paper. Our experience with newsroom culture and practice began with identifying the location of the headquarters of NPL which is Malawi's second largest print newspaper (Gunde, 2015; Sharra, 2020). Since its inception in 1993, NPL has been operating in this area which also houses its competitor: *Times Group*. Ginnery Corner is an industrial site

A. Sharra (✉)
Department of Political Studies, University of Witwatersrand, Johannesburg, South Africa

Centre of African Studies, University of Edinburgh, Edinburgh, UK

T. Tembo
Journalism and Media Studies, Malawi University of Business and Applied Sciences, Blantyre, Malawi
e-mail: ttembo@mubas.ac.mw

© The Author(s), under exclusive license to Springer Nature Switzerland AG 2025
A. Sharra, U. Akpojivi (eds.), *Technologies and Media Production Cultures*, Palgrave Studies in Journalism and the Global South, https://Doi.org/10.1007/978-3-031-78582-5_5

85

adjacent to Mandala, where the African Lakes Corporation established its headquarters during the colonial era (Visonà, 2017). Since then, it is a home of major institutions which include institutions of higher learning, referral hospitals and headquarters of major media organisations. NPL has grown from a publisher of an eight-page biweekly newspaper to a publisher of four print newspapers—*The Nation, Weekend Nation, Nation on Sunday* and *Fuko*—and an online edition, Nation Online (Gunde, 2015). It operates in an all-glass structure located on the second floor of a two-storey building.

From the main entrance of the newsroom, one is able to see all corners of the building. The newsroom section is made up of three main parts: a big open space stocked with laptops and desktop computers, five single-person lockable rooms, meeting room, phone call room, small open space with desk-top computers and the library. The lockable rooms are for the very senior newsroom editors for *The Nation, Weekend Nation* and *Nation on Sunday* print newspapers and the managing editor and deputy chief executive officer. The big open space is for reporters while the smaller one is the design section and is connected to the library. The reporters sit together with senior reporters who include investigative journalists and section heads of all the papers. Others in the group are Fuko (print) and Online desk editors.

We arrived at NPL offices at around 11am and we found a number of desks and offices empty. Few minutes later, a group of staff members emerged from the other side of the building with notepads and pens in their hands. Some walked straight to their desks while others stopped by the desks of their reporters. The latter group was heard inviting its reporters to their offices. These were editors and section heads returning from the editorial diary meeting where they discuss pitches of news stories of the day. They were giving the reporters feedback on their pitches. Traditionally, reporters meet their section heads in the morning and pitch their news ideas. After the meeting, they email the story pitches to the section heads who then compile all the pitches for the desk and take them to the editorial meeting where all section heads and senior editors meet to discuss the pitches. It is also at this meeting where they agree on stories for the front and back pages of the newspapers.

At reporters level, everyone was busy with some leaving their desks to a phone call room to contact their news sources while others jumped into a pool transport downstairs to cover news events. Several others were busy on their computers putting their news stories together. Those returning from covering events were seen going straight to their editors' desks to update them on the news story they were working on. In toned voices, some reporters would shout the name of their editors from their desks, *ndatumiza*, which literary means, 'I have sent you the news story' and the editor would respond with a 'thumbs up' or a 'thank you'. A similar kind of interaction was noted across the newsroom, particularly between editors and designers. We saw editors handing over to designers pieces of papers with sketches which presented how they wanted the published pages to look like. In this chapter, we are interested in this newsroom interaction between reporters, editors and designers. While what we saw may not capture in its entirety systems in other newsrooms, the template that guides newsroom work at NPL is representative of what happens in many traditional newsrooms in Africa. This chapter is interested in this aspect of journalism practice at office level to present empirical evidence of how the recent advancements in technologies for newsrooms are transforming newsroom culture and practice in the Global South. NPL as a case study captures a range of rationales for understanding traditional newsroom in Malawi and beyond. Apart from being one of the two oldest print newspapers that have been in operation for more than three decades, its newsroom structure and systems, according to its deputy chief executive office, Alfred Ntonga, were inspired by *The Times* of England, which was the favourite newspaper of its founder, the late Aleke Banda.

We are particularly interested in how technologies are impacting 'newsroom organisational processes'. By newsroom organisation processes we mean the routine processes of news production in print newsrooms. These routines are not universal in nature and we focus on what happens at NPL only. We call these routine processes 'journalism culture and practice' which as Moyo (2013, p. 216) puts it are "values and routines that have always characterized news production, distribution and consumption over the years". This approach captures the illustration used above and allows us to see the routine activities in NPL newsroom as journalism culture and practice. These activities are "based on a routinisation logic that amounts to certain established norms and practices" (Moyo, 2013, p. 216; Schudson, 2003) which happen in a space where journalists are guided by both professional and organisational norms and values that regulate the profession (Tuchman, 1978; Moyo, 2013). Throughout the paper, we use journalism culture and practice to mean routine print newsroom activities like news writing, editing, design and staff appraisals.

The timeliness of this study is that it comes when most literature on the global south focus on how technologies are impacting newsrooms in negative ways, citing issues like shrinking newsrooms due to declining revenues. We argue that technologies are also transforming newsrooms in positive ways (El Gody, 2016). For instance, they have promoted the digital first concept, keeping many print newspapers in business in countries like Malawi and Egypt (Sharra, 2023; El Gody, 2016). In this chapter, we investigate how NPL is deploying digital technologies to improve productivity and efficiency in the newsroom. We focus on its recent attempt to digitalise and automate its whole editorial system, through the adoption of News-Wrap software in 2014. The software was purchased to automate all processes of the organisation from newsroom to marketing. However, this chapter focuses on newsroom only. The software was phased out in the newsroom in 2017 and there are plans to resume using it.

With News-Wrap software, reporters, editors and designers interact and communicate online with no or few paperwork involved. We investigate whether (and in what ways) NPL's decision to procure News-Wrap software transformed the news production process. Our point of departure is to understand what motivated the procurement of the News-Wrap after more than two decades in the business and whether it achieved the intended purpose thus far. Drawing on this, we investigate how the News-Wrap was implemented, embraced by staff, performed and transformed news production processes. We employ the theory of structure, systems theory and structuration theory to understand how different aspects of news production processes were affected by the software. This includes talking to the leadership of the newsroom and users (editors and reporters) to understand how News-Wrap impacted their work.

DIGITALISATION OF NPL NEWSROOM

Journalism practice worldwide has always been shaped by technological developments. However, the third and fourth industrial revolutions caused major disruptions in news production processes. For print media and television, the need to move from delayed to instant publication of news stories through live broadcast of news meant a shift in ways of doing business. For instance, we saw the emergence of what scholars have theorised as 'hybrid newsrooms' characterised by what Prenger and Dueze call "dual management system", a newsroom system that addresses both online and traditional needs of journalism (2017). While televisions have easily moved to 24-hour broadcasts, print newspapers rely on social media platforms and websites to publish briefs while working on detailed articles for the print version. These hybrid newsrooms are common in legacy media newsrooms where organisations embrace digital technologies to be the first to publish online while working on a detailed news story for the traditional platforms (Hendrickx, 2020). The International Centre of Journalists (ICFJ) observes that there is a rapid growth of hybrid newsrooms and a decline in conventional newsrooms across the world. In its recent report, it notes that between 2017 and 2019, hybrid newsrooms grew from 40% to 45%, while traditional newsrooms declined by almost 6% from 27% (ICFJ, 2019). What is more unique about these hybrid newsrooms is their high dependence on technologies to produce and disseminate news. This has also been used as evidence of the growing use of technologies by journalists (Beckett & Yaseen, 2023). What is, however, missing in the analysis is a close examination of the kinds of technologies being adopted in hybrid newsrooms in the global south, including the ways they are transforming newsroom processes, particularly journalism culture and practice.

In Malawi, the adoption of new technologies and the transition to a hybrid newsroom system has been gradual and somewhat abrupt and unplanned. So far, there is no well documented literature that captures how legacy media like radios, televisions and print media have embraced hybrid newsroom system. Nonetheless, few scholars have noted how some legacy media have utilised digital tools to expand their traditional newsrooms over the years. For instance, using a case study of Malawi's oldest radio station, Capital Radio, Last Moyo demonstrates the complexities that shadow the embracement of technologies in legacy media by arguing that the "presence or absence of technologies in newsrooms apart from the material questions of affordability, reflects the decisions of powerful actors that shape media institutions" (2013, p. 217). The actors, as Moyo notes, include the Malawi Regulatory Authority (MACRA) and the policies that empower it to regulate the use of digital technologies in broadcast media. Moyo observes that Capital Radio's digital platforms architecture comprised computers and mobile phones. He says these tools facilitated the consistent use of technologies by journalists before the media organisation opened a website and social networking sites (Moyo, 2013, p. 219).

NPL adopted the hybrid newsroom system in the early 2000s and has teams that produce material for both online and print platforms (Sharra, 2023). In 2023, NPL celebrated its 30th anniversary with a new partnership with iHub online, a dynamic media technology start-up for content creation (Phiri, 2023). Their collaboration is to produce digital content using various technologies (Phiri, 2023). This is the first partnership in Malawi between a legacy media organisation and an independent new media organisation. The partnership also demonstrates the organisation's continued efforts to digitise its systems and processes and be the leading institution in digital news production. However, although this partnership is outstanding, the organisation's most historic intervention happened in 2014 when it purchased a software called News-Wrap. Through the software, NPL became the first hybrid newsroom in Malawi and Sub-Saharan Africa to attempt to digitise its whole newsroom process from reporters to editors and designers allowing automation and artificial intelligence (AI) to be at the centre of its work. This paper focuses on News-Wrap intervention. It examines the processes that led to the purchase of the software, how it was implemented, embraced by newsroom personnel and, more importantly, transformed journalism culture and practice in NPL's newsroom.

Newsroom as an Organisational System

This chapter adopts three complementary theories; organisational theory, systems theory and structuration theory, to understand how News-Wrap was implemented at NPL and affected the newsroom processes. We pay attention to issues of structure, formalisation of processes and individual and group roles that define the everyday business in a newsroom. We study NPL's newsroom as an organisational system allowing us to focus on its editorial processes "that characterize the organization as a whole" (Tolbert & Hall, 2015, p. 16), and how News-Wrap as a technological intervention affected editorial processes. The organisational theory analyses organisational structures in terms of their complexity, formalisation and centralisation of power (Tall & Hall, 2016, pp. 43–57). These aspects help us to show how complexity, in terms of individual, group and organisational needs in the face of News-Wrap, affected its overall implementation. Previous studies have shown how these three aspects of power structure in an organisation like a newsroom affect the implementation of new interventions in newsrooms. For instance, in the United States, David Ryfe shows how *The Daily Times* management's decision to produce more enterprise news over daily news failed due to "deep structure of daily newsgathering, coupled with the inability and/or unwillingness of reporters and editors to bear the costs of altering this structure" (2009, p. 665).

This illustrates the need to pay attention to social structures in an organisation as it captures how different aspects of an organisation can frustrate the success of an intervention even when power is formalised and centralised.

Systems theory, on the other hand, captures the hierarchical elements that make up the organisation structure and how roles of different actors facilitate the organisation's functioning. We treat the newsroom as an 'organised social system' (Josephi, 2000, p. 79) where different actors play various roles in a systematised organisational structure. Ruhl's (1979) work highlights the functional structures of the newsroom and argues that journalistic operations are steered by pre-programmed decision-making (Rühl, 1979). We analyse the newsroom as a self-referential system of journalism (Ruhl, 2004, p. 7) paying attention to "values and routines that characterise news production system" (Moyo, 2013, p. 216). This is done from an organisational perspective because, as Schudson (1995, p. 12) notes, journalism "is not the sum of individual subjective experience but the source and structure that give rise to them" (1995, p. 12). Structuration theory follows the postulation that sees "technology and society in interaction" (Orlikowski, 1992). Originally coined by Giddens (1984), Orlikowski's modification of the concept explains technology's 'duality' by looking at how it is "constructed by actors working in a given social context" and 'flexibility' by focusing on the "capacity of users to interpret, appropriate and manipulate technology in various ways" (1992, p. 409). Simply put, "technologies do not have effects built into them, because it is always a question of how particular technologies come to be institutionalized in particular ways" (Mare, 2013, p. 19). Thus, "interaction of technology with organizations must be understood dialectically, as involving reciprocal causation, where the specific institutional context and the actions of knowledgeable, reflexive humans always mediate the relationship" (Orlikowski, 1992, p. 423).

Methodologically, this study takes an ethnography approach that involved experiencing the newsroom culture and practice first hand in NPL newsroom and interviews with newsroom personnel. A two-day ethnography in November 2023 was conducted at the NPL's newsroom headquarters in Blantyre where all editors are based. This was to appreciate how the routine editorial activities are conducted and contrast them with News-Wrap process. One-on-one and phone interviews were conducted with ten staff members (four senior editors, two technical journalists and four reporters) selected randomly based on experience. These individuals were around during the time of implementing News-Wrap and at the time of the interviews, they had spent more than ten years in the organisation. The staff members we spoke to are categorised into three: management, editors and reporters. By management, we refer to individuals who represent the whole newsroom at management level. For instance, in this study we spoke to the deputy CEO who heads the newsroom and Technical Editor who is in-charge of technical issues in the newsroom. By Editors, we mean all staff members who supervise junior reporters. In NPL newsroom, they are clearly distinguished through the use of terms like Section Heads which cover individuals who edit a section of a newspaper, and they include Copy Editors, Technical Editors meaning those who supervise technical journalists or designers, and finally Brand Editors, those who are in charge of a whole newspaper. The questions were framed around understanding what they know about News-Wrap, how they were engaged, its implementation, what they think contributed to its withdrawal and whether they can support its return.

NEWS-WRAP ENTERS NPL NEWSROOM

NPL has always been in the forefront of adopting new technologies and this is largely attributed to its participation in international conferences. For instance, NPL established its first website in 1998, thus, after one of its former editors, Gracian Tukula, had attended a six-week training under the auspices of the Netherlands Management Cooperation programme in Europe (Sharra, 2023). Since then, the organisation has adopted several technologies to improve its editorial system. The Online Desk, which now has a Social Media Policy, is among the departments that have embraced several new AI technologies for digitalisation of the newsroom (Nation Publications Limited, 2020), leading to automation of most of its activities. Recent investments in automation at NPL are aimed at utilising online platforms to sustain print newspaper, a new way of running traditional media in the digital age (Lewis & Cushion, 2009; Cushion & Lewis, 2009; Sharra, 2023; Moyo, 2013).

> What happens at NPL is that sometimes we learn from others. Malawi, we are kind of an enclosed society, but whenever opportunities come to travel, we do go out and learn from others. We got the News-Wrap idea when our CEO, Mbumba Banda, attended the WAN-IFRA Summit in Europe, and we said look, this is exciting and we should try it. (Personal interview, A. Ntonga, November 23, 2023)

During the early years of the website, they used to post news stories that are in print online around midday. They were uploaded late in the night and then posted manually. Later on, they adopted AI technologies to upload the news articles and set them to be published automatically at a particular time. This has simplified the work of online editors, allowing them to post news online at the same time as the traditional copy goes to print. The delayed publication of online paper is to ensure all copies of the print newspaper are sold. At the time of the study, the organisation had several software programmes for different desks particularly Online, Design and Library sections. News-Wrap, however, stands out as one of the first AI software programmes to have attempted to automate all editorial processes in the newsroom. According to NPL's deputy chief executive officer who also heads the newsroom, Alfred Ntonga, the idea to adopt News-Wrap came from the WIN-IFRA Summit and appreciation of how the software could transform their newsroom processes.

In 2014, the organisation hired a team from India called 4Cs to install and implement NewsWrap at NPL. Although this chapter focuses on newsroom, News-Wrap was adopted to automate processes in all the departments of the organisation. In the newsroom, News-Wrap installation started with Blantyre where NPL's headquarters is based. The organisation has bureau offices in two other regions of the country and the offices are in Lilongwe and Mzuzu cities. Ntonga says News-Wrap was adopted to automate the newsroom systems.

There were multiple factors that made us think we should get that way, one of them was the need to automate our newsroom processes and NewsWrap does that so well. Automation makes life easier on certain things that are of routine nature. You know process of production can be a bit cumbersome, and if not done properly, you can have many people working on things that are of routine nature. This comes with costs. So, as an organisation, we were trying to see where the machine could do some tasks and allow humans to concentrate on things that could bring tangible returns by the end of the day. That's the advantage of automation. (Personal interview, A. Ntonga, November 23, 2023)

NPL's Technical Editor Andrew Mtupanyama, who was at the centre of the implementation of the News-Wrap software, captured both the key objective and how it was structured at implementation stage.

> News-Wrap is like an integrated news production system. Everyone inputs the content on the same platform, but the users have got different access rights. For instance, a reporter would just upload the text and then the Editor of that desk would be able to access the report. So even before this person has completed the story, the Editor would be able to know that this person has done maybe 8 paragraphs and would be able to follow the progress of the story, but the editor cannot do anything before it is submitted. The Editor [section head] will only be able to view. Once submitted, the Editor can now have access and start editing. (Personal interview, A. Mtupanyama, November 24, 2023)

What News-Wrap mainly did was to digitalise and automate the news production process. Thus, all the roles played by reporters to editors, then technical journalists and managing editors to designers were performed online and, in a space where management could see who was doing what. It replaced what we saw the day we visited the newsroom. Reporters were no longer emailing and informing their editors that they have submitted the news article. Similarly, editors were not moving around with hard copy papers to the copy editors or designers. Everyone was working in the system.

> It's a smart system. At editors level, the editor submits to the designers and copy editors. Thus, the designer will see the headline, byline, text, picture and caption. So instead of the designer coming back to the Editor to say you haven't given me a caption etc, everything will be there. If you forget when uploading, the system will ask you that you are uploading a picture but there is no caption the same way an email will ask you that you are sending an email without a subject. So, the software ensures there is a smooth flow of the work because the newspaper is about time, so you don't have to be asking each other the obvious questions. Simply put, NewsWrap ensures all the elements that are supposed to be there for a print newspaper are there. (Personal Interview, A. Mtupanyama, November 24, 2023)

From this, we see how NPL tried to digitise its newsroom process and allowed the staff members at all levels to interact through a software in ways that ensured each actor plays the expected roles online. Both Mtupanyama and Ntonga say the other objective was to improve efficiency in the newsroom processes. They said the system ensures responsibility at individual level. For instance, it is easy to track the origin of an error that ended up in the published article. It records whatever one does in the system.

In the event where an editor introduced errors to the news story and the errors have given rise to legal issues, the system is there to help address issues which could have been addressed through reports and arguments, but the system will just fish out the original copy of the reporter and show the edited version. Similarly, if three people have edited the same copy, the system will show where the error originated from. If you submit to the Section Head, then it will be sent to the Copy Editor. The Copy Editor may add some background which may not be relevant, and if the problem comes from the background which may not be factual, then we would know that this background was added by the Copy Editor. So, it takes the responsibility of blaming everything on the reporter to the actual person who introduced an error. (Personal Interview, A. Mtupanyama, November 24, 2023)

Not only that, but the software was also useful with staff appraisals. Since all records were kept online, the management was able to see contributions by each staff member and prevented cases in which seniors reward employees they like most. Ntonga said News-Wrap was also preferred to enhance efficiency and objectivity in the way they look at things, and to encourage reporters to work hard, knowing they will be judged and rewarded fairly.

We are not only crammed in one place. Apart from Blantyre, we have Mzuzu and Lilongwe offices. Each office has reporters who produce stories, and it is very important that where we need to increase the numbers or reduce the numbers of staff, it's based on controllable data. At the same time, it is also important that whenever we want to reward, we should not just reward people because there are numbers, but we should be able to objectively assess productivity. New-Wrap is able to do that in an objective way looking at the various roles each person plays in the production system. (Personal interview, A. Ntonga, November 23, 2023)

Mtupanyama said that on a weekly basis News-Wrap produces a report on what each desk has done. The newsroom structure relies on a group of employees headed by a Section Head. They are responsible for producing particular pages and they are allocated time or what are called Print Runs, to ensure their pages are sent to print. News-Wrap captures all this process and produces a report that shows what was done by who and at what time.

For instance, if it is a Wednesday paper, the first 'print Run' will have Political Index, which is a pullout. This one will be the first to be printed on the machine and the deadline is 10am on Monday. These pages must be done a day before production. The system will note that this page was submitted late to the next level and when producing the report, it will indicate that this section had these delays. So instead of producing reports which may look like witch-hunting because if I don't like you, I can just add 30 minutes and make your page look like it has delayed, but this one is a fair judge. It helps our seniors to see where the problems are and how to address them. (Personal interview, A. Mtupanyama, November 24, 2023)

Both Ntonga and Mtupanyama, as well as other senior staff members, said that News-Wrap was seen as a saviour that would have cut down some of the costs. They cited a process that they still believe costs the organisation a lot of money through printing. Once the reporters submit their news articles, the editor prints out the final copy and gives it to the copy editor who indicates areas for corrections on the paper using a marker pen. The copy editor sends it back to the editor, who fixes the errors and print it again and submits to the copy editor for approval. This process continues until the copy editor and editor are happy with the story. The same process happens between the editor and designers. Once designers have finished designing a paper, they print it out and give the editor and this process continues until the editor and managing editor are satisfied that the page is ready for print. It is then sent to the Technical Editor, who prints out a sample and have the responsible designers and any other sign to say they saw the final copy. The Technical team also records manually the time when they got the article from the editor and completed by the designer and sent it out to print.

Based on this discussion, it is evident that News-Wrap was mainly adopted to digitise the newsroom process to allow the staff members to coordinate through an automated system that allocates roles based on one's hierarchy in the newsroom. It also captured all details of what every newsroom member was contributing to the process which simplified the process of generating evidence and assessing staff productivity. According to Ntonga and Mtupanyama, each staff member had access rights to the system. For instance, reporters, once they are happy with their news story, would release it to the Section Head. Similarly, a Section Head would release it to the Copy Editor, and the Copy Editor back to the Section Head, who then sends it to the Technical Journalist for design and Editor for approval. The Editors work closely with the Managing Editor and Editor-in-Chief.

Figure 5.1 shows the flow of roles. News-Wrap had those connections in the system and responsible officers would only wait for pop-ups to perform their roles. Each individual has rights that limit what they can see in the system. Those at the senior level, like the Editor, Managing Editor and Editor-in-Chief, have exclusive rights to see what is happening at all levels.

One of the major findings was that all interviewees believed the software achieved the intended goals even at partial implementation. For instance, the management personnel said they were able to see what was happening in the system and could identify gaps in production processes and make timely decisions. There was also a cut on stationery and printing costs, including production time, although this was affected by those not using the software for various reasons. Some reporters said the system helped them to see the changes made to their stories which became an easy learning process as they could refer back to the articles stored in the system. One of the Designers, Matteus Mapiko, praised the policing element in the News-Wrap and speculated that this may be one of the reasons it is no longer in use.

> News-Wrap is really smart, and it helped in facilitating control of production and encourage efficiency at all levels. We work with deadlines in the newsroom. Each page has a specific time to be ready. Thus, each newsroom personnel is allocated specific times to perform particular routine roles. This

Fig. 5.1 Work flow pathway. (Source: Fieldwork 2023)

made every individual do their job on time and pass it over to the next person, thereby creating efficiency in production. However, some saw this as a trap that would expose their inefficiencies. Another issue is that it reduced the need for other people's roles in the newsroom and this created job insecurity to many. (Personal interview, M. Mapiko, November 24, 2023)

Ntonga said that, overall, there are many things to celebrate about News-Wrap despite its short lifespan at NPL. He said there is no way a big newsroom like NPL can avoid new technologies like AI and said this justifies the organisation's decision to invest heavily in News-Wrap. He, however, said that because of their experience with News-Wrap and the rhetoric around AI, their approach to adopting AI and any other automated newsroom systems is to ensure they are complemented by humans. He insisted that he looks forward to the day when "AI will be integrated fully into our newsroom processes so that routine works are done quickly and more efficiently". Ntonga believes this will come with many advantages including improved news headlines.

A Failed Intervention?

It was during the third year of implementing News-Wrap at NPL that the organisation decided to scale down and eventually revert to its traditional system. At the time of this publication, it had been six years since the decision was made but the organisation insists, they only suspended it to put its house in order and resume its implementation later. Simply put, the software faced many challenges which are unique to African newsrooms and this reminds us that African journalism has codes and principles that differ from the normative Western view (Nyamnjoh, 2005, 2010; Akpojivi & Fosu, 2020). In this section, we discuss some of the factors that led to its discontinuation. We argue that implementation of News-Wrap was affected by three main challenges. The first is that the decision-making process at management level was not inclusive and it ignored or delayed engaging voices that could have helped in making timely decisions which could have saved some of the resources spent. The second is poor quality equipment that could not support News-Wrap. The third one is reception at user level. By user level, we mean everyone that was expected to use the software at newsroom.

The first major challenge that affected the sustainability of News-Wrap at NPL was that the management hurried in signing contracts with 4Cs before sufficiently engaging its technical team to understand how well the software could be implemented at NPL, including the feasibility of the intervention in a developing newsroom like this. Two issues emerge here. The first is that during the entire full implementation period of News-Wrap, 4Cs team from India was in Malawi and NPL covered their costs. There was no clear arrangement for the team to train local staff to take over its implementation within the shortest period of time which proved costly on the part of investor. According to Ntonga, one of the major factors that led to its withdrawal was that the team from India took long to finish the installation, and thus, its sustainability depended on the team being on the ground which was not feasible economically. We also noted that even if NPL decides to resume using News-Wrap today, they will still need 4Cs to come back which is a costly arrangement considering that they also pay for the software.

Secondly, the procurement did not pay attention to issues of compatibility which slowed the whole installation processes. Other issues arose while 4Cs team was already on the ground. They realised NPL's computers were too old to support the News-Wrap software. The internet speed was also slow. NPL also ended up investing heavily in creating a reliable database. We noted that although all staff use computers, the nature and type of computers for departments vary. In the newsroom, reporters used computers that can only support writing news stories on Microsoft Word document. Departments such as library and technical are stocked with powerful computers that can support software like In-Design Studio. This arrangement made things worse and delayed the full implementation of the software.

> We discovered some challenges when the software was already here. For instance, you really need faster internet and modern computers to handle the software. In some parts of our newsroom, the computers we had were incompatible with the software. I should say there were many things that militated against our interests, and to try to improvise, it took us long. We also had issues with the terminal particularly for reports filing a news story outside the newsroom. For example, if a reporter is in Mzuzu and filing a story using a shared terminal, it was difficult to know who is filing the story. Thus, for staff like me, I would only start to see the story from the Editor who is editing it because normally, editors have a terminal. Thus, it would be the Editor's terminal registering instead of the reporter. Honestly, there were just so many factors militating against what we wanted to achieve really (Personal interview, A. Ntonga, November 23, 2023).

Mtupanyama added that compatibility issues affected its total implementation especially in the newsroom. He said that they ended up having some staff members using the software and others not. The most affected group was that of journalists, particularly those using personal computers or office computers that did not meet the software compatibility. One of the senior editors, Aubrey Mchulu, said efforts to improvise did not produce expected results. Among others, he said, they set aside some computers to be used by members of particular desks so that each team has a reliable computer for uploading their materials. However, this only slowed the production further, making reverting to traditional system inevitable.

> Each desk, like The Business or Current News Desk had one or two computers. Thus, the reporters on desk would only log in, if they were to use NewsWrap. Unfortunately, this led to delays in production. When this problem was realised, we changed to restrict News-Wrap for producing front and back pages of the newspaper. This did not help, and we eventually reverted to the traditional system. (Personal interview, A. Mchulu, November 24, 2023)

We argue that such challenges could have been avoided had the management engaged its local team to understand the capacity for a new intervention. We found that both technical team and reporters were not involved. Most newsroom members only responded to what they were told to do. For instance, Mtupanyama said he learnt about the software when 4Cs was in Malawi. This means there was no exchange of notes between 4Cs and NPL's Technical team on what the installer wanted for the software to work. We argue that if the 4Cs and the head of technical department were engaged from the onset, issues of compatibility could have been addressed before commissioning the project. This also speaks to the issue of continued westernisation of African newsrooms through adoption of western ideas without paying attention to the local context (Nyamnjoh, 2010).

> The CEO went to India and visited a publication there. So, she was impressed with the way News-Wrap was helping in speeding up the production process. So, 4Cs was invited to implement the software. In my case, I was just told that there is a team from India with a new innovation, and you are invited. So, we got into the meeting, and we were told good things about News-Wrap, and we went ahead to implement what our managers wanted. (Personal interview, A. Mtupanyama, November 24, 2023)

The gravity of this problem can be seen in the specifications that 4Cs wanted against what NPL had. Mtupanyama said that 4Cs recommended a minimum of i5 Generation computers. NPL had some computers which met the condition, but they were old versions with reduced performance. He said most of the computers they had were from Pentium Generation and incompatible with the software.

We also noted that Mtupanyama was among the first newsroom members to be introduced to the software because of his position as the Technical Editor. We also noted that he and other senior editors were very passionate about the software. This is seen in how they supported the implementation of the software despite several shortfalls. However, it took months for most of the staff members to understand what was happening in the organisation. Most of them were engaged at the implementation stage. Interestingly, some reporters said they never used the system until its suspension. This speaks to the whole issues of inclusivity and engagement when coming up with interventions in an organisation. Ryfe and other social theorists note that "the immediate experience of actors in a social situation is with one another and not with abstract structures" (2009, p. 675). Actually, they do not "experience social structures so much as they experience interpretation of those structures" (Wiley, 1994; Ryfe, 2009, p. 675). We argue that NPL's newsroom staff were mainly constrained by the structure of the system which demanded them to do journalism differently using a software that was just imposed on them and paid little attention to pertinent issues that define their day-to-day business. Most of the interviewees wondered how they would effectively support a system that was going to affect how they do their job when they were not engaged from the onset, at a time when they were complaining of poor equipment in the newsroom. For instance, some of them said that the newsroom had less than ten computers in good shape, that were not accessible to everyone.

There were also mixed reactions to how each of the individuals was introduced to the software, with some saying the process was more informal. Macdonald Bamusi, a Copy Editor at NPL, said the News-Wrap training was informal particularly between Technical and editorial team.

The training was a bit informal. The formal part was done between the buyer and suppliers. The supplier sent its technical team who interacted with NPL's technical team, they trained each other. Now the passing on of knowledge from the technical people to the editors was not very formal and it took a bit of time for us to appreciate the importance, even the processes. (Personal interview, M. Bamusi, November 24, 2023)

Mercy Malikwa, who at the time of the interview was no longer working for NPL but was around during the entire time of the software, said that she benefited from desk-specific orientation. She said during the first days, it was mandatory for everyone to use News-Wrap, and every person had an account. She admitted that the story may be different from one staff to another because the interface of the software varied and also NPL has workers based in its bureau offices. Those on Features Desk had a different interface compared to those on Current News and the orientation she got was specific to Features Desk, where she worked. Random interviews with employees based in bureaus show that they were not trained, and that the software was not installed at their offices. This means News-Wrap was mainly used at the headquarters. Nonetheless, some reporters at the headquarters said they did not receive any training and did not even use the software.

One of the senior reporters who has been with the organisation for more than a decade, Lucky Mkandawire, said he knew about the software but due to lack of computers in the newsroom, he use his personal laptop. While the organisation was able to install News-Wrap in personal laptops, he did not benefit from it because his laptop was not meeting the software's specifications. For this reason, he did not use the software throughout its lifespan despite being in the newsroom during the time of News-Wrap. Theorists of organisational studies highlight the need to pay attention to organisational structures when attempting an intervention. Tolbert and Hall (2015) call organisation structures as "complexity" in an organisation. Their argument is that an organisation has three aspects: individuals, groups and organisation. It is the roles of individuals and groups that result in achieving the ultimate goal of an organisation. In this case, although the decision to automate the whole newsroom had the potential to achieve high returns in the long run, NPL's failure to tap into the interests of different individuals and groups in the organisation, including their specific needs, affected the realisation of the goals. Certainly, the staff were restrained by their interpretation of the social structures. They believed News-Wrap implementation was rushed and would not work. This was more evident during the visit to NPL headquarters. Our ethnography reveal that some journalists were not interested and did not support the system, and it explains the challenges of adopting top-down approaches to policy that ignore society's unique needs (Nyamnjoh, 2005, 2010). For instance, some journalists said they didn't know there was News-Wrap when they were around when it was introduced and implemented. We also noted that even when the organisation arranged to install the software in personal laptops, some journalists snubbed the offer and for this reason they did not directly engage with the software.

LOOKING INTO THE FUTURE

Although News-Wrap failed, the organisation believes they learnt lessons which will inform future decisions in adopting new technologies. They argue that while News-Wrap can be seen as a failure, their contract with 4Cs is still intact and plans are there to roll it out fully in the near future once compatibility issues are addressed.

> We have stopped using it until the computer situation is improved but we still have the software in our system. The partnership is still there, and the contract is intact, of course some aspects have been put on hold since we are not using it fully. All the individual accounts and the server are intact. We heavily invested in the servers, so we can't just abandon it. I think we were also affected by Covid-19 because some of the partners who used to give us computers on regular basis like the Chinese Embassy, haven't come to give us with gifts. The Covid-19 situation also affected business, so we haven't been able to improve on the computers. We are now behind in terms of the technology advancement, and we've put it on hold hoping that once we get back on our feet, we will be able to start again. (Personal interview, A. Mtupanyama, November 24, 2023)

However, according to Mtupanyama, this will involve starting all over due to many changes that have happened in the organisation. He says they will start by training staff members because many newsroom members are no longer with the organisation. Ntonga insists suspension of News-Wrap should not be taken as a failure because it was partially implemented.

> Three issues affected this project: lack of faster internet, good computers and of course the knowledge. We take News-Wrap as a work in progress. We are not afraid of trying something new, put it on hold and wait for another day. This is in NPL's spirit. We will definitely get over this and automate our newsroom. (Personal interview, A. Ntonga, November 23, 2023)

These sentiments are shared by many staff members in the newsroom. They see automation as the future of newsrooms and journalism. When asked whether they would support News-Wrap on its return, almost every interviewee expressed optimism and believes the issues that affected its full implementation will have been addressed.

It's a modern way of doing business in the newsroom, I would strongly recommend News-Wrap. But it goes down to the investors that we have in the media industry. They want you to use low quality computers as long as you produce a story, and that's okay with them. But if you look at the media landscape now, it is digital. We need gadgets that can simplify our work. We are now required to do many things at once. We are multitasking all the time. So, I would strongly recommend NewsWrap again. (Personal interview, M. Bamusi, November 24, 2023)

Mchulu concurs with Bamusi, saying that as long as the computer and other issues noted are addressed, it is important for NPL to bring back News-Wrap. He also spoke highly of NPL's commitment to investing in technologies, saying that the organisation demonstrated commitment by buying the software and also meet costs of hosting the installers in Malawi for more than two years. He said News-Wrap is something worth having in a modern newsroom. While this case cannot be said to be representative of all media organisations in Malawi and Africa, NPL's experience with News-Wrap sheds light on the challenges of adopting technologies in developing print newsrooms, especially at the time when print sales are dwindling and surviving on limited resources. We cannot also say the challenges NPL face mirror the situation in the country and region as whole. As scholars such as Mabweazara (2014) and Gody (2016) have argued elsewhere against such blanketing, we treat this case as a starting point to think about how different newsrooms adopt technologies, including the ways they affect the newsroom. More broadly, the chapter also takes us back to the debate around digital divide, particularly how as Mare (2013) notes "issues of access to technologies in their diverse forms shape and constrain the news agenda of local newspapers". Understanding these issues with such an open mind can help other newsrooms in Malawi and beyond to plan and prepare for new technologies rather than experiment with technologies that require huge investments.

CONCLUSION

This study has investigated the processes through which a software called News-Wrap found its way into the newsroom of Malawi's leading print and online newspaper, NPL, and how it was implemented, and staff engaged with it. We demonstrated that the software was adopted to help in automating the newsroom processes, reduce workload and improve efficiency in the organisation. It was withdrawn completely from the newsroom in 2017 after more than two years of implementation, but with plans to resume its use in the future. The findings also show that the decision to procure the software was inspired by experience of how it works elsewhere, particularly in India. Although newsroom is universal in its nature, context and standards are barely universal (Akpojivi & Fosu, 2020). We examined the key decision-making processes and argued that the software failed to achieve the expected results because some decisions were rushed and key voices in the newsroom were not involved. Interests of different groups of staff members were also not given the necessary attention and this affected the user experience at different levels. One of the key factors that frustrated the intervention was poor quality of facilitates, particularly computers and internet speed. The computers were of old generation and not compatible with the software. Lack of expertise was another factor that made the investment unattainable as the software required the installers to be in Malawi during the two years of installation. All these challenges point to the key issues that hamper the penetration of new technologies in newsrooms in developing economies and present lessons that can inform future investments of this nature in developing newsrooms.

REFERENCES

Akpojivi, U., & Fosu, M. (2020). African Language Journalism in Ghana and the Quest for Quality and Sustainable Broadcast Journalism: An Investigation of Peace FM. In *African Language Media*, 204–223. Routledge. https://www.taylorfrancis.com/chapters/edit/10.4324/9781003004738-17/african-language-journalism-ghana-quest-quality-sustainable-broadcast-journalism-ufuoma-akpojivi-modestus-fosu

Beckett, C., & Yaseen, M. (2023). *Generating Change: A Global Survey of What News Organisations Are Doing with AI.* United Kingdom: London School of Economics. www.chrome-extension://efaidnbmnnnibpcajpcglclefindmkaj/https://static1.squarespace.com/static/64d60527c01ae7106f2646e9/t/656e400a1c23e22da0681c46/1701724190867/Generating+Change+_+The+Journalism+AI+report+_+English.pdf

Cushion, S., & Lewis, J. (2009). Towards aFoxification'of 24-Hour News Channels in Britain? An Analysis of Market-Driven and Publicly Funded News Coverage. *Journalism, 10*(2), 131–153.

El Gody, A. (2016). The Use of Information and Communication Technologies in Three Egyptian Newsrooms. In *Digital Technologies and the Evolving African Newsroom* (pp. 78–98). Routledge. https://api.taylorfrancis.com/content/chapters/edit/download?identifierName=doi&identifierValue=10.4324/9781315741826-6&type=chapterpdf

Giddens, A. (1984). *The Constitution of Society: Outline of the Theory of Structuration.* University of California Press. https://books.google.co.uk/books?hl=en&lr=&id=x2bf4g9Z6ZwC&oi=fnd&pg=PR9&dq=.+1984.+The+Constitution+of+Society:+Outline+of+the+Theory+of+Structuration.+Berkeley+and+Los+Angeles:+University+of+California+Press.&ots=jPUR0ous8E&sig=K5baFiQodfihR633bfd6ygCYkK0

Gunde, A. M. (2015). The Political Role of the Media in the Democratisation of Malawi: The Case of the Weekend Nation from 2002 to 2012.

Hendrickx, J. (2020). Trying to Survive While Eroding News Diversity: Legacy News Media's Catch-22. *Journalism Studies, 21*(5), 598–614.

ICFJ. (2019). The State of Technology in Global Newsrooms. 2. www.chrome-extension://efaidnbmnnnibpcajpcglclefindmkaj/https://www.icfj.org/sites/default/files/2019-10/2019%20Final%20Report.pdf

Josephi, B. (2000). Newsroom Research: Its Importance for Journalism Studies. *Australian Journalism Review, 22*(2), 75–87.

Lewis, J., & Cushion, S. (2009). The Thirst to Be First: An Analysis of Breaking News Stories and Their Impact on the Quality of 24-Hour News Coverage in the UK. *Journalism Practice, 3*(3), 304–318.

Mabweazara, H. M., Mudhai, O. F., & Whittaker, J. (2014). Introduction: Online Journalism in Africa: Trends, Practices and Emerging Cultures. In *Online Journalism in Africa* (pp. 1–14). Routledge. https://api.taylorfrancis.com/content/chapters/edit/download?identifierName=doi&identifierValue=10.4324/9780203382530-1&type=chapterpdf

Mare, A. (2013). New Media Technologies and Internal Newsroom Creativity in Mozambique: The Case Of@ Verdade. In *Digital Technologies and the Evolving African Newsroom*, 13–29. Routledge. https://api.taylorfrancis.com/content/chapters/edit/download?identifierName=doi&identifierValue=10.4324/9781315741826-2&type=chapterpdf

Moyo, L. (2013). The Digital Turn in Radio: A Critique of Institutional and Organizational Modeling of New Radio Practices and Cultures. *Telematics and Informatics, 30*(3), 214–222.

Nation Publications Limited. (2020). *Social Media Policy.* Nation Publications Limited.

Nyamnjoh, F. B. (2005). *Africa's Media, Democracy and the Politics of Belonging.* Zed Books. https://books.google.com/books?hl=en&lr=&id=0Tr6EUTxQ WYC&oi=fnd&pg=PA1&dq=Frances+Nyamnjoh%E2%80%99s+book+Africa+ Media+and+Democracy&ots=v-eqAKazaE&sig=PLjrrzUWET4NmKDMu0h Gi9UJ6yg

Nyamnjoh, F. B. (2010). De-Westernizing Media Theory to Make Room for African Experience. In *Popular Media, Democracy and Development in Africa* (pp. 35–47). Routledge. https://www.taylorfrancis.com/chapters/edit/10.4324/9780203843260-9/de-westernizing-media-theory-make-room-african-experience-francis-nyamnjoh

Orlikowski, W. J. (1992). The Duality of Technology: Rethinking the Concept of Technology in Organizations. *Organization Science, 3*(3), 398–427. https://doi.org/10.1287/orsc.3.3.398

Phiri, C. (2023, September 3). NPL Partners Malick Mnela's Ihub Online Tv for Events Live Streaming. Online edition. https://www.247malawi.com/npl-partners-malick-mnelas-ihub-online-tv-for-events-live-streaming/

Prenger, M., & Dueze, M. (2017). 12 A History of Innovation and Entrepreneurialism in Journalism. *Remaking the News: Essays on the Future of Journalism Scholarship in the Digital Age* (p. 235).

Rühl, M. (1979). Die Zeitungsredaktion Als Organisiertes Soziales System (The Newspaper Editorial Office as an Organized Social System). *Fribourg: Universitätsverlag.*

Ruhl, M. (2004). Positioning Journalism Research in World Society. *Journalism Research in an Era of Globalization.*

Ryfe, D. M. (2009). Broader and Deeper: A Study of Newsroom Culture in a Time of Change. *Journalism, 10*(2), 197–216. https://doi.org/10.1177/1464884908100601

Schudson, M. (1995). *The Power of News.* Harvard University Press. https://books.google.co.uk/books?hl=en&lr=&id=jr9V0ku5rzoC&oi=fnd&pg=PA1 &dq=Schudson+(1995,12)is+not+the+sum+of+individual+subjective+experie nce+but+the+source+and+structure+that+gives+rise+to+them&ots=RYUYOB lZCW&sig=YAV4fxw_funawjGKVeGIToqHXg4

Schudson, M. (2003). The Sociology of News. *New York.* https://scholar.google.com/scholar?cluster=2948761692924443840&hl=en&oi=scholarr

Sharra, A. (2020). Eyes of the Society: How Malawian Journalists Utilize Question Time during Political Press Briefings. *African Journalism Studies, 41*(3), 49–64.

Sharra, A. (2023). "Digital First" as a Coping Measure for Malawi's Print Newspapers. In *New Journalism Ecologies in East and Southern Africa: Innovations, Participatory and Newsmaking Cultures,* (pp. 113–132). Springer.

Tolbert, P. S., & Hall, R. H. (2015). *Organizations: Structures, Processes and Outcomes*. Routledge. https://api.taylorfrancis.com/content/books/mono/download?identifierName=doi&identifierValue=10.4324/9781315663388&type=googlepdf

Tuchman, G. (1978). Making News: A Study in the Construction of Reality. https://espace.library.uq.edu.au/view/UQ:735008

Visonà, M. B. (2017). Gifts from Our Elders: African Arts and Visionary Art History. *African Arts, 50*(3), 1–7.

Wiley, N. (1994). *The Semiotic Self*. University of Chicago Press.

CHAPTER 6

The Illusion of Change: Unveiling News Production and Consumption Dynamics in Zimpapers News Hub

Samuel Anesu Muzhingi and Jennings Joy Chibike

INTRODUCTION

In the dynamic realm of global media, the swift progression of digital technologies has catalysed a transformative era, reshaping the landscape of information dissemination and consumption globally (Jiang et al., 2022; Rosmani et al., 2020). In the context of Zimbabwe in recent years, there has been the mushrooming of digital media platforms and the utilisation

---

S. A. Muzhingi (✉)
William Allen White School of Journalism and Mass Communications, The University of Kansas, Lawrence, KS, USA

Daystar University, Athi River, Kenya

J. J. Chibike
Language, Media and Communication Studies, Lupane State University, Bulawayo, Zimbabwe

Media, Communication, Film and Theatre Arts, Midlands State University, Gweru, Zimbabwe

© The Author(s), under exclusive license to Springer Nature 109
Switzerland AG 2025
A. Sharra, U. Akpojivi (eds.), *Technologies and Media Production Cultures*, Palgrave Studies in Journalism and the Global South,
https://doi.org/10.1007/978-3-031-78582-5_6

of new media for journalistic purposes (Munoriyarwa & Chibuwe, 2022). Munoriyarwa and Chibuwe (2022) posit that there has been a rise of start-up media houses which are dominating digital spheres and posing a serious threat to already established media outlets. More so, Tshabangu and Salawu (2022) attribute this to the fact that established media outlets, though they are beginning to have new media presence, are not vigorously using digital spheres. Moyo (2009) poignantly notes that digital media outlets concerned with Zimbabwe such as *NewZimbabwe.com* and *Kubatana.net* emerged as a result of the environment in the country which stifles the minority, opposition political parties and general diversity as this is seen as embracing counter-hegemonic motives. While these online platforms are being seen as alternate public spheres in Zimbabwe, Tshabangu and Salawu (2022) posit that they still feel the ripple effects of being stifled and muzzled in various ways by the government. It can, therefore, be seen that even though the digital media landscape is growing in Zimbabwe, outlets independent and critical of the government face restriction while those linked to the government have not vibrantly used its digital presence to maximum use in the new dispensation (Tshabangu & Salawu, 2022)

The ascent of the digital revolution has not only sparked inquiries into the pivotal role of digital platforms in moulding public discourse and democratic engagement but has also generated extensive scholarly discourse on these subjects (Harcup, 2023; Dragomir & Thompson, 2014; Allan & Matheson, 2004). Scholars like Harcup (2023) have further delved into the intersection of journalism ethics and academic discussions, particularly in the context of digital media's impact on the metamorphosis of journalism practices and the consumption of cultural artefacts. Research by Xu and Zhang (2022), Rosmani et al. (2020), and Albarana (2010) has explored the transformation of journalism and news consumption in the digital epoch, revealing a reconfiguration of journalistic processes. However, this chapter contributes to the ongoing scholarship on digital media and journalism by narrowing its focus to news applications, specifically the Zimbabwe Papers (Zimpapers) News Hub, a previously unexplored domain. Through the perspectives of both journalists and users of the application, this chapter investigates the intricate dynamics of news production and consumption. It delves into the methods employed by journalists in creating news for the application, unravelling the intricate process of content generation. Simultaneously, it scrutinises how audiences engage with and absorb information from this platform, drawing comparisons with their interactions with traditional news media. This exploration seeks to answer questions surrounding how journalists navigate the digital landscape to produce content for this unique platform and how audiences, in turn, navigate this digital space for information consumption.

The significance of this study lies in its scrutiny of journalists' role in crafting news for applications and users' patterns of media consumption within the realm of computer-generated applications. This exploration aims to discern whether journalistic practices and media consumption are truly evolving in the digital age, with a specific emphasis on news applications as opposed to websites, an aspect that has been insufficiently addressed in previous scholarship. By shedding light on these dynamics, this study contributes to enhancing journalism practices within the context of the Fourth Industrial Revolution.

BACKGROUND

Zimbabwe's media landscape evolution is intricately tied to historical, political, and economic changes. The pursuit of independence in 1980 aimed to establish a democratic media environment, yet persistent colonial shadows, as highlighted by Tshabangu and Salawu (2022), significantly shaped the trajectory of the media landscape. Colonialism's enduring impact continued to influence media operations, reinforcing established norms and power structures (Msindo, 2009).

Msindo (2009) points out how press institutions like the *Rhodesia Herald, Chronicle, Sunday Mail, Sunday News*, and *Financial Gazette* played a crucial role during the colonial era, promoting the interests of the white ruling elite. They not only disseminated information but also acted as conduits for promoting European culture and denigrating African culture, perpetuating negative portrayals of Africans (Mukasa, 2003). Media consumption at this time was marked by a controlled flow of information directed by colonial authorities, marginalising indigenous perspectives.

An examination of media consumption during the colonial epoch reveals a landscape where information dissemination was precisely regulated, reinforcing the colonial power structure (Mukasa, 2003). Journalistic practices operated within a framework restricted by colonial authorities, limiting access to diverse and objective information (Msindo, 2009; Mukasa, 2003). Censorship and control dictated practices, moulding a narrative aligned with the colonial agenda (Mukasa, 2003). Journalistic practices during colonial times, as Msindo (2009) and Mukasa (2003) note, were inherently biased, serving the interests of the ruling elite, constrained by censorship. The information landscape was manipulated to reinforce the colonial narrative, perpetuating stereotypes, and marginalising indigenous voices.

This historical context forms the foundation for understanding shifts in media consumption and journalistic practices post-independence. Digital platforms have emerged in response to the challenges posed by colonial influences, economic constraints, and the legacy of traditional media. This chapter examines the evolution of digital journalism in Zimbabwe, focusing on platforms like Zimpapers News Hub. It aims to unravel how historical challenges, including colonial influences, economic constraints, and the legacy of traditional media, have shaped the trajectory of digital journalism in the country, shedding light on its tangible impact in reshaping Zimbabwe's media landscape.

Zimpapers News Hub

Zimpapers News Hub established in 2021 is an application facilitated by Zimbabwean media company Zimpapers. Zimpapers, which is largely, owned by the government houses various newspapers, radio stations and television channels such as *Business Daily, Umthunywa, Chronicle, Herald, Kwaedza, Sunday Mail, Sunday News, CapiTalk FM, Star FM, Diamond FM*, and *ZTN Prime*. The Zimpapers Hub Application offers a one-stop shop for all news from the various publications, radio stations, and television channels from Zimpapers. The application found on the Play Store and Apple Store is now the second most-used application after Twitter in Zimbabwe. Not only is the application a source of news but also a platform for business transactions as it carries business information and allows one to import goods.

Digital Journalism in Zimbabwe

Digital journalism has undergone a transformative evolution in Zimbabwe, fundamentally altering the landscape of media and news consumption dynamics (Mapuvire, 2022). New media platforms in Zimbabwe exemplify the impact of digital advancements, providing real-time updates and diverse analyses that broaden the availability of news and foster extensive discussions within the public sphere (Mhiripiri & Mutsvairo, 2014).

Scholars such as Nyamnjoh (2019) and Yzer and Southwell (2008) express optimism about new communication technologies addressing issues in marginalised societies, challenging the traditional dominance of print newspapers and radio. However, a critical examination of the implications of this shift, particularly on state-backed platforms is warranted, as underscored by Steensen et al. (2019).

With the emergence of the internet, Zimbabwe now boasts of multiple online media outlets ranging from blogs to online radio stations (Moyo, 2007). These online media platforms were largely subaltern public spheres which uplifted and amplified the voice of the marginalised and peripheralised in Zimbabwe and examples include *Studio 7*, *New Zimbabwe.com*, and *Voice of the People* (Mhlanga & Mpofu, 2014). Contemporary society has seen the rise of online media start-ups that seek to amplify the voice of the subaltern, minority and repressed such as the *Centre for Technology and Innovation* (Madzinisa et al., 2022) and *Zimdaily.com* (Mano, 2022). It thus can be seen that digital journalism in Zimbabwe came through as an avenue for the "pressed" to air out their grievances.

According to Mabweazara (2011), not only did digital journalism in Zimbabwe widen the communicative space but also allowed for improved journalism practice. Madzinisa et al. (2022) argue that digital spheres have allowed journalists to converse deeply with news sources in the process simplifying the news-gathering process. Mabweazara (2020) argues that due to the advent of digital spheres and ICTs journalists have seen themselves adopting gadgets such as phones to navigate their profession.

Digital media in Zimbabwe has also seen the rise to prominence of citizen journalists and unattached journalists (Ncube, 2019). They have gloriously taken up the task of creating and disseminating information through various social media platforms such as Jacob Ngarivhume and Hopewell Chin'ono (Nyoka & Tembo, 2022). These have led to the decentring of the creation of information as most people now subscribe to these celebrity journalists over established scribes and media outlets particularly those liked to the state (Matingwina, 2018). However, Tufekci (2017) warns against trusting these sources as they sometimes propagate biased information.

New Media and Media Consumption Patterns

In the ever-evolving landscape of journalism, the digital age has ushered in transformative practices that distinguish themselves from traditional counterparts (Karaoglu, 2022). The consumption of new media has also undergone metamorphosis in the digital age as alluded to by Karaoglu (2022) who notes that the consumption of news media is now located on social media platforms such as Twitter (X). This is further substantiated by Cherian (2015), who points out that most people now read news on their phones and no longer subscribe to traditional forms of the media such as hardcopy newspapers.

It seems ICT has attracted young people as Elarashi and Gunter (2012) note that the youth in Libya generally prefer consuming technology devices such as phones and advanced screens. However, Meraz (2009) attests that these mobile phones and social media platforms that attract the youth have forced consumers to use their personal discretion due to information overload in ascertaining whether the information being consumed is correct or not. In the same vein, Nordenson (2008) states that in the consumption of media online, audiences now craft their own background to stories sometimes the stories are not detailed. Holton and Chyi (2012) argue that those who do not have background information for particular stories sometimes skip news stories online.

Due to digital media being characterised by gossip, rumours and unverified information, media consumers have adopted a filtering style of reading news online (Pentina & Tarafdar, 2014). Those who do not have the filtering ability will opt to stay away from news altogether as they desist from paying for news from traditional media sources such as newspapers and television (Lee et al., 2016).

Social Constructionist Approach to Technology

The social constructionist approach to technology provides a pertinent theoretical lens for understanding the intricate interplay between society, culture, and technology, particularly in the context of the Zimpapers News Hub and its impact on news consumption in Zimbabwe. This framework, as Djordjevic et al. (2016) and van Baalen et al. (2016) posit, is not merely a neutral tool but is actively shaped and interpreted by social and cultural contexts, and, in turn, it influences the way society perceives and interacts with information.

The social constructionist approach is central to this chapter's exploration of how the Zimpapers News Hub has transformed, if at all, news consumption patterns within Zimbabwe. By adopting this framework, the study acknowledges that the development, implementation, and reception of digital news applications are deeply influenced by the sociopolitical dynamics, historical legacies, and cultural norms specific to the Zimbabwean context. The framework enables a comprehensive analysis of how societal and cultural factors shape the adoption and utilisation (Djordjevic et al., 2016) of the Zimpapers News Hub, revealing insights into the complexities of digital journalism within the nation's unique environment.

The social constructionist approach illuminates how societal beliefs and cultural values influence the way journalists create news content for the Zimpapers News Hub and how audiences interpret and engage with this information (Djordjevic et al., 2016; van Baalen et al., 2016). By recognising the socially constructed nature of technology (Djordjevic et al., 2016), the study delves into the underlying cultural factors shaping news production and consumption habits. This framework is instrumental in unravelling the platform's role in fostering democratic ideals within the Zimbabwean society. By exploring how technology is socially constructed within the democratic framework, the study evaluates the Zimpapers News Hub's contribution to public discourse and inclusive democratic engagement, acknowledging the unique sociopolitical realities that influence these processes.

In summary, the social constructionist approach to technology provides a robust theoretical foundation for this chapter, offering a comprehensive understanding of how the Zimpapers News Hub is socially constructed, perceived, and utilised within the unique sociopolitical fabric of Zimbabwe. By embracing this framework, the study advances our comprehension of digital journalism's complexities, contributing valuable insights to both academic discourse and practical applications within the evolving media landscape of Zimbabwe.

Methodology

This research adopted a qualitative research approach, employing in-depth interviews to scrutinise the transformative influence of the Zimpapers News Hub on news dissemination and consumption in Zimbabwe. As defined by Teherani et al. (2015), qualitative research serves as an inquiry method designed to delve into and comprehend people's beliefs, experiences, behaviours, and social phenomena. Leveraging in-depth interviews facilitated a comprehensive exploration of the Zimpapers News Hub's transformative impact on news creation and consumption in Zimbabwe. The study targeted a purposive sample of 20 participants, encompassing journalists from various Zimpapers newspapers and users of the Zimpapers

News Hub. Participants were selected purposively based on their relevance to the research questions, ensuring diverse perspectives within the Zimbabwean media landscape. Semi-structured interviews guided participants in sharing insights, experiences, and perceptions related to their engagement with the Zimpapers News Hub, utilising open-ended questions to encourage candid expression.

This study employed a dual approach to sampling, integrating purposive sampling and snowball sampling methods. Purposive sampling, as outlined by Palinkas et al. (2015), involves the deliberate selection of individuals with characteristics or experiences pertinent to the research questions. Simultaneously, snowball sampling initiates with an initial participant and relies on referrals to enlist additional participants, forming a network of individuals with shared experiences or perspectives (Kirchherr & Charles, 2018). Purposive sampling is crucial for intentionally selecting participants directly involved with the Zimpapers News Hub, ensuring insights from individuals knowledgeable about the application. This method aligns with the study's specific research objectives, providing a focused and targeted approach to participant selection. On the other hand, snowball sampling captures diverse perspectives within a network of Zimpapers News Hub users and journalists, leveraging existing connections to include participants not easily accessible through traditional methods. This method facilitates the exploration of a broad range of experiences, ensuring a comprehensive understanding of the topic and enriching the depth of qualitative data.

The amalgamation of purposive and snowball sampling endeavours to compile a varied and nuanced set of perspectives, augmenting the comprehensiveness and depth of research findings. Stringent ethical considerations, including informed consent and participant confidentiality, will be strictly observed throughout the research process. Participants will be provided with clear information about the study's objectives, their rights, and the confidentiality of their responses. Informed consent will be obtained from all participants, ensuring their voluntary participation in the study.

This qualitative methodology enables a thorough exploration of the Zimpapers News Hub's influence on the media landscape in Zimbabwe, aligning with the chapter's objectives to unveil the complexities of digital journalism in this specific regional context. The inclusion of diverse participants and the systematic analysis of their perspectives furnished valuable insights into the transformative impact of the Zimpapers News Hub on news creation and consumption in Zimbabwe.

ANALYSIS

This chapter aims to unearth how journalists produce news for the Zimpapers hub application and how consumers also consume news on this digital application. Sampled journalists had it that content creation and production precisely that involving news is still for the application still resonates with that of traditional media. Additionally, empirical data demonstrate that the consumption patterns, though they have changed some patterns, are still similar to those that characterised the consumption of traditional media. These findings will be discussed in detail in the next sections.

Journalist's Opinions: Content Creation and Production for Zimpapers News Hub

The majority of journalists' interviews revealed that the process of content creation and production of the Zimpapers hub is similar to that of traditional media. In light of this participant 7 states that

> Chronicle Journalist, personal interview, November 7, 2023: "Sourcing news for the application is still done the same way we do for the newspapers, radio and television outlets. We physically go out there to look for stories. We attend court sessions, gatherings, and sports matches to gather news. So not much has changed."

The participant here spectacles the fact that the sourcing of news has not been revolutionised in the digital gage. News for the Zimpapers hub application is coursed exactly the same way in which journalists source news for traditional media outlets. This, therefore, dents Steensen et al. (2019) argument that internet-based communication has altered journalists' cultures. In light of this, the argument here is that digital spheres have not changed the way journalists source news. Thus, journalists' culture and practices of news sourcing for Zimpapers hub remain the same as those that were there before the advent of the application. Against this background, it is crystal clear that in the context of Zimpapers hub traditional journalistic cultures still remain viable within the era of digital journalism.

Adding on issues of sourcing is Participant 1, who states that even interviewing has not changed that much. In light of this, the participant states that

> Herald Journalist, personal interview, November 10, 2023: "We still largely use face-to-face interviews whenever we are looking for information. You find us on the site interviewing potential sources of information."

However, Participant 3 claims that now there is a hybrid style of sourcing for information. In light of this, the participant said:

> Sunday News, personal interview, November 7, 2023: "As much as we still heavily rely on face-to-face interviews and traditional phone calls and emails sometimes, we also use Zoom conferences to interview sources. These interviews can be done from anywhere at any time both the journalists and interviewees are comfortable."

Participant 5 weighed in on this issue of sourcing and stated that

> Sunday Mail Journalist, personal interview, November 10, 2023: "Even though we are sourcing information for digital platforms we still prioritise the views of the elite and downplay those of the common man. So, nothing much has changed. The bottom-up approach we thought would be brought by digital media will surface is a fallacy."

The participants here bring to the fore important issues when it comes to interviewing. A majority of the participants indicate that interviewing styles and techniques remain the same for that of traditional media and Zimpapers News Hub. Online spheres and spaces are only used whenever there is a need for supplementary information. In terms of the actual interviewing for the news application, there has not been a metamorphosis of the practice as it still takes up a top-down approach where the elite are given more prominence over the general populace. Therefore, this shows that journalism cultures and practices have not changed; journalists who write for online media platforms such as Zimpapers News Hub still stick to the medieval style of journalism.

Despite the shift to a digital platform, participants consistently highlighted the enduring nature of traditional writing practices, reinforcing the continuity of established journalistic norms. The participants consistently emphasised the persistence of traditional writing practices, such as the inverted pyramid structure as highlighted by Participant 7:

6 THE ILLUSION OF CHANGE: UNVEILING NEWS PRODUCTION... 119

> Chronicle Journalist, personal interview, November 7, 2023: "In the ever-evolving landscape of digital journalism, one thing remains steadfast for us at Zimpapers News Hub—the fundamentals of storytelling. We adhere rigorously to the inverted pyramid structure, ensuring that crucial information is presented upfront, just as we would in our traditional print media counterparts."

The affirmation that "fundamentals of storytelling remain the same" (Participant 7) underlines the steadfast adherence to established conventions in the crafting of news content. This continuity suggests that, at its core, the essence of storytelling and journalistic writing remains unchanged in the transition to Zimpapers News Hub. The social constructionist approach emphasises that technology is shaped by social and cultural contexts. In this context, the persistence of traditional writing practices, such as the inverted pyramid structure, suggests that Zimpapers News Hub is socially constructed within the framework of established journalistic norms (Djordjevic et al., 2016).

Adding on issues of writing style is Participant 10, who states that even writing has not changed that much while acknowledging adaptations to digital consumption habits. The acknowledgement that "the essence of storytelling remains" implies that, despite adjustments for digital readership, the core principles of journalistic writing have not undergone fundamental changes. This supports the notion that evolution is more about adaptation than a complete overhaul of writing styles. In light of this, the participant states that:

> B Metro Journalist, personal interview, November 7, 2023: "While embracing the digital age, we've learned to navigate the terrain without compromising the essence of storytelling. Crafting concise headlines has become an art form for us, recognizing the habits of online readers who tend to skim through content. This adaptation allows us to meet the demands of the digital era without losing the soul of our journalistic narrative."

The literature on the enduring nature of traditional writing practices aligns with this finding, emphasising that certain journalistic norms persist even in the digital landscape (Harcup, 2023). The continuity in traditional writing practices reflects a socially constructed approach to technology, where Zimpapers News Hub is embedded within the cultural and social context that values established journalistic norms.

However, Participant 3 claims that the only change has been the integration of multimedia elements and viewed it as an augmentation rather than a change. The integration of multimedia elements was framed as a complement to written content rather than a replacement. Participants recognised the importance of visuals and multimedia in enhancing the reader's experience, but this did not signify a departure from traditional writing styles. Instead, it demonstrated an augmentation of written content to align with the multimedia-rich nature of digital platforms. In light of this, the participant said:

Herald Journalist, personal interview, November 10, 2024: "Embracing the multimedia-rich nature of digital platforms, we've revolutionised our approach at Zimpapers News Hub. We've seamlessly integrated visuals, infographics, and video snippets into our articles. This augmentation enhances the reader's experience while maintaining the integrity of our written content, a testament to our commitment to evolving without abandoning our traditional roots."

The social constructionist approach suggests that technology, in this case, multimedia integration, is socially constructed and influences the way society interacts with information. The emphasis on evolution without abandoning traditional roots aligns with the idea that Zimpapers News Hub is adapting to the multimedia-rich nature of digital platforms within the sociocultural context of Zimbabwe (Djordjevic et al., 2016). In the same breadth, Li et al. (2022) note how multimedia integration in journalism acknowledges the importance of adapting traditional practices to the multimedia-rich nature of digital platforms. Hence, this finding supports the literature by illustrating that Zimpapers News Hub's integration of multimedia elements represents an evolution in response to the demands of digital platforms, while still honouring traditional journalistic practices.

Consumption of News on Zimpapers News Hub

1. Time of News Consumption: Morning, Lunch, and Evening

Findings revealed that consumption of news has not changed much since the digital news adoption. In light of this, Participant 8, a journalist said:

UMthunywa Journalist, personal interview, November 9, 2023: "Our observation is that readers on Zimpapers News Hub maintain a traditional reading rhythm. There's a notable surge in engagement during morning, lunch, and evening hours, aligning with established patterns of news consumption."

This was supported by a user, Participant 12, of Zimpapers News Hub:

Zimpapers News Hub user, personal interview, November 6, 2023: "I find myself checking the Zimpapers app at specific times of the day. Morning coffee on my way to work, lunch break, and winding down in the evening, while I'm stuck in traffic going home. It's like a ritual, similar to how I used to grab the newspaper at these times."

The finding aligns with existing literature emphasising the habitual nature of news consumption (Harcup, 2023). The traditional reading times in the morning, during lunch breaks, and in the evening reflect the enduring influence of established media routines even in the digital era (Jiang et al., 2022). The persistence of these temporal patterns supports the conclusion that consumption habits on Zimpapers News Hub mirror those of traditional media, underscoring a continuity in temporal engagement.

2. Headlines First: Determining Which Stories to Read

News consumers are still attracted to reading a story because of the headlines. Headlines are used to grab the attention of readers and it is still the same for the digital world as claimed:

Herald Journalist, personal interview, November 12, 2024: "Analysing user interactions, it's evident that the majority gravitate towards headlines first. The headlines serve as a gatekeeper, guiding readers to choose which stories to delve into. This behaviour mirrors the traditional approach of skimming through newspaper headlines."

A reader, Participant 18, also confirmed what the journalist claimed:

Zimpapers Hub user, personal interview November 6, 2023 "When I open the Zimpapers app, the first thing I do is check the headlines. It sets the tone for my reading. If something grabs my attention, I'll read the whole article. But it's the headlines that decide where I invest my time."

The preference for checking headlines first resonates with the literature highlighting the importance of headlines in digital journalism (Pritchard et al., 2022). Headlines serve as gatekeepers, influencing the reader's decision to engage further, echoing traditional skimming behaviours (Harcup, 2023). This aligns with the conclusion that Zimpapers News Hub consumers follow a pattern reminiscent of traditional media, where headlines play a pivotal role in guiding their reading choices.

3. *Sequencing of News Categories: Top Stories, Sports, and Business Last*

In exploring the sequencing of news categories on Zimpapers News Hub, both journalists and readers shed light on their perspectives, revealing a striking resemblance between the digital platform and traditional media preferences. This finding, aligned with the second objective, underscores the familiarity emphasised by journalists in the structure of news consumption, while readers express comfort in a pattern that echoes the conventional arrangement of news sections in traditional newspapers. This is what Participant 9 had to say:

> Sunday News Journalist, personal interview, November 7, 2023 "The sequence of news consumption on Zimpapers News Hub closely mirrors traditional media preferences. Users tend to start with top stories, venture into sports news next, and conclude with business updates. It's a pattern reminiscent of how news sections are structured in traditional newspapers."

A user, Participant 14, reiterated the journalist's sentiments:

> Zimpapers Hub user, personal interview, November 6, 2023: "I've noticed I follow a pattern when navigating the Zimpapers app. I want to know the top stories first especially politics, maybe catch up on sports in the middle, and wind down with business news. It's comforting how the layout aligns with what I'm used to in the traditional paper."

The sequencing of news categories echoes the traditional newspaper structure, where top stories often take precedence (Harcup, 2023). This aligns with the hierarchical arrangement of news content in traditional media (Li et al., 2022). The observed pattern reinforces the conclusion that Zimpapers News Hub users follow a sequence that mirrors traditional news consumption, supporting the notion of continuity in media habits.

4. *Reader Interaction and Feedback*

In exploring the dynamics of user interaction and feedback on Zimpapers News Hub, Participant 6 noted a designated space within the platform where users can input their comments or reviews. This observation unveils a potential avenue for user engagement, highlighting a platform feature designed to facilitate direct participation from the audience. Participant 6 notes:

> Sunday News Journalist, personal interview, November 7, 2023: "Our platform intentionally provides users with a designated space to express their opinions and contribute feedback. This deliberate effort aims to create a channel for direct engagement, allowing users to actively participate in shaping the discourse around the news."

However, most participants who are users of the platform professed otherwise. In light of this, Participant 20, a user of the platform, expressed frustration with the feedback feature:

> Zimpapers Hub user, personal interview, November 6, 2023: "Despite the platform's claim of providing a space for user comments, my attempts to engage have been met with disappointment. I've posted comments on various articles, sharing my perspectives and suggestions, but they seem to vanish into thin air. It makes me question the transparency and authenticity of this supposed interactive space. If user comments are indeed filtered or not visible, it raises concerns about the platform's commitment to fostering genuine dialogue. The opacity in the feedback process undermines the idea of user participation and casts doubt on the effectiveness of this feature in truly reflecting public sentiment."

The findings on Reader Interaction and Feedback present a nuanced picture of Zimpapers News Hub's user engagement features. Participant 6 highlights intentional efforts to create a space for user comments, reflecting the platform's design to facilitate direct audience participation. However, Participant 20's frustration introduces a significant discrepancy, raising questions about the transparency and authenticity of the feedback mechanism. This discordance aligns with concerns from the literature about filtered or invisible user comments on digital platforms. This tension contradicts the optimistic views expressed by scholars such as Nyamnjoh (2019) and Yzer and Southwell (2008) regarding new communication technologies addressing issues in marginalised societies and challenging traditional media dominance. Zimpapers News Hub's potential opacity or filtering of user comments may contribute to a perception of the platform as censorial or elitist, counteracting the intended benefits of digital media in fostering inclusive dialogue. In conclusion, these findings contribute to the broader discourse on user participation in the digital age, emphasising the imperative of transparent and authentic interactive features that align with sociocultural contexts and user expectations.

DISCUSSION

The discussion unveils a striking consistency between the findings from Zimpapers News Hub participants and existing literature, emphasising the endurance of traditional media habits amid digital transformation. Despite the technological shift, established practices like temporal engagement, headline reliance, and sequential news consumption persist, indicating a resilience in traditional patterns. This synthesis reinforces the overarching conclusion that Zimpapers News Hub's journalistic practices and audience habits have, for the most part, resisted substantial change in the digital age.

The application of the social constructionist approach to technology enriches the theoretical framework, offering insights into how societal beliefs and cultural values shape news consumption habits. The findings validate this perspective by highlighting the deep-rooted nature of traditional media practices within the digital platform. The sustained patterns of temporal engagement and the continued significance of headlines underscore the socially constructed essence of news consumption on Zimpapers News Hub, influenced by ingrained habits and cultural norms.

In summary, the empirical evidence not only aligns with but also enhances the theoretical framework, providing context-specific support for how Zimpapers News Hub reflects and perpetuates traditional media habits within the Zimbabwean context. This analysis contributes meaningfully to the ongoing discourse on the interplay between technology, media practices, and cultural continuity in the digital age.

CONCLUSIONS

The chapter was poised at examining how journalists create and produce information for the Zimpapers News Hub app. It was also aimed at exploring the consumption patterns of news on the Zimpapers Hub application. The study unravelled that journalists' behaviours and cultures that were predominant in the era where traditional media was dominant still exist in the digital era. For the Zimpapers News Hub application, journalists still abide by what contemporary scholars celebrating the power of digital media call medieval practices. The sourcing patterns, interview cultures, and writing styles remain the same. Speaking to the second objective, empirical digital suggests that the consumption of news on the application resonates with that of traditional media. The chapter realised that in terms of time, stories that are consumed first and checking headlines first still characterise the reading patterns of consumers. Therefore, the chapter concludes that journalistic practice and consumption patterns and styles have remained the same and there is no outright change in the digital era. However, there is still a need for more studies to verify and modify this argument. Future scholarship on this research terrain can focus on other DSTV application information production and consumption patterns in Zimbabwe.

REFERENCES

Albarana, A. B. (2010). *The Transformation of the Media and Communication Industries*. Ediciones Universidad de Navarra, S.A. (EUNSA). ISBN: 978-84-8081-999-2

Allan, S., & Matheson, D. (2004). Online Journalism in the Information Age. *Savoir, Travail and Société, 2*(3), 73–94.

Cherian, J. (2015). Emergence of Digital Publishing – A Great Challenge to The Print Publications. *Procedia Economics and Finance, 23*, 576–586. https://doi.org/10.1016/S2212-5671(15)00361-5

Djordjevic, B., Spirtovic, O., & Acimovic, D. (2016). Social Constructivism and Technology. *International Journal of Business and Social Science, 7*(11). ISSN 2219-1933.

Dragomir, M., & Thompson, M. (Eds.). (2014). *Mapping Digital Media*. Open Society Foundations. ISBN: 978-1-910243-03-9

Elarashi, M., & Gunter, B. (2012). Patterns of News Media Consumption Among Young People in Libya. *Journal of African Media Studies, 4*(2), 173–191.

Harcup, T. (2023). The Struggle for News Value in the Digital Era. *Journalism and Media, 4*(3), 902–917. https://doi.org/10.3390/journalmedia4030058

Holton, A. E., & Chyi, H. I. (2012). News and the Overloaded Consumer: Factors Influencing Information Overload Among News Consumers. *Cyberpsychology, Behavior, and Social Networking, 15*(11), 619–624.

Jiang, X., Mao, T., & Tian, J. (2022). The Application of Digital Technology in the Complex Situation of News Dissemination from the Perspective of New Media Art. *Computational Intelligence and Neuroscience, 2022.* https://doi.org/10.1155/2022/1685430

Karaoglu, G. (2022). News Production and Consumption Practices in Online Journalism: A Cross-Platform Review. *Selçuk Ün. Sos. Bil. Ens, 48,* 184–194.

Kirchherr, J., & Charles, K. (2018). Enhancing the Sample Diversity of Snowball Samples: Recommendations from a Research Project on Anti-dam Movements in Southeast Asia. *PLoS ONE, 13*(8). https://doi.org/10.1371/journal.pone.0201710

Lee, S., Kim, K., & Koh, J. (2016). Antecedents of News Consumers' Perceived Information Overload and News Consumption Patterns in the US. *International Journal of Contents, 12*(3), 1–11.

Li, K., Zhou, C., Benitez, J., & Liao, Q. (2022). Impact of Information Timeliness and Richness on Public Engagement on Social Media During COVID-19 Pandemic: An Empirical Investigation Based on NLP and Machine Learning. *Decision Support Systems, 162,* 113752. https://doi.org/10.1016/j.dss.2022.113752

Mabweazara, H. M. (2011). The Internet in the Print Newsroom: Trends, Practices and Emerging Cultures in Zimbabwe. In D. Domingo & C. Paterson (Eds.), *Making Online News: Newsroom Ethnographies in the Second Decade of Internet Journalism* (pp. 57–69). Peter Lang.

Mabweazara, H. M. (2020). Towards Reimagining the Digital Divide: Impediments and Circumnavigation Practices in the Appropriation of the Mobile Phone by African Journalists. *Information, Communication and Society, 24*(3), 344–364.

Madzinisa, N., Lunga, C., & Ndlovu, M. (2022). News in the Digital Age: A Case Study of CITE as a Digital Public Sphere in Zimbabwe. *African Journalism Studies, 46*(6), 1–19.

Mano, W. (2022). Between citizen and Vigilante Journalism: ZimDaily's Fair Deal Campaign and the Zimbabwe Crisis. *Communicare: Journal for Communication Studies in Africa, 29*(1), 57–70.

Mapuvire, D. H. (2022). Social Media and Behaviour in Zimbabwe: A Case of the Ruwa Youths in Harare. *Journal of Public Administration and Development Alternatives, 7*(2), 18–34.

Matingwina, S. (2018). Social Media Communicative Action and the Interplay with National Security: The Case of Facebook and Political Participation in Zimbabwe. *African Journalism Studies, 39*(1), 48–68.

6 THE ILLUSION OF CHANGE: UNVEILING NEWS PRODUCTION... 127

Meraz, S. (2009). Is There Elite Overload? Traditional Media to Social Media Influence in Blog Networks. *Journal of Computer-Mediated Communication*, *14*(3), 682–707.

Mhiripiri, N. A., & Mutsvairo, B. (2014). Social Media, New ICTs and the Challenges Facing the Zimbabwean Democratic Process. Retrieved February 27, 2024, from https://www.igi-global.com/chapter/social-media-new-icts-and-the-challenges-facing-the-zimbabwe-democratic-process/90778

Mhlanga, B., & Mpofu, M. (2014). The Virtual Parallax: Imaginations of Mthwakazi Nationalism – Online Discussions and Calls for Self-determination. In A. Solo (Ed.), *Handbook on Research on Political Activism in the Information Age* (pp. 129–146). IGI Global.

Moyo, D. (2007). Alternative Media, Diasporas and the Mediation of the Zimbabwean Crisis. *Ecquid Novi: African Journalism Studies*, *28*(1), 81–105.

Moyo, L. (2009). Repression, Propaganda and Digital Resistance: New Media and Democracy in Zimbabwe. In O. Mudhai, W. J. Tettey, & F. Banda (Eds.), *African Media and the Digital Public Sphere* (pp. 57–71). Palgrave Macmillan.

Msindo, E. (2009). 'Winning Hearts and Minds': Crisis and Propaganda in Colonial Zimbabwe, 1962–1970. *Journal of Southern African Studies*, *35*(3), 663–681. https://www.jstor.org/stable/40283283

Mukasa, S. D. (2003). Press and Politics in Zimbabwe. *African Studies Quarterly*, *7*(2), 3.

Munoriyarwa, A., & Chibuwe, A. (2022). Journalism Beyond the Coup: Emerging Forms of Digital Journalism Practices in Post-coup Zimbabwe. *Digital Journalism*, *10*(7), 1198–1218.

Ncube, L. (2019). Digital Media, Fake News and Pro-Movement for Democratic Change (MDC) Alliance Cyber-Propaganda during the 2018 Zimbabwe Election. *African Journalism Studies*, *40*(4), 44–61.

Nordenson, B. (2008). Overload! Journalism's Battle for Relevance in an Age of Too Much Information. *Columbia Journalism Review*, *47*(4), 30.

Nyamnjoh, F. B. (2019). Digital Humanities Keynote. In *Conference on the Theme of Complexities. Utrecht University, The Netherlands*, 9–12 July, pp. 1–8.

Nyoka, P., & Tembo, M. (2022). Dimensions of Democracy and Digital Political Activism on Hopewell Chinono and Jacob Ngarivhume Twitter Accounts Towards the July 31st Demonstrations in Zimbabwe. *Congret Social Sciences*, *8*(1), Article 2024350.

Palinkas, L. A., Horwitz, S. M., Green, C. A., Wisdom, J. P., Duan, N., & Hoagwood, K. (2015). Purposeful Sampling for Qualitative Data Collection and Analysis in Mixed Method Implementation Research. *Administration and Policy in Mental Health*, *42*(5), 533. https://doi.org/10.1007/s10488-013-0528-y

Pentina, I., & Tarafdar, M. (2014). From 'Information' to 'Knowing': Exploring the Role of Social Media in Contemporary News Consumption. *Computers in Human Behavior, 35*(4), 211–223. https://doi.org/10.1016/j.chb.2014.02.045

Pritchard, A. J., Silk, M. J., Carrignon, S., Bentley, R. A., & Fefferman, N. H. (2022). Balancing Timeliness of Reporting with Increasing Testing Probability for Epidemic Data. *Infectious Disease Modelling, 7*(2), 106–116. https://doi.org/10.1016/j.idm.2022.04.001

Rosmani, A. F., Mutalib, A. A., & Sarif, S. M. (2020). The Evolution of Information Dissemination, Communication Media and Technology in Malaysia. *Journal of Physics, 1529*. https://doi.org/10.1088/1742-6596/1529/2/022044

Steensen, S., Grøndahl Larsen, A. M., Hågvar, Y. B., & Fonn, B. K. (2019). What Does Digital Journalism Studies Look Like? *Digital Journalism, 7*(3), 320–342. https://doi.org/10.1080/21670811.2019.1581071

Teherani, A., Martimianakis, T., Stenfors-Hayes, T., Wadhwa, A., & Varpio, L. (2015). Choosing a Qualitative Research Approach. *Journal of Graduate Medical Education, 7*(4), 669–670. https://doi.org/10.4300/JGME-D-15-00414.1

Tshabangu, T., & Salawu, A. (2022). Alternative Media, Repression and the Crisis State: Towards a Political Economy of Alternative Media in Post-Mugabe Zimbabwe. *Journal of Asian and African Studies, 1*–15. https://doi.org/10.1177/00219096221106090

Tufekci, Z. (2017). *Twitter and Tear Gas: The Power and Fragility of Networked Protest.* Yale University Press.

Van Baalen, P., van Fenema, P., & Loebbeeke, C. (2016). Extending the Social Construction of Technology (SCOT) Framework to the Digital World. *Reframing the Social Construction of Digital Ecosystems.* Thirty Seventh International Conference on Information Systems, Dublin. Retrieved November 28, 2023, from, https://core.ac.uk/download/pdf/301370166.pdf

Xu, Z., & Zhang, C. (2022). The Dissemination Effect of Human-Computer Interactive Advertising News—Using the Theory of Media Audience and Emotion Management. *Frontiers in Psychology, 13*. https://doi.org/10.3389/fpsyg.2022.959732

Yzer, M. C., & Southwell, B. (2008). New Communication Technologies, Old Questions. *American Behavioral Scientist, 52*(1). https://doi.org/10.1177/0002764208321338

PART II

Journalism and Social Media Platforms

CHAPTER 7

Traditional Media and New Technologies: Facebook Radio Programming in Uganda

Fred Max Adii and Fred Kakooza

INTRODUCTION

Digital technologies have transformed the media sector at the global level and influenced trends in Africa, particularly the broadcasting media sector in Uganda (Srinivasan & Diepeveen, 2018, p. 2; Chibita, 2016, p. 30). The liberalisation of the broadcasting sector in Uganda and the rise in digital technologies, including mobile phones and the Internet, facilitates a convergence of the traditional radio medium and new media including social media (Srinivasan & Diepeveen, 2018, p. 2). Digital technologies have forced traditional radio stations to adopt both digital and analogue broadcasting to remain accessible and relevant to their audiences (Laor et al., 2017, p. 951). To encourage this bond with their listeners, radio stations rely on traditional radio broadcasts, and many add-ons from other

---

F. M. Adii
Digital Platforms, Vision Group Media Company, Kampala, Uganda

F. Kakooza (✉)
Journalism and Communications, Makerere University, Kampala, Uganda
e-mail: fred.kakooza@mak.ac.ug

© The Author(s), under exclusive license to Springer Nature Switzerland AG 2025
A. Sharra, U. Akpojivi (eds.), *Technologies and Media Production Cultures*, Palgrave Studies in Journalism and the Global South, https://doi.org/10.1007/978-3-031-78582-5_7

131

new media, including websites and Facebook live streams, as well as inviting listeners to call-in and answer quiz questions, and ticket giveaways for live events hosted by the radio station (Spangardt et al., 2016, p. 69). While previously, listeners participated in radio programming through visits to the radio station, letter writing, or telephone call-ins, smart mobile phones and the Internet have offered opportunities for audience interaction with radio stations (Zelenkauskaite & Simoes, 2015, p. 1657; Bonini, 2014b, p. 2; Willems, 2013, p. 226). The different social media channels enable the constant delivery of content directly to the listeners (Mediatool, 2023). Freeman et al. (2012, p. 17) posit that social media including Facebook enables more connectivity and interactivity between radio stations and their listeners, thereby improving brand awareness and loyalty.

Digital platforms have expanded consumer choice and control, whereby radio stations are able to distribute multi-media content, reaching new audiences and yielding higher commercial sales (Bonini et al., 2014a, p. 98; Freeman et al., 2012, p. 3). There is a blurring of lines between traditional and digital media forms in the promotion of broadcast content through interaction, feedback, and content creation which allows the audience new listening experiences (Mediatool, 2023; Kurtul, 2013). Such affordances have consolidated the growth of the global broadcast and media technology. It is against this background that Ewart and Ames (2016, p. 92) suggest that more research is needed to understand how audiences use websites and social media to engage and participate in radio programming. For instance, Laor et al. (2017, p. 951) analysed radio presence on websites in Israel and found that stations have started live streaming their radio broadcasts, offering select segments of their programmes, and maintaining engagement with their listeners. The websites can preserve and strengthen ties between radio stations and their listeners in both traditional and online spheres, as listeners are not dependent on any line-up and can listen to the programmes anytime, anywhere around the world (Steinfeld & Laor, 2019, p. 198; Laor et al., 2017, p. 951).

Freeman et al. (2012, p. 6) assessed the relation between broadcast and social media in the United States, Germany, and Singapore and found that driving listeners to the broadcast products seems to be a major objective of most of radio station's Facebook efforts in all three countries. Another study by Laor and Steinfeld (2018, p. 1) explored Israeli radio stations' activities on Facebook and found that stations and their listeners turn to Facebook mostly for promotional purposes and least for interaction, without utilising the full range of opportunities this platform offers them. Laor

(2019, p. 80) found that radio programme activity on Facebook expands the reach of radio stations, promoting higher levels of interaction with listeners beyond the broadcast schedule. Bonini et al. (2014a, p. 96) note that Facebook is far more used by radio producers than Twitter, most certainly since it was integrated into radio production routines before Twitter. Although radio stations in developed countries have leveraged Facebook's connective and interactive potential, there is a paucity of studies in the context of developing countries (Boscha, 2013, p. 29). This chapter focuses on the use of Facebook in radio programming in the Ugandan context.

LITERATURE: CONTEXTUALISING BROADCASTING IN UGANDA

Across Africa, the liberalisation of the media sector and the rapid rise in mobile phone use are facilitating a convergence of traditional radio broadcast and digital technologies. These trends in Africa are influenced by global transformations in the media sector brought about by digital communication technologies (Srinivasan & Diepeveen, 2018, p. 2). Since the liberalisation of Uganda's broadcast sector in the 1990s, the sector has witnessed considerable growth (Chibita, 2016, p. 30; Ogola, 2016, p. 93), and today radio stations can be found in some of the remotest parts of the country (Ogola, 2016, p. 93). Between 1992, when the broadcast sector was liberalised, and 2004, the broadcast sector grew from one to 80 radio stations broadcasting in various languages (Chibita, 2016, p. 30). As of 2020, there were 202 operational private/commercial radio stations whose programming has become more global and commercialised as local radio stations have to compete for audiences with regional and global media (Chibita, 2016, p. 30). With such competition for audience among the radio stations in Uganda, there is a need to find alternative ways of reaching new audiences as well as maintaining the audience base.

Radio and Digital Media in Uganda

Studies show that traditional media, including radio stations, have been embracing social media with a growing number of them using Facebook and Twitter. For instance, Bonini et al. (2014, p. 96) note that Facebook is far more used by radio producers than Twitter, most certainly since it was integrated into radio production routines before Twitter. The current digital media landscape in Uganda is characterised by notable growth driven by increased Internet penetration and widespread smartphone adoption (Mirembe, 2015). Uganda has approximately 2.8 million digital media users, constituting 5.9% of the total population of about 47 million people (Uganda Bureau of Statistics, 2022). A substantial portion of these users belong to the youth demographic, who have widespread access to smartphones and the Internet. Social media platforms like Facebook, Twitter, WhatsApp, and Instagram are widely used in Uganda. These platforms play a significant role in communication, information sharing, and social interactions. Despite the growth of digital media, challenges such as the digital divide among urban and rural areas in terms of reach, gender divide, limited access, affordability of data, online privacy, and security continue to impact the digital media landscape in Uganda (Davis et al., 2012). In conclusion, the evolving state of digital media use in Uganda is a reflection of global trends shaped by technological advancements, cultural shifts, and economic considerations.

In as much as social media are pervasive, little is known about how radio stations use Facebook in programming (Zelenkauskaite & Simoes, 2015, p. 1657) in developing countries. While radio stations in developed countries have leveraged Facebook's connective and interactive potential, there is a paucity of studies in the context of developing countries (Boscha, 2013, p. 29). In the Ugandan context, this study examines the use of Facebook in programming at 94.8 XFM to establish the opportunities and strategies and how this has affected the broadcasting landscape. The broadcasting landscape in Uganda is dominated by the Vision Group and the Nation Media Group (Namusoga, 2017, p. 88; Chibita, 2016, p. 52). The Vision Group has a wide portfolio of products and services including daily newspapers, magazines, printing services, online presence, five television stations, and six radio stations including 94.8 XFM (Vision Group, 2018; Lugalambi, 2010, p. 15).

Radio has remained relevant and ever-present in Uganda due to the bond stations have built with their audience over time (McMahon, 2021, p. 1). Indeed, Spangardt et al. (2016, p. 71) argue that radio stations do not just want audience members to listen to their programmes; rather, they want to create a real bond. To encourage this bond of loyalty from listeners, they argue that radio stations rely not only on their actual radio broadcast, by inviting listeners to call-in and answer quiz questions, or win tickets for live events staged by the station, but also on many add-ons from new media, such as websites, blogs, podcasts, and social media. They note that presenters invite listeners to visit the station's website and like or share content on their social media platforms. Freeman et al. (2012, p.17) argue that contests on Facebook facilitate "Likes" and connect more listeners to the station.

Starkey and Crisell (2010, pp. 661–662) outline the ways in which digital technology has affected the traditional radio medium. First, digital technology such as the Internet has created a new habitant for radio. Laor and Steinfeld (2018, p. 1) argue that the Internet provides a variety of broadcasting platforms such as online streaming, fragmented content segments of radio programmes, as well as previously aired programmes, available on-demand. They note that radio stations now add to their websites a variety of interactive content, for instance, online programme archives and podcasts, in addition to integrating major sharing platforms such as Facebook and Twitter with the site. And so, in concurrence with traditional radio broadcasts, new radio trends, which promote audience participation and interaction with content, have emerged (Laor & Steinfeld, 2018, p. 1).

Berry (2014, pp. 3–4) argues that the future of radio is not the Internet as a means of sending programmes to the listeners but as a tool creating a hybridity in the programme-making process and the listening experience. This hybridity offers previously unavailable opportunities that should be considered within the context of programme production and distribution. Digital technology resulted in an expansion in the modes of radio reception. In addition to dedicated receivers, it allowed listeners to consume radio on television sets, desktop and laptop computers, and mobile communications (Starkey & Crisell, 2010, pp. 661–2). More listeners turn to radio on smartphones, streaming devices, and computers and interactions take place through a keyboard or touch screen. Listening to radio content is no longer just an aural or visual activity; it is increasingly haptic with people touching their screen multiple times to open an app, access schedules, and turn to a station to listen to their favourite radio show, live or on-demand (Bonini, 2020, p. 15). Moreover, Starkey and Crisell (2010, pp. 661–2) argue that the collective impact of these developments has been twofold. There has been a fall in the cost of broadcast transmission and thus a widening of access to it. Today, almost anyone can start a radio station and reach a worldwide audience.

In view of the expansion in the modes of reception, there has been something of a convergence of radio with other media. Nearly every radio station has its own website and social media platforms, and many provide photos and video clips containing material that is supplementary to the broadcasts or webcams that deliver to the listener's computer and phones images and videos of the broadcasters in the studio. For the time-shifted consumption of programmes, there are also podcasts of special programmes, which can be downloaded to iPods, phones, and computers.

Social Media and Radio Programming

Social media are Internet-based channels that provide radio stations and their listeners an opportunity to share information, interact, and engage with each other (Rafeeq & Jiang, 2020, p. 3). Social media, including Facebook, have enabled listeners to share information and their opinions and thoughts with the radio station (Miller, 2019, p. 7). Radio producers are encouraging interaction by posting content that appeals to the audience's desire for information and entertainment (McMahon, 2019, p. 157). In a study of online comments of news items posted on the Facebook pages of radio stations, Al-Rawi (2016, p. 50) found that the audience is more engaged with posts that encourage discourse on broad issues, interacting with quotes, and entering contests and less with reading breaking news. In an analysis of the presence of programmes on Facebook and Twitter, Galán-Arribas et al. (2018, p. 1) focused on the number of posts, formats, and forms of interaction and found that some programmes have many followers while others have very few. The number of posts radio stations makes is as diverse as the forms of interaction. They concluded that the use of social media by radio stations is very heterogeneous and does not reflect patterns of use.

Mashud and Ofori-Birikorang (2018, p. 15) examined how radio stations in Ghana use social media in news production and found that social media have been useful in enhancing journalistic practice and audience interactivity and engagement. Boscha (2013, p. 35) explored South African community radio stations' use of social media, including Facebook and Twitter, and found that social media use is often linked to the socio-economic status of the region in which the stations are located. Stations in affluent or urban areas might have audiences that access social media via their mobile phones or even on their desktops. With the proliferation of social media in radio contexts, Zelenkauskaite and Simoes (2015, p. 1657) analysed the interaction between 223 Italian radio stations and their audience across three social media platforms, including Facebook, Twitter, and Google+. They found that radio stations utilise multiple platforms; yet the interactions were limited to content redistribution and repetition.

The Affordance Theory

In exploring the use of Facebook in radio programming at 94.8 XFM, the affordance theory was employed. The theory has been used for studying the uses and consequences of social media technology (Pozzi et al., 2014, p. 1). While articulating the original tenets of the affordance theory, Volkoff and Strong (2017, p. 2) and Schrock (2015, p. 1229) explain that a goal-oriented actor perceives an object in the environment in terms of how it can be used, what it "affords" the actor in terms of action possibilities for meeting that goal, and not as a set of characteristics or features that are inherent to the object and independent of the actor. Hafezieh and Eshraghian (2017, p. 2) explored how the concept of affordance has been employed in social media research to uncover the effects of social media affordances. They found that while the concept was employed in various ways to study social media technologies, some studies focused on the user's perceptions or actualisation of affordances and others explored the affordances that social media provide for users or the implications of such affordances.

Moreover, Volkoff and Strong (2017, p. 2) explained two main themes in technology-related fields. One is that affordances arise from the relationship between users and technology and are not of the technology itself. Another is that affordances relate neither to actual actions nor to the objects or states but to action possibilities for goal-oriented actors. Therefore, affordances are possibilities for goal-oriented action, emerging from the relation between social media technology and users, considered in terms of technology features afforded to specific groups of actors (Pozzi, et al., 2014, p. 2). A single technology can result in multiple action possibilities because individuals or radio stations in the case of this study have agency in how they use it; possibilities are finite and relatively stable in comparison to user practices or habits (Schrock, 2015, p. 1230). Proponents of the theory acknowledge its potential for studying the complex relationship between technologies and actors by considering the functional and relational aspects of affordances as possibilities for action (Volkoff & Strong, 2017, p. 2). Moreover, Bucher and Helmond (2018, p. 4) reflect on affordance as a key concept for understanding and analysing social media technology and the relations between the technology and its users.

Therefore, Facebook affords action possibilities for goal-oriented actors in a sense that radio stations have the opportunity to create fan pages for themselves or for their programmes, connecting the radio station and/or programmes with its listeners. Boscha (2013, p. 35) notes that various programmes on radio stations often set up their own Facebook pages, which can be "Liked" by the fans. This increases opportunities to interact with their audience. In a study of how Facebook is used as a platform for interaction between radio stations and their listeners, McMahon (2019, p. 161) argues that interaction is required from both the radio station and the audience. Programme hosts/presenters interact with the audience by regularly posting stimulating or engaging content that will appeal to their listeners. The listeners are also active by visiting the radio station's Facebook page and engage with content through emoji reactions, shares, or comments. The interaction on the radio station's Facebook page is indicated by the number of likes, comments, emojis, and shares the posts received (Boberg et al., 2020, p. 6). Interaction with user posts contributes to the station's popularity, and so do updates on Facebook during programmes (Laor & Steinfeld, 2018, p.1).

Radio stations have started streaming live on Facebook, offering select segments of their programmes (Laor, 2019, p. 81; Laor et al., 2017, p. 951). Radio stations are benefiting from the prolonged programme life in that the audience may listen to segments or entire programme on-demand, after its original airing, as many times as possible (Laor et al., 2017, p. 963). Facebook extends radio's listening range, eliminating the constraints of limited frequency reception ranges. In this sense, digital broadcasting complements and even replaces the analogue radio broadcast (Laor, 2019, p. 81). Moreover, radio stations have gone on to become increasingly multi-media-based (Laor et al., 2017, p. 951). The programme content on Facebook may be accompanied by image, audio, video, or a graphic. Facebook is an easier platform for user-generated content, as radio station listeners can upload texts, photos, and videos in a very fast and intuitive way (Bonini et al., 2014, p. 90). In a study of traditional radio use of social media, Steinfeld and Laor (2019, p. 194) analysed content published on Facebook pages of radio stations in Israel and found that commercial radio content is more promotional, privileging internal station events and calls for action. It can, therefore, be concluded that radio stations have leveraged Facebook's potential in achieving their traditional goals.

Methodology

This study used a case study research design to investigate the use of Facebook in radio programming. The case study design was considered because the focus of the study was to answer "how" and "why" questions (Wedawatta et al., 2011, p. 6). This in-depth inquiry required a qualitative approach in order to understand the contexts or settings in which participants in a study address a problem or an issue (Creswell, 2013, pp. 47–48). In collecting data for the study, direct observation realised through field notes and in-depth interviews through interview guides were used among programme hosts/presenters, programme producer, music scheduler, aggregation manager, deputy programme controller, digital manager, and station manager at 94.8 XFM. Purposive sampling of respondents was done to provide an in-depth understanding of the use of Facebook in radio programming at 94.8 XFM by examining how Facebook has been used in programming, how the platform has affected programming, and suggesting how it can be used in radio programming. The sample included eight personnel at 94.8 XFM who were engaged in the study. The majority (seven) were male and one was female which pointed to a gender disparity that was beyond the scope of this study to ascertain how such a gender imbalance affected the use of Facebook in radio programming or it pointed to the digital skills gap in relation to gender in the use and access to Facebook technology.

Findings

94.8 XFM has been in the market for over 14 years. It started its operations on August 1, 2007, as Vision Voice FM, an English news-focused radio station, but was rebranded to XFM in 2011 to focus on urban entertainment. The radio broadcasts on 94.8 FM and covers Kampala and surrounding urban areas. The online digital broadcast is on www.xfm.ug. However, the radio station uses social media as an alternative channel to reach its audience. The platforms include: Facebook at www.facebook.com/xfmug, Twitter at www.twitter.com/xfmug, Instagram at www.instagram.com/xfmug, and a WhatsApp line at +256750948948 for their in-radio programming. As of August 15, 2021, the station's Facebook page had 238,496 followers, Twitter had 133,700 followers, and Instagram had 22,700 followers. By observation on Facebook, the profile photo of the radio was typically the branded logo image and the associated graphic of the cover picture to mark 10 years of the station's existence. The station uses the cover picture to reveal more information, the hosts/presenters, logo image, and radio app downloadable on Google Play or App Store.

The findings indicate that Facebook has been used in radio programming at 94.8 XFM in the following ways: connecting with the audience, interacting/engaging with the audience to reach new audience, posting multi-media content, streaming live audio/video, conducting research, and advertising or promoting products and services. Through the Facebook page, the hosts/presenters also used their personal pages to connect with listeners during programmes. Moreover, individual programmes did not have Facebook pages because the station wanted to keep the audience connected to its page rather than scatter them in programme pages. "This is because collectively we have bigger numbers as opposed to every show at the station having its own Facebook page" (Respondent 1, personal communication, July 10, 2021). Further, 94.8 XFM uses Facebook in radio programming to interact with listeners. Both the station and its listeners used the platform to interact beyond the programme airing times and in ways that could not be done by phone calls or text messages. As one respondent said, "Many listeners found it easier to interact with the radio station via Facebook without using phone calls that require one caller at a time" (Respondent 2, personal communication, July 8, 2021). The station posts questions about topical issues, such as news, entertainment, or fashion trends, and the listeners interact with the station by giving their feedback and sharing their thoughts and opinions about the topical issues.

The station uses Facebook in programming to reach new audiences by positing multi-media content. The hosts/presenters helped reach new listeners by promoting the radio station on Facebook through streaming live programmes and events and posting video and audio clips of programmes. According to one respondent, "The hosts/presenters encouraged listeners to follow the station's page, post comments and like programmes of their interest" (Respondent 2, personal communication, July 8, 2021). Another respondent noted, "We can record a video interview and post it on Facebook, so that listeners can [view]. This will attract comments and likes from the audiences even after the radio show" (Respondent 3, personal communication, July 11, 2021). For instance, an interview video clip with Sheila Gashumba, (a local celebrity) about her new boyfriend had 359 comments and the video clip had 464,000 views. Facebook provides listeners a new experience of consuming radio content by seeing and listening to their favourite hosts/presenters or guests in the studio. As a result, the platform has promoted radio personalities, making them popular among listeners. And when they leave the station or are unable to work, the station's page provides listeners with the platform to voice their concerns and express their frustration that requires feedback.

The station uses Facebook to carry out research on its audience and competitors. Facebook was seen as a great tool to keep an eye on competitors by just visiting their pages. "Sometimes we are able to know what our competitors are doing by looking at their Facebook posts" (Respondent 4, personal communication, August 10, 2021). The station uses Facebook to conduct audience research to discover not only trending topics and songs but also to measure the relevance of the songs played on radio. For example, the hosts/presenters request the audience to tell them whether a particular song is worth playing on-air or not. The other way the radio station discovered trending songs was by asking listeners to send their song requests (Respondent 3, personal communication, July 11, 2021). Moreover, 94.8 XFM uses Facebook in radio programming as an advertising and promotional tool. By posting the programme line-up, hosts/presenters, and guests hosted on-air, Facebook promotes the station's programmes, events, and contests at low costs. "At the top of the hour, listeners are updated on Facebook about what is coming up in the next hour. If there is a topic to be discussed, it will be posted on [the station's] Facebook page and listeners can contribute to the discussion" (Respondent 2, personal communication, July 8, 2021).

Further, it was established that using Facebook in radio programming has promoted citizen journalism where the online radio audience publishes news content by commenting on the station's status updates, tagging and sharing the news. It was observed that followers share latest news updates as comments on 94.8 XFM's Facebook page, and in order to promote citizen journalism, 94.8 XFM regularly requested followers to send in news updates as comments on their Facebook page. Facebook was also used to update listeners in cases of crises, accidents, breaking news, or sudden changes in programming by "posting the headlines on the station's page and providing details of the story in the news bulletin" (Respondent 5, personal communication, August 10, 2021). Therefore, the platform has altered how radio broadcasters break news and how journalists collect information from sources. As noted, "The journalists can obtain information and immediate responses from sources online" (Respondent 1, personal communication, July 10, 2021).

Using Facebook in radio programming at 94.8 XFM has resulted in the growth of followers who are presented to advertisers as potential customers. For example, one respondent noted, "We are able to tell that because our followers on Facebook have been growing steadily over time" (Respondent 6, personal communication, July 9, 2021). As a result of the growing number of programme followers/fans, the platform has created business opportunities for the station and its listeners. As a result, advertisers have given revenue to 94.8 XFM through advertising on the station's Facebook page, thus providing an alternative source of revenue for 94.8 XFM. At 94.8 XFM, Facebook space is sold in combination with on-air space and 10% of the total advertising revenue was from social media— Facebook and Twitter. "Facebook alone contributed 5% of XFMs annual revenue amounting to twenty-two million five hundred Uganda shillings" (Respondent 7, personal communication, July 9, 2021) which is approximately 6000 US dollars. Facebook made it easy for advertisers to get added value on traditional radio advertising.

DISCUSSION

Adapting the affordance approach to social media technology in terms of how Facebook can be used, looks at what the platform "affords" radio stations and their listeners in terms of action possibilities for meeting their desired goals (Volkoff & Strong, 2017, p. 2; Schrock, 2015, p. 1229). The Facebook pages of radio stations that Freeman et al. (2012, p. 4) examined were similar in that they obviously had to conform to the basic Facebook layout. The profile of 94.8 XFM was a branded logo image and associated graphic of the cover picture to mark 10 years of the radio's existence. The menu links included "Home, About, Posts, Photos, Videos, Live, Events, and Community." Freeman et al. (2012, p. 4) argue that the menu links are customisable and radio stations can add or remove them to create a unique experience, although it was observed that 94.8 XFM had not customised its menu links which meant that they still had opportunities of customising the menu action buttons.

While it is important to consider the basic features of Facebook, Caers et al. (2013) argue that it is even more important to consider how the platform is actually being used by radio stations and their audiences. Steinfeld and Laor (2019, p. 206) contend that Facebook is used by radio stations primarily as an extension of their radio broadcasts. Therefore, radio stations have recognised Facebook's potential in achieving their traditional goals. Respondents identified the following goals of using Facebook in radio programming at 94.8 XFM: connect with the audience, interact/engage with the audience, reach new audience, post multi-media content, stream live audio/video, conduct research, and advertise or promote products and services. These findings confirm the observation by Bonini et al. (2014, p. 98) that radio stations use Facebook in programming for five main reasons, namely, strengthening connections with their regular listeners; increasing opportunities to interact with their audience; reaching new audience; transforming radio into a multi-media platform; and increasing distribution of content, making it easily accessible for a longer time.

Facebook features afford goal-oriented actors, such as radio stations and their listeners, the action possibilities for meeting their goals. The most common affordance on Facebook is the ability to "Like" (Hayes et al., 2016, p. 171). For instance, the "Like" feature affords the listeners an action possibility of clicking the button and automatically connecting them with the radio station because every comment or liking action on that very comment will send an alert to the listener thus linking them and the station. The majority of radio stations, including 94.8 XFM, use Facebook pages in a way that allows anyone to follow them with a single click of the "Like" button and without any need for administrator approval (Laor et al., 2017, p. 962). The number of "Likes" the radio station's page has is an indicator of the number of listeners who receive status updates about the page in their newsfeed. The number of likes is an indicator of the page's potential audience reach (Boberg et al., 2020, p. 6). Besides, listeners receiving status updates in their newsfeed affords 94.8 XFM the opportunity of growing their follower base on Facebook.

At 94.8 XFM, it was observed that the hosts/presenters started their shows by posting a status update on the station's Facebook page to introduce the programme. These posts were normally accompanied by multi-media content, such as images, audio, videos of the hosts/presenters, guests in the studios, or celebrity artists. Steinfeld and Laor (2019, p. 200) note that posts with multi-media content attract more engagement than text-only or text and hyperlink posts. Multi-media content on Facebook has been used by 94.8 XFM in programming to interact and/or engage with listeners. Interaction is required from both the radio station and the audience (McMahon, 2019, p. 161), therefore, the station has to regularly post stimulating or engaging content that will appeal to their listeners. Listeners also need to be active by engaging with content through emoji reactions, shares, or comments. The main way that 94.8 XFM interacted with listeners was by posting multi-media content, and streaming audio/video broadcasts. It was reported that 94.8 XFM uses Facebook for breaking news by posting headlines on the station's page and providing details of the story in the bulletin. Listeners also share and tag breaking news on the station's Facebook page. Mashud and Ofori-Birikorang (2018, p. 18) found that listeners post news items on radio station's pages, drawing attention to such content by way of sharing and tags. These stories are then verified and incorporated into the news bulletin or shared on the radio station's various social media platforms. Therefore, Facebook has altered not only how radio broadcasters break news but also how journalists collect information from sources.

The result of using Facebook in radio programming has been the emergence of the social media audience. There has been a general growth in fans/followers on social media and listeners of the radio broadcast. Indeed, Bonini (2020, p. 14) argues that the radio station audience must be understood as the sum of its listeners and those who follow it on social media platforms including Facebook. While the former audience receive radio broadcast in the traditional way, the latter audience receive online broadcast and are connected to the host/presenter with each other via the station Facebook page. The relationship between the programme hosts/presenters and listener as well as between listener and listener is now closer. Indeed, Bonini (2014b, p. 14) argues that Facebook considerably modifies both the vertical relationship between the host/presenter and listeners and the horizontal relationship between each listener. The attachment between the listeners and hosts/presenters is now closer than before. Laor (2019, p. 80) argues that the radio broadcast and live stream on Facebook tends to create for the listener a feeling of intimate and personal interaction with the host/presenter. This feeling of trust translates into listeners conceiving radio not only as authoritative but also as reliable and reflecting real social conditions. McMahon (2021, p. 4) argues that any loss of focus on providing that consistent, trusted voice in the audience's everyday life would be of detriment to the entire station or programme. Listeners leave negative comments on the station's Facebook page when the presenter/host is unable to work or leaves the radio station. This is because they have a platform to express their frustration.

Related to the issue of the social media audience are the business opportunities that Facebook has created for the radio station. While social media represent the station's true social capital that is visible, Bonini (2020,

p. 14) argues that they also constitute the economic capital of the station. Even if the social media audience don't generate a tangible economic value like the traditional radio audience do, it generates a significant amount of reputational capital. The difficult economic circumstances have forced radio stations to devise new and cost-effective ways of generating income by utilising social media including Facebook in a bid to enhance their audience and revenues (McMahon, 2019, p. 157). 94.8 XFM is a commercial enterprise, which relies on commercial revenue via advertising, sponsorship, and investment incomes (Vision Group, 2018, p. 19). Facebook has been used by 94.8 XFM to highlight advertisers and sponsors by uploading their logos and messages for the audience to view products/services advertised on-air and, thus creating additional space and added value to advertisers.

Being a global network, Facebook is the best platform for promoting radio programmes, events, and contests. Facebook has enabled 94.8 XFM to carry out promotional events and other competitions at very low costs. Laor and Steinfeld (2018, p. 1) found that both station and listeners turn to Facebook for promotional purposes. Many listeners contribute to conversations on the station's Facebook page by promoting products. It was also observed that 94.8 XFM promotes its programmes, events, or products by posting the programme line-up, the hosts/presenters, or the guests hosted on-air. This observation was consistent with the argument by Pilitsidou et al. (2019, p. 25) that social media including Facebook are being used by radio stations as a means of promoting their programmes to increase their rating. Facebook has also promoted radio personalities and programmes, because listeners get to see them being posted on the radio station's Facebook page. As Laor (2019, p. 81) notes, the platform enhances accessibility of programme hosts/presenters, since listeners are more likely to engage with them.

Conclusion

The findings revealed that 94.8 XFM uses Facebook in radio programming for connection, interaction, audience growth, multi-media content production, streaming audio/video, research, advertising, promotion, and update purposes. It is important for radio professionals to enhance their use of social media to improve radio programming of commercial stations. It was further established that the use of Facebook in radio programming resulted into citizen journalism, content production by audience, and radio becoming a visual medium, as well as fostered growth in audience, advertising revenue, and promotion of station products. While the benefits of using Facebook in radio programming are undoubtable, these can be harnessed through a robust social media strategy that allows for the employment of a social media manager, audience engagement, and production of interactive multi-media content.

REFERENCES

Al-Rawi, A. (2016). Understanding the Social Media Audiences of Radio Stations. *Journal of Radio & Audio Media, 23*(1), 50–67. https://doi.org/10.108 0/19376529.2016.1155298

Berry, R. (2014). The Future of radio is the internet, not on the internet. In *Radio: the Resilient Medium: Papers from the Third Conference of the ECREA Radio Research Station (pp. 3–16)*. Centre for Research in Media and Cultural Studies, Sunderland, ISBN 099298050X

Boberg, S., Quandt, T., Schatto-Eckrodt, T., & Frischlich, L. (2020b). *Pandemic Populism: Facebook Pages of Alternative News Media and The Corona Crisis—A Computational Content Analysis.* (No. 1).

Bonini, T. (2014a). Doing radio in the age of Facebook. *The Radio Journal – International Studies in Broadcast & Audio. Media, 12*(1&2), 73–87. https://doi.org/10.1386/rjao.12.1-2.73_1

Bonini, T. (2014b). The New Role of Radio and Its Public in the Age of Social Network Sites. *First Monday, 19*(6). https://doi.org/10.5210/fm.v19i6.4311

Bonini, T. (2020). Radio Audiences: More Vocal than Ever Before. In A. Bardon, K. Markelova, & C. Xiaorong (Eds.), *The UNESCO Courier* (pp. 14–15). UNESCO. https://en.unesco.org/courier/2020-1/radio-audiences-more-vocal-ever

Bonini, T., Fesneau, E., Perez, I. G., Luthj, C., Jedrzejewski, S., Pedroia, A., Rohn, U., Sellas, T., Starkey, G., & Stiernstedt, F. (2014). Radio Formats and Social Media Use in Europe—28 Case Studies of Public Service Practice. *The Radio Journal—International Studies in Broadcast & Audio Media, 12*(1&2), 89–106. https://doi.org/10.1386/rjao.12.1-2.89_

Boscha, T. (2013). Social Media and Community Radio Journalism in South Africa. *Digital Journalism, 1*(2), 29–43. https://doi.org/10.1080/2167081 1.2013.850199

Bucher, T., & Helmond, A. (2018). The Affordances of Social Media Platforms. In J. Burgess & T. P. A. Marwick (Eds.), *The SAGE Handbook of Social Media* (pp. 33–253). Sage Publications.

Caers, R., De Feyter, T., De Couck, M., Stough, T., Vigna, C., & Du Bois, C. (2013). Facebook: A Literature Review. *New Media & Society, 15*(6), 982–1002. https://doi.org/10.1177/1461444813488061

Chibita, M. B. (2016). Indigenous Language Media and Freedom of Expression in Uganda. In A. Salawu & M. B. Chibita (Eds.), *Indigenous Language Media, Language Politics and Democracy in Africa* (pp. 28–56). Palgrave Macmillan.

Creswell, J. (2013). *Qualitative Inquiry and Research Design: Choosing among Five Approaches.* SAGE Publications, Inc.

Davis, C. H. F., Canche, M. S. G., Deil-Amen, R., & Rios-Aguilar, C. (2012). *Social Media in Higher Education: A Literature Review and Research Directions.* Arizona: The Center for the Study of Higher Education at the University of Arizona and Claremont Graduate University.

Ewart, J., & Ames, K. (2016). Talking text: Exploring SMS and e-mail use by Australian talkback radio listeners. *The Radio Journal – International Studies in Broadcast & Audio Media, 14*(1), 91–107. https://doi.org/10.1386/rjao.14.1.91_1

Freeman, B. C., Klapczynski, J., & Wood, E. (2012). Radio and Facebook: The Relationship between Broadcast and Social Media Software in the U.S., Germany, and Singapore. *First Monday, 17*(4). https://doi.org/10.5210/fm.v17i4.3768

Galán-Arribas, R., Herrero-Gutiérrez, F.-J., & Martínez-Arcos, C.-A. (2018). Social Networks as a Promotional Space for Spanish Radio Content. The Case Study of the On-demand Programming of Cadena SER and COPE. In F. J. García-Peñalvo (Ed.), *Proceedings of the 6th International Conference on Technological Ecosystems for Enhancing Multiculturality (TEEM 2018)* (pp. 1–6). ACM.

Hafezieh, N., & Eshraghian, F. (2017). Affordance Theory in Social Media Research: Systematic Review and Synthesis of the Literature. In *Twenty-Fifth European Conference on Information Systems (ECIS), Guimarães, Portugal* (pp. 1–12).

Hayes, R. A., Carr, C. T., & Wohn, D. Y. (2016). One Click, Many Meanings: Interpreting Paralinguistic Digital Affordances in Social Media. *Journal of Broadcasting & Electronic Media, 60*(1), 171–187. https://doi.org/10.1080/08838151.2015.1127248

Kurtul, G. (2013). Digital Connections Redefined With User-Generated Content (UGC). *NMQ Digital.* Available: https://nmqdigital.com/blog/user-generated-content

Laor, T. (2019). "Hello, is There Anybody Who Reads Me?" Radio Programs and Popular Facebook Posts. *International Journal of Interactive Multimedia and Artificial Intelligence, 5*(7), 80–87. https://doi.org/10.9781/ijimai.2019.10.003

Laor, T., Galily, Y., & Tamir, I. (2017). Radio Presence in Online Platforms in Israel. *Israel Affairs, 23*(5), 951–969. https://doi.org/10.1080/1353712 1.2017.1345420

Laor, T., & Steinfeld, N. (2018). From FM to FB: Radio Stations on Facebook. *Israel Affairs.* https://doi.org/10.1080/13537121.2018.1429544

Lugalambi, G. W. (2010). *Public Broadcasting in Africa Series: Uganda* (D. P. G. Mwesige & H. Bussiek, Eds.). Open Society Initiative for East Africa.

Mashud, Z., & Ofori-Birikorang, A. (2018). Social Media and Radio News Production: A Study of Selected Radio Stations in Ghana. *New Media and Mass Communication, 68,* 15–26.

McMahon, D. (2019). The economic, social & cultural impact of the social network site Facebook on the Irish radio industry 2011–2016. Thesis. https://doi.org/10.48773/926z6

McMahon, D. (2021). In Tune with the Listener: How Local Radio in Ireland has Maintained Audience Attention and Loyalty. *Online Journal of Communication and Media Technologies, 11*(3), e202112. https://doi.org/10.30935/ojcmt/11085

Mediatool. (2023). Broadcast Trends in the Digital Age. Retrieved March 15, 2023, from https://mediatool.com/blog/broadcast-media

Miller, S. (2019). Citizen Journalism. *Oxford Research Encyclopedia of Communication.* https://doi.org/10.1093/acrefore/9780190228613.013.786

Mirembe, D. (2015). *The Threat Nets Approach to Information System Security Risk Analysis.* University of Groningen, SOM Research School. https://doi.org/10.1057/9781137547309

Namusoga, S. (2017). *The Framing of Homosexuality by Two Ugandan Newspapers: An Analysis of the New Vision and Daily Monitor (PhD thesis).* University of KwaZulu-Natal.

Ogola, G. (2016). African Journalism: A Journey of Failures and Triumphs. *African Journalism Studies, 36*(1), 93–102. https://doi.org/10.1080/23743670.2015.1008175

Pilitsidou, Z., Tsigilis, N., & Kalliris, G. (2019). Radio Stations and Audience Communication: Social Media Utilization and Listeners Interaction. *Issues in Social Science, 7*(1). https://doi.org/10.5296/iss.v7i1.14743

Pozzi, G., Pigni, F., & Vitari, C. (2014). Affordance Theory in the IS Discipline: A Review and Synthesis of the Literature. *AMCIS 2014 Proceedings, Savannah, United States.* https://aisel.aisnet.org/AMCIS2014

Rafeeq, A., & Jiang, S. (2020). Breaking News of Disasters: How Stuff.co.nz and NZHerald.co.nz Used Facebook and Twitter in the 2016 Kaikoura Earthquake Coverage in New Zealand. *Media and Communication Studies.* https://doi.org/10.1080/23311886.2020.1731121

Schrock, A. R. (2015). Communicative Affordances of Mobile Media: Portability, Availability, Locatability, and Multimediality. *International Journal of Communication*, *9*, 1229–1246.

Spangardt, B., Ruth, N., & Schramm, H. (2016). "… And please visit our Facebook page, too!" How Radio Presenter Personalities Influence Listeners' Interactions with Radio Stations. *Journal of Radio & Audio Media*, *23*(1), 68–94. https://doi.org/10.1080/19376529.2016.1155710

Srinivasan, S., & Diepeveen, S. (2018). The Power of the "audience-public": Interactive Radio in Africa. *The International Journal of Press/Politics*, 1–24. https://doi.org/10.1177/1940161218779175

Starkey, G., & Crisell, A. (2010). Hear today and on tomorrow: the future of news and 'news talk ' in an era of digital radio. In *The Routledge Companion to News and Journalism* (pp. 661–667). Routledge. https://journalism.utexas.edu/sites/default/files/sites/journalism.utexas.edu/files/attachments/reese/baresch-hsureese-chapter.pdf

Steinfeld, N., & Laor, T. (2019). New Arenas or More of the Same? Public and Commercial Radio Stations on Facebook. *Journal of Radio & Audio Media*, *26*(2), 194–209. https://doi.org/10.1080/19376529.2018.1431890

Uganda Bureau of Statistics. (2022). *The 2022 Statistical Abstract*. https://www.ubos.org/wpcontent/uploads/publications/05_20232022_Statistical_Abstract.pdf

Vision Group. (2018). *Resilience and recovery. Annual Report 2018/2019*. New Vision Printing and Publishing Company, Kampala Uganda.

Volkoff, O., & Strong, D. (2017). Affordance Theory and How to Use It in IS Research. In R. D. Galliers & M.-K. Stein (Eds.), *The Routledge Companion to Management Information Systems* (First, pp. 1–14). Routledge. https://doi.org/10.4324/9781315619361

Wedawatta, G., Ingirige, B., & Amaratunga, D. (2011). Case Study as a Research Strategy: Investigating Extreme Weather Resilience of Construction SMEs in the UK. *ARCOM Doctoral Workshop, International Conference on Building Resilience*, 1–9. http://usir.salford.ac.uk/id/eprint/18250/

Willems, W. (2013). Participation—In What? Radio, Convergence and the Corporate Logic of Audience Input through New Media in Zambia. *Telematics and Informatics*, *30*, 223–231. https://doi.org/10.1016/j.tele.2012.02.006

Zelenkauskaite, A., & Simoes, B. (2015). User Interaction Profiling on Facebook, Twitter, and Google+ across Radio. *48th Hawaii International Conference on System Sciences*, 1657–1666. https://doi.org/10.1109/HICSS.2015.199

CHAPTER 8

The Algorithmic Power and Subtitles in African Language on Facebook Peripheral News Outlets: Language Policy and Practices

Limukani Mathe

INTRODUCTION

Digital journalism practice in indigenous languages has become ubiquitous on social networking sites (SNSs) prompting scholarly inquiry on what journalism is and what it should be. The significant part of African journalism practice in indigenous languages is how local content thrives on Western-based digital technologies as peripheral actors compete or align in the pursuit of establishing journalistic boundaries. These peripheral actors are considered non-traditional players (individual or organisations) that operate on the margins or outside the boundaries of traditional journalism yet part of the broader communication ecology in the news making (Cheruiyot et al., 2021; Mutsvairo & Solgado 2020; Roberts 2019; Vos & Thomas 2023). The discursive text on peripheral news outlets is often in indigenous languages reflecting non-traditional style of

---

L. Mathe (✉)
Research Focus Area: Social Transformation, North-West University, Potcheftroom, South Africa

© The Author(s), under exclusive license to Springer Nature Switzerland AG 2025
A. Sharra, U. Akpojivi (eds.), *Technologies and Media Production Cultures*, Palgrave Studies in Journalism and the Global South,
https://doi.org/10.1007/978-3-031-78582-5_8

news making (Mathe 2024). It is, therefore, important to analyse how such content in indigenous languages thrives as journalism content on English-dominant websites spaces.

This chapter focuses on peripheral news outlets by non-traditional actors through Facebook pages which we view as non-mainstream or peripheral. One can debate that peripheral news outlets are not non-mainstream yet distinct from legacy media as they exploit a non-standard language in news making. This chapter seeks to analyse how editors or administrators of these Facebook news pages thrive on Western-owned websites as they circumvent the English algorithm to disseminate content in indigenous languages through subtitles or captions. The study answers the following questions: how do editors or administrators of indigenous-language Facebook news pages circumvent the English algorithm and how does the local language get monitored and regulated by Facebook.

There is limited scholarship on the issue of language and algorithmic power on digital spheres, especially on peripheral "non-mainstream" news pages. Several studies explore the issues of digital colonialism through Google language translation tool, and other various digital tools of the internet. These studies note that there have been algorithmic power imbalances between the English Western technology or the Anglo-centrism of cyberspace and the African Multilingual internet users in the Global South (Arora 2019; Mignolo 2007; Waisbord & Mellado 2014; Willems & Mano 2016). Predictive language technologies on Google have been criticised for promoting language imbalances through content moderation in various cultural and linguistic settings, creating dilemmas for the multilingual internet users. Thus, Afrocentric studies call for the internet decolonisation to promote global multilingual inclusivity (Mpofu & Salawu 2020) because global language policy and practices privilege the English Algorithm through filtering language variations at the expense of indigenous languages in Africa (Chonka et al., 2023).

In their study, Chonka et al. (2023) show that the Google predictive language technology wrongly moderates African languages by politicising and gendering keywords in Amharic, Kiswahili and Somali. Taking a different approach, this study analyses how Zimbabwean indigenous-language "non-mainstream" news outlets thrive on English-dominant Facebook website. There are numerous Zimbabwean "non-mainstream" news outlets on Facebook and most of these disseminate content in major indigenous languages such as Shona and Ndebele. Non-mainstream or peripheral news outlets on social media include *iHarare.com* and

Hatirare263, Zimbolive, ZimCeleb mainly publishing in Shona language. Shona is widely spoken in Zimbabwe and commands a sheer size of digital capital (Mathe & Motsaathebe 2024a, 2024b). We, therefore, opted for Facebook news outlets disseminating content in Shona, namely, *iHarare. com* and *Hatirare263*, which have highest numbers of followers. The *iHarare.com* page has 67,400 followers while the *Hatirare263* page has 30,100 and these numbers keep increasing.

Peripheral News Outlets in Indigenous Language

The impact of digital technologies has shifted political and cultural ways of news production (Mano 2007; Mutsvairo & Salgado 2022; Mabweazara & Mare 2021). Peripheral news outlets are now ubiquitous on social media (Cheruiyot et al. 2021). The disruptive nature of peripheral journalism in the African media ecology presents new arenas for academic inquiry (Holton & Belair-Gagnon 2018; Cheruiyot et al., 2019), as these peripheral actors continue to transgress and supplant traditional boundaries of journalism practice (Eldridge 2019; Baack 2018; Cheruiyot et al., 2019) with new language stylistics in news making.

From a traditional perspective, professional journalism standard practice has been based on ethics and objective reporting. Legacy media, namely radio, television and print, have been well-known for their "standard journalism" practice (Yarmohammadi, 2010; Novo 2011, p. 34) as "mainstream" and by "mainstream journalists". These set the boundary work of what has been known as journalism before the advent of new media and non-mainstream news outlets. The advent of the internet, specifically social media, enabled the visibility of new actors in the journalism field. Non-traditional actors sometimes viewed as interlopers and intralopers occupy the digital space and disrupt narratives by mainstream media. Social media is increasingly becoming utilised for content creation to report, inform and engage audiences (Mathe 2023). It is, therefore, necessary to consider how such forms of journalism practice continue to thrive in the Africa media ecology, especially on digital platforms. There is a need to explore the specifics, especially on the nature of journalism practice and media production, on English-dominant spaces. Many studies focus on the crisis that the journalism field continues to face with the impact of digital technologies (Cheruiyot et al., 2019, 2021; Eldridge 2019; Baack 2018); however, little has been done to investigate how non-traditional actors disseminate content in indigenous languages and how their journalistic practice circumvents the English algorithm. Cheruiyot et al. (2021) lament insufficient scholarly attention on the narratives, outputs and practices by significant journalistic actors in Africa's communication ecology. We also note that there has been insufficient focus on how journalistic actors in the African communication ecology overcome language regulations on Facebook

A Facebook page can be managed in different ways, for instance, a page can be controlled by administrators while everyone follows, likes and comments on posts but without the privilege of posting directly on the timeline as this privilege is only reserved for administrators. Another Facebook page involves a group page where users can join and have the freedom to post on the timeline and comment on other posts. A controlled Facebook page is one whereby administrators function as editors of the page with the privilege of administration just like WhatsApp groups. The editors of the page have the privilege to post main content while followers of the page can only comment, share or like the posts. Although criticised as "amateurish", "phony" and "bad imitator" of mainstream journalism (Goldstein & Rotich 2008; Siegel 2008), the indigenous-language peripheral news outlets can exploit community language relevant to audiences (Zelizer 1993; Jaffe 2009). The most interesting feature of indigenous-language "non-mainstream" peripheral journalism is the refection of readers' cultural context. Language in journalism can reflect the socio-cultural context of the media and the audiences (Motssathebe 2018; Mathe & Motsaathebe 2023).

The challenge now and then is the dominance of English on digital platforms. Western-owned social networking sites (SNSs) are controlled by the algorithm which promotes language imbalances and moderates content due to linguistic settings (Chonka et al. 2023; Arora, 2019; Mignolo, 2007; Waisbord & Mellado 2014; Willems & Mano 2016). These language imbalances by the Western-based and controlled internet perpetuate digital coloniality which also seems problematic for indigenous-language media platforms in Africa. The English algorithm normally prefers English news outlets at the disadvantage of non-English-language platforms. The problem is Africa, unlike China, does not have an Afrocentric cyberspace but depends on Western big media technologies such as X (formerly known as Twitter) and Meta. Such challenges of indigenous language segregation have led to a rhetoric call for an Afrocentric multilingual cyberspace (Mpofu & Salawu 2020).

We are of the perspective that the multilingual Afrocentric cyberspace is important because it will promote language policy and practice for indigenous-language platforms. From an interpretive community perspective, discursive text reflects even the language of the media, journalists and audiences (Zelizer 1993; Jaffe 2009). Also, from the perspective of peripheral journalism, we note that community and journalism are intertwined, reflecting the daily discursive text or language of the community. Therefore, in terms of the relationship between community and journalism, several scholars have shown how the media continually renovates to accommodate the ever-changing language of the community, even online audiences. In this light, indigenous-language media is also abandoning the standard language but transmuting to eccentric code-switching, slang and colloquial language of readers' everyday discourses (Mpofu 2023; Chan 2018). Code mixing is defined as the hybridisation and deviation of language opposite to standard journalism writing (Chan 2018). In this respect, the well-known standard journalism writing has been disrupted by new digital journalism ecologies (Yarmohammadi, 2010; Novo 2011; Cheruiyot et al. 2021).

Given this background of digital technologies and indigenous languages, we focus on how *iHarare.com* and *Hatirare263* circumvent the English algorithm to disseminate content in indigenous languages through subtitles or captions and how indigenous languages get monitored and regulated. Zelizer (2012, p. 181) shows that the interpretive community "retains a collective and authoritative voice" that makes media and journalists contribute to readers' everyday discourses. In other words, the "non-mainstream" news outlets convey shared beliefs, ideologies and identities through language (Jaffe 2009). Language also underpins "not only linguistic form and use, but also the very notion of the person and the social group" (Woolard 1998, p. 3), providing "a basis for shared values, practices, and ideologies" even in African journalism (Carpenter & Sosale 2019: 284). Such linguistic discourses are "a marker of how journalists see themselves as journalists" and their journalistic role is legitimised or reinforced by telling society its news (Zelizer 1993, p. 28).

FACEBOOK AND THE ALGORITHM

Algorithm refers to how the computerised software communicates or conditions instructions in a certain sequential order (Knuth 1998; Bucher 2016). In other words, algorithm refers to how machine-readable instructions transmit messages on the computer to accomplish a specific task. Algorithm implies how the "software conditions our existence" (Thrift 2005, p. 138). In the context of Facebook, algorithms refer to how the algorithm selects and directs content on the media user's newsfeed for consumption. Media and communication studies have begun to query the power, relevance and accountability of the algorithm and the logic that feeds content on user's newsfeed (Beer 2013; Gillespie 2014; Diakopoulos 2015; Bucher 2012, 2016; Christin 2017; van Dijck 2013). Due to social media use, algorithms have become a part of media users' everyday lives as content gets channelled for their attention and consumption (Deuze 2012). Media users can spend the day scrolling and browsing the internet through social media streets (newsfeeds) using digital technologies (smartphones and computers). Thus, some studies note that power dynamics are shaped and engendered by the algorithm as a "software conditions our existence" (Thrift 2005, p. 138); conditions and moderating content to varying degree (Kitchin & Dodge 2011, p. ix). On the other hand, other studies show that media users can also influence the algorithm through Facebook likes and comments, as shown by McKelvey (2014) that counter-publics and mediators can reshape the algorithm. Leong (2020) discusses how social media networks can be domesticated through the algorithm.

According to van Dijck (2013), media users influence the algorithm on Facebook through sharing, friending and liking as this generates more "algorithmically mediated interactions" within a discursive community. The user interactions with the discursive community, therefore, generate ordinary effects reflective of everyday life algorithms (Bucher 2016). The everyday life algorithms have also made Facebook users aware of the ordinary effects in such a way that they manipulate or circumvent to determine favourable content for themselves (Bucher 2016). Even journalists are becoming knowledgeable in adhering to algorithmic accountability functions (Diakopoulos 2015). In what Diakopoulos (2005) calls "algorithmic accountability reporting", Bucher (2016) argues that journalists now deliberately characterise their power and delineate their biases and mistakes in their reporting. In this light, this study probes how indigenous-language "non-mainstream" Facebook news pages circumvent the English algorithm to generate their own algorithmic power through indigenous-language subtitles or captions.

It is vital to note that Facebook has a policy that regulates user language and interaction. One of the fundamental regulations of Facebook is against hate speech (Facebook, 2024). As extracted, Facebook policy is:

> … we define hate speech as a direct attack against people- rather than concepts or institutions -on the basis of what we call protected characteristics: race, ethnicity, national origin, disability, religious affiliation, caste, sexual orientation, sex, gender identity and serious disease. We define attacks as violent or dehumanising speech, harmful stereotypes, statements of inferiority, expressions of contempt, disgust or dismissal, cursing and calls for exclusion or segregation. We also prohibit the use of harmful stereotypes, which we define as dehumanising comparisons that have historically been used to attack, intimidate or exclude specific groups, and that are often linked with offline violence. (Facebook, 2024)

By doing so, Facebook protects its users from hate speech. It has a facility where victims of hate speech such as refugees, immigrants, migrants, asylum seekers and others can report incidences of hate speech and attack. Such affordances regulate the platform leading to suspension or blocking of the account perpetuating hate speech. For instance, Donald Trump's Facebook account was permanently banned on the grounds of promoting violence and xenophobia. Facebook policy also prohibits the use of slurs and "certain words or phrases" that violate other people's rights. More so, Facebook removes content presumed as hate speech without the user indicating the intent or the interpretation of such content.

Given the complexities of language differences in the Global North and South, this chapter questions how Facebook positively moderates words or phrases that are not in the glossary of English or the algorithm, as predetermined by the software. As asserted by Mpofu and Salawu (2020), such language gaps demand the localisation of the internet for multilingual inclusivity. Afrocentric studies call for the decolonisation of the internet that privileges the English algorithm (Chonka et al., 2023; Waisbord & Mellado 2014; Willems & Mano 2016).

DECOLONIAL THEORY

Pertaining to language challenges, Afrocentric scholars have been calling for the decolonisation of the internet. The concept of decoloniality aims to counter the impact of colonialism, and neo-colonialism argues that though colonialism ended, coloniality is still ongoing. Many studies conceptualise "coloniality" as the continuance of colonial patterns of administration and power (Quijano 2000; Grosfoguel 2007; Maldonado-Torres, 2007). According to Maldonado-Torres (2011, p. 2),

> the decolonial turn does not refer to a single theoretical school, but rather points to a family of diverse positions that share a view of coloniality as a fundamental problem in the modern age, and of decolonisation or decoloniality as a necessary task that remains unfinished.

Decoloniality is an epistemic interrogation as it questions all aspects of innovation, including media and communication (Moyo 2020). African scholarship is now challenging Western theories as it seeks to break away from theories that seem to be irrelevant to the African context. Nyamnjoh (2011) argues that the theory of African media has been more dependent on Western theoretical concepts that emphasise the liberal democratic approach. Although communication theory has evolved, most theories are criticised for failing to incorporate African cultural contexts (Obonyo 2011). On the other hand, Mohammed (2021, p. 22) notes that indigenous African knowledge is offering tools to think "freely and break out of the mould that the northern canon constricts us in".

In the context of the internet, the Google Translate tool was the first to be questioned by many African scholars for its inappropriate translation of English to African languages. Although Google has thrived to incorporate African languages, some scholars note that the practicality of localised Google falls short of accurate translations with English being the dominant language (Mpofu & Salawu 2020; Chonka et al. 2023). Mpofu and Salawu (2020, p. 76) put it plainly that "elements of linguistic imperialism and electronic colonisation concepts are deployed to explain African language use on the Internet, in the context of English language dominance in Zimbabwe and the global digital divide". Their argument stems from the fact that the global multilingual context of Google promotes language policy and practices that favour the English language. They argue that the localisation of the internet should not render indigenous languages second to English—promoting the Western language as a yardstick for language translation (Mpofu & Salawu 2020). Just as shown by Chonka et al. (2023), the Google Translate tool wrongly moderates and politicises African languages by gendering keywords.

The same phenomenon is common with social media and the algorithm. Since Facebook is a Western technology, the logic of the algorithm is primarily English dominant as it moderates and feeds content on users' newsfeeds (Beer 2013; Gillespie 2014; Diakopoulos 2015; Bucher 2012, 2016; Christin 2017; van Dijck 2013). It is in this endeavour of decoloniality that some studies have reflected on the localisation or domestication of social media through the media user's influence of the algorithm. Some studies have shown that the algorithm can be reshaped to promote local content if users retweet, like and share local content (McKelvey 2014; Leong 2020). The problem is that it is not clear if Facebook moderates indigenous languages in the same manner it regulates English in terms of policy and practice.

METHODOLOGY

This study makes use of a qualitative methodological triangulation. A qualitative content analysis was applied on Facebook posts of two Facebook news pages, *Hatirare263* and *iHarare.com*, within a Zimbabwean discursive community. The selection of Facebook pages under study was influenced by the algorithm because they appeared the most on researchers' joint account newsfeed. It is noteworthy that the algorithm can channel any information to the newsfeed that is liked or shared by other users within the discursive network. However, the algorithm did not influence the selection of posts for analysis because the content was manually browsed on *Hatirare263* and *iHarare.com* Facebook pages. It is important to note that *Hatirare263* and *iHarare.com* are controlled Facebook pages where administrators are the only ones who post while followers only comment, like and share. Although the browsing of *Hatirare263 and iHarare.com* Facebook timelines (through a joint Facebook researchers' account) occurred between 16 October 2023 and 19 November 2023, posts collected were dated as far as December 2021 to November 2023.

A purposive selection of posts on the timeline only focused on posts in Shona. Only Facebook posts in Shona language with code-switching to English were collected for study since the objective was to explore posts in indigenous language. This means some posts in English only were not selected for the study. Thus, a corpus of 267 Facebook posts (mainly focusing on captions or subtitles) in indigenous languages were collected for analysis. Thus, this study features some of the Facebook captions or subtitles reflecting content in indigenous language to demonstrate how

160   L. MATHE

the English algorithm is circumvented. The study ethically makes use of texts without showing images of the subjects involved in the story. The unity of analysis was the Facebook post in discursive indigenous language text.

We employed follow-up in-depth interviews with the administrators of *iHarare.com* and *Hatirare263* to extract perspective from their experience of the algorithmic power, content creation and dissemination of content in indigenous language. The interviews were carried out after a qualitative content analysis of Facebook posts as this determined the designing of the semi-structured interview guide, as shown in Appendix A. The interviews were conducted via WhatsApp text messages for convenience retrieved from Facebook page's profile contact numbers. The chapter does not reveal the names of administrators as we did not seek to reveal their identities.

FINDINGS

The findings of the study are presented in three categories, namely, localising social media and reshaping the algorithm, circumventing the English Algorithm and poor regulation of content in indigenous languages. These three categories reflect a qualitative content analysis of Facebook posts in indigenous languages and administrators' perspectives on the issues of the algorithmic power, language policy and practice as we answer the following questions: how do editors or administrators of Facebook news pages circumvent the English algorithm as they disseminate content in indigenous languages through subtitles or captions and how does the Shona language get monitored and regulated

Localising Social Media and Reshaping the Algorithm

Unlike Leong (2020) who uses the term "domesticating" social media through the algorithm, we use the term "localising" social media through the algorithm. By localising, this chapter refers to the activity of generating algorithmic interactions through liking, sharing, friending and commenting on content in indigenous or local languages. By localising content, we refer to engaging local content unlike domesticating content which also includes liking, sharing and engaging international content. As van Dijck (2013) puts it, media users can reshape the algorithm on social media by sharing, following, friending and liking, the findings of this study acknowledge that audience engagement on "non-mainstream" news outlet promotes localisation of content, thereby influencing more local audience traffic. The *Hatirare263* administrator argued that the "page posts content in Shona language because it identifies with the majority and attracts good traffic that circumvents the English algorithm".

As peripheral news outlets, *iHarare.com* and *Hatirare263* reflect the community's daily language. The code-switching and the lingo in Facebook post largely Shona slang as non-standard language reflected in words such as "*Amapedza masports*" (he did it), the "gaffa" (the leader)—resonating with the audience. As shown in Fig. 8.1, the page elicits audience engagement through discursive post "*Maona here zvaitwa ne Gaffa*" (did all see what has been done by the Gaffa?). The post provoked 644 likes and 179 comments reflecting audience engagement on the page.

Fig. 8.1 iHarare.com Facebook post (webcam screenshot). (Source: iHarare.com)

The administrators of *Hatirare.com* and *iHarare263* agreed that their pages distribute content that reflect the voice of the community. The use of everyday language attracts the audience and generates more engagement. Often Shona is used in mix with English as subtitles or captions to an image, poster or video attracting more audience engagement seen by the readers' comments in the commentary forum. According to *Hatirare263* administrator, "the code-switching and mixing of Shona and English somehow strikes a balance between brevity and providing enough context to ensure the audience understands the content because our audience loves such kind of style as it increases engagement on posts". Literature has shown that discursive communities or platforms reflect even the language of journalists, audiences and the media (Zelizer 1993; Jaffe 2009). The editor of *iHarare.com* added that the algorithm is designed in such a way that it channels content for people in the specific region or country as determined by their language: "the higher the number of people who follow the page, the greater the visibility and posts in Shona trend more in Zimbabwe than other languages".

The administrators of *iHarare.com* and *Hatirare263* noted that newsmaking is sometimes informed by stories from audience engagement or gossip from the readers' comments. Thus, audience engagement on the commentary section inspires more stories and promotes the algorithm making the page more visible to followers and users. Thus, localising social media and influencing the algorithm involves following the page and engaging the content for the algorithm to channel-related content to the media user. One of the administrators noted that using Shona as the indigenous language for the audience promotes more engagement for the target audience as they follow up YouTube and website links for more content. For instance, Fig. 8.2 by *iHarare.com* uses caption to explain the story of a car stolen while the owner was meeting a woman. The poster attracted readers' attention and people could follow such stories through YouTube links or website to get the full story.

The findings of the study show more likes and engagement happen, especially on scandal-based or tabloid stories relating to the context and proximity of the reader. As put by the administrator of *Hatirare.com*, "our code-switching and tabloid stories, creates a perception in followers that the page, media house or content creator is not elitist but identifies with the ordinary individuals who follow the page".

Fig. 8.2 iHarare.com Facebook post (webcam screenshot). (Source: iHarare.com)

Circumventing the English Algorithm

According to the perspective of administrators, the algorithm does not suppress frequent post distribution of content. The more the page gets active the more the visibility of content to the followers and media users within the discursive network. On the other hand, *iHarare.com* and *Hatirare263* circumvent the English algorithm and language regulation because meaning in indigenous language is hardly interpreted. Administrator of *Hatirare263* opined:

> It is better to use street lingo which cannot be interpreted by Google translator. Even if someone reports the post it is not going to be taken down or page blacklisted as the algorithm cannot decode the meaning of the words.

Figure 8.3, written in Shona, talks about an artist by the name Silent Killer. It reads "*hazvichisiri trend kwatova kupisa chaiko, ipai munhu sando dzake*" (Silent Killer is trending, kudos to him). The language is in slang such as the terms "*kupisa*" meaning trending and "*sando dzake*" meaning give him kudos. The text reflects code-switching with the English word as "trend".

Code-switching and mixing in Shona and English reflects the informal discursive text that has become a common feature in former British colonies. The code-switching and mixing, however, shows how English remains dominant even in indigenous-language platforms, as shown in Fig. 8.3. The colloquial language with deployment of indigenous

164 L. MATHE

Fig. 8.3 iHarare.com Facebook post (webcam screenshot). (Source: iHarare.com)

language and English is, as argued by Mpofu and Salawu (2020, p. 76), that "elements of linguistic imperialism and electronic colonisation concepts are deployed to explain African language use on the internet, in the context of English language dominance in Zimbabwe and the global digital divide". Nonetheless, the colloquial language seems to be working to the advantage of indigenous-language forums as it circumvents the regulation of hate speech because Facebook sometimes cannot deduce meaning in indigenous languages, making it problematic to regulate content in indigenous languages. Mpofu and Salawu (2020) and Chonka et al. (2023) have shown that Western-based web applications wrongly interpret African languages.

Thus, the submissions through the interviews pinpoint that Shona-driven captions or titles draw more audience traffic than English captions. The administrator of *iHarare.com* added:

> the appeal of the mother language to the human especially the African is a grossly underrated superpower. It is also far easier to use more modern colloquial lingo relevant to the reader to increase traction and traffic towards the website or article or post.

While English remains dominant in former British colonies, this study finds that English is only used in code-switching and mixing for the purposes of inclusivity for a multilingual audience or page followers who do not proficiently speak in Shona. While it is easy to catch audience attention or traffic by using the mother language (Shona), the administrator of *Hatirare263* submitted that "we also avoid making our page purely or limiting to only to Shona speaking people, hence we always revert to mixing of English and Shona (reflecting the street lingo)", as shown in Fig. 8.4. Figure 8.4 reflects the mixing of English and Shona.

Fig. 8.4 *Hatirare263* Facebook post (webcam screenshot). (Source: *Hatirare263*)

"Inyaya yei nhai wangu, titaurirane?!" (what is the issue, we can talk about it). On the other hand, the administrators of *Hatirare263* and *iHarare.com* acknowledged that Facebook is to some extent strict on language because if the page or post is reported for hate speech it can be blacklisted or deleted by Meta. This confirms Facebook policy against hate speech, violence, dehumanising speech, harmful stereotypes, statements of inferiority, expressions of contempt, disgust or dismissal, cursing and calls for exclusion or segregation (Facebook, 2024). Notwithstanding regulation and policy on language, administrators highlighted that the competition is about audience reach and engagement, and posts in indigenous language elicit more local engagement.

Poor Regulation for Content in Indigenous Languages

The drawback, as informed by the findings of the study, is that Facebook struggles to regulate content in indigenous languages. The administrator of *iHarare.com* noted that Facebook regulations are more effective for content in English than African indigenous languages. It is noteworthy that often Facebook hides most of the readers' comments because the algorithm fails to pick up the meaning of the language. Another response by the administrator of *iHarare.com* notes that "something that is not vulgar in Shona gets flicked as Facebook mistaken it as vulgar". This shows the complexity of language and practice in a Western-based and English-dominant web application. Some of the comments from the administrators of *iHarare.com* and *Hatirare263* pages are presented below:

> Facebook has to rely on translators which have no capacity to fully define the insults. Most insults are usually written in slang or shorthand and there is no way the algorithm can deduce meaning so as to find out if the content is in violation of community guidelines.
> Facebook depends on reports, if there would be any reports against our page or posts but it is rare and their algorithm does not pick our language.
> Facebook has not developed much in detecting Africa language. The Algorithm is not that strict to indigenous languages as compared to English.

The above statement shows how Western-based technology struggles to deal with African indigenous languages. Administrators view the internet as open and freely accessible to anyone connected through digital technologies. From this perspective, they did not necessarily believe that the internet perpetuates colonialism rather can be used for different purposes. Some of the perspectives include "the internet does not limit anyone or any geographic area from self-expression because particular people or regions can develop their own self focused platforms and applications that identify with their needs and in their own languages". As shown by digital journalism studies, various forms of journalism emerged and can still emerge through the internet (Cheruiyot et al. 2021).

On the other hand, responses to the interview reflect uncertainties on the effectiveness of a multilingual African internet or social media algorithm. One of the participants believed that an indigenous language-based web application will still face challenges to interpret diverse African languages:

> indigenous language focused web applications and platforms will be intrinsically limited in distribution because of the ubiquitous nature of African languages and the platforms will be limited to the regions or people that speak the particular language.

It was perceived that a Shona-based web platform to be specific will only be limited to Shona-speaking people and will not have any reach or interaction with non-Shona-speaking people. This means "out of 1.2 billion people in Africa the Shona domiciled application will only reach less than 12 million people who speak Shona, which then works against the ethos of the world wide web which is by nature wide reaching". Participants believed Africa can still use English to their own advantage through code-switching and mixing to the understanding of their audience. Thus, English works as an advantage in such a way that a Shona in Harare can interact with a Yoruba in Nigeria and a Somalia using English. On the other hand, English can work as a disadvantage if the web application does not promote indigenous languages. The administrator of *Hatirare263* argued that "there is no particular disadvantage to African languages given that Africans can develop their own social media that speak to their needs and language considerations".

DISCUSSION

African communities are already decolonising the internet by reshaping and influencing the algorithm through liking, sharing and following non-mainstream indigenous language platforms. The argument is the very

Western-based technologies such as Facebook can be manipulated for local or African indigenous people interactions as they form discursive networks. We define local interactions through indigenous-language platforms as localising social media to suit the agenda and the language of the local community. The drawback, however, is that dependence on Western-based technologies for African interactions seems disadvantageous in terms of language policy and regulation. The Western-based web applications are incapable to detect violent content in indigenous languages as they do with the English language. The current colloquial lingo that "non-mainstream" news outlets cannot be easily regulated by Facebook. By so doing, the Western-based technology becomes incompetent and irrelevant to the context of African ever-changing language, hence making effective language regulation impossible. Thus, the evolving nature of journalism in the African media ecology is challenged by the lack of a friendly global application that can promote and appreciate the practice of peripheral journalistic activities.

The argument above leads to the decolonial narrative for African-based social networking sites that can effectively regulate hate speech in indigenous languages. However, the problem is that Africa is also complex with a multiplicity of languages to be regulated or monitored in one single space of audience interaction. It becomes difficult, therefore, to say the colloquial lingo by non-mainstream indigenous languages will be effectively regulated by an African-based technology without the media control of the very language speakers. In this case, this chapter calls for a multilingual-based technology reflective of African diversity that is schooled within African localities of language interactions. While Mpofu and Salawu (2020) agree with this notion of a multilingual internet, our argument is that multilingualism should be effective and relevant enough to regulate indigenous language, not necessarily to be like Google that wrongly moderates or translates indigenous languages (Chonka et al. 2023). The notion of an African multilingual technology should not only be in theory but in practice as to encompass the vast African languages. Taking such a direction is also problematic given the complexity of involving diverse language speakers. Perhaps community-based internet technology should be taken into consideration for the effective and specific language practice and policy, but this will also limit the notion of a global web application.

Having discussed the above, we submit that the Western-based Facebook (Meta) can be localised to the advantage of indigenous or local people through their engagement in the discursive network. This means

African indigenous language communities should be able to form their own social media pages in their mother languages. The indigenous language pages, however, should be promoted, liked, shared, followed and friended to circumvent the English algorithm and its coloniality. Just as shown by findings, *iHarare.com* and *Hatirare263* attract audience traffic by posting in Shona and eliciting audience engagement. This means without audience reach and engagement, indigenous-language platforms cannot survive the English algorithm. Another point to take note of is that the majority of languages like Shona have a better digital import for local audience reach; hence, major African languages have high chances of competing with the English algorithm. Rather than having a limited Afrocentric web application, we conclude that Facebook can enable Africans to contribute towards multilingual language tools that can easily monitor and policy indigenous languages.

Conclusion

This chapter discussed the complexity of language policy and practice on Western-based platforms such as Facebook. Analysing the use of indigenous language on *iHarare.com* and *Hatirare263*, the study explored how social media can be localised through the reshaping of the Facebook algorithm, as administrators circumvent the English algorithm as well as language regulations. The key findings of the study show that social media such as Facebook can be localised as users shape the algorithm. However, the main challenge is that Facebook is not well equipped to regulate hate speech in indigenous languages, thus depending on other users to report the use of hate speech. In conclusion, we note that a Facebook multilingual tool by Africans is needed to sufficiently regulate language violation in indigenous languages.

From a theoretical perspective, this study notes that a locally based website will be globally limited if only for African languages and culture. Although the decolonisation perspective calls for Afrocentric websites, it is important to note that Africa has diverse languages, which means some languages might dominate others. On the other hand, media users may need to access global content on the given website. This chapter argues that local content can be prioritised if we are to decolonise the internet. Some perspectives on decolonisation ignore the existing global impact and the interactivity of diverse cultures through social networking sites (SNSs) such as Facebook. Thus, this study notes that content can be localised if we are to go local on the same website. Any media user has the ability to like, share and comment on local content since Facebook provides such affordances.

The limitation of this study is that it only features perspectives from Facebook page administrators. There is a need to explore the interaction of audiences on the commentary forum whether they use indigenous language or English. On the other hand, a study is also needed to explore media users' social media literacy concerning the influence of the algorithm. This chapter, therefore, recommends future research focusing on the media users' awareness and literacy about the algorithm. Future studies should explore media user's perspectives on what they understand as domestication or localisation of social media sites in indigenous language and finding out how they circumvent the English algorithm to unpack the level of social media literacy in terms of the algorithm.

APPENDIX 1

(a) How does the Western-based technology (Facebook) disadvantage African languages?
(b) By liking, retweeting and sharing content in indigenous language, does it promote the algorithm and your page?
(c) How do you evaluate the competition between non-mainstream pages in English and Others in Shona?
(d) Does mixing English and Shona work to the advantage of the page?
(e) In terms of policy or ethics, does Facebook policy vulgar in Shona?
(f) Can one insult or abuse people in Shona without being penalised by Facebook?
(g) Is there an ethical policy gap between English and Indigenous language. Probe from your experience what have u noticed?
(h) Would you recommend decolonising the internet, for instance having an African based internet that policies indigenous languages?

REFERENCES

Arora, P. (2019). *The Next Billion Users: Digital Life Beyond the West.* Harvard University Press.

Baack, S. (2018). Practically Engaged: The Entanglements Between Data Journalism and Civic Tech. *Digital Journalism, 6*(6), 673–692. https://doi. org/10.1080/21670811.2017.1375382

8 THE ALGORITHMIC POWER AND SUBTITLES IN AFRICAN LANGUAGE... 171

Beer, D. (2013). *Popular Culture and New*. The Politics of Circulation. Palgrave Macmillan.

Bucher, T. (2012). Want To Be on the Top? Algorithmic Power and the Threat of Invisibility on Facebook. *New Media &Society, 14*(7), 1164–1180. https://doi.org/10.1177/1461444812440159

Bucher, T. (2016). The Algorithmic Imaginary: Exploring the Ordinary Affects of Facebook Algorithms. *Information, Communication & Society, 20*(1), 30–44.

Carpenter, J. C., & Sosale, S. (2019). The Role of Language in a Journalistic Interpretive Community Building on Indonesia's "biggest scoop ever". *Journalism Practice, 13*(3), 280–297. https://doi.org/10.1080/17512786.2018.1463865

Cheruiyot, D., Baack, S., & Ferrer-Conill, R. (2019). Data Journalism Beyond Legacy Media: The Case of African and European Civic Technology Organisations. *Digital Journalism, 7*(9), 1215–1229.

Cheruiyot, D., Wahutu, J. S., Mare, A., Ogola, G., & Mabweazara, H. M. (2021). Making News Outside Legacy Media: Peripheral Actors within an African Communication Ecology. *African Journalism Studies, 42*(4), 1–14. https://doi.org/10.1080/23743670.2021.2046397

Chonka, P., Diepeveen, S., & Haile, Y. (2023). Algorithmic Power and African Indigenous Languages: Search Engine Autocomplete and the Global Multilingual Internet. *Media, Culture & Society, 45*(2), 246–265.

Christin, A. (2017). Algorithms in Practice: Comparing Web Journalism and Criminal Justice. *Big Data & Society, 4*(2), 1–14. https://doi.org/10.1177/2053951717718855

Deuze, M. (2012). *Media life*. Polity.

Diakopoulos, N. (2015). Algorithmic Accountability: Journalistic Investigation of Computational Power Structures. *Digital Journalism, 3*(3), 398–415. https://doi.org/10.1080/21670811.2014.976411

Eldridge, S. A. (2019). Where Do We Draw the Line? Interlopers, (Ant)agonists, and an Unbounded Journalistic Field. *Media and Communication, 7*(4), 8–18.

Facebook, 2024. *Community Standards. Facebook Transparency Centre*. Retrieved on 26 April, 2025. Available on https://transparency.meta.com/en-gb/policies/community-standards/

Gillespie, T. (2014). The Relevance of Algorithms. In T. Gillespie, P. Boczkowski, & K. Foot (Eds.), *Media Technologies: Essays on Communication, Materiality, and Society* (pp. 167–194). MIT Press.

Goldstein, J., & Rotich, J. (2008). *Digitally Networked Technology in Kenya's 2007–2008 Post-election Crisis*. Harvard University.

Grosfoguel, R. (2007). The Epistemic Decolonial Turn: Beyond Political-Economy Paradigms. *Cultural Studies, 21*(2–3), 211–223.

Holton, A. E., & Belair-Gagnon, V. (2018). Strangers to the Game? Interlopers, Intralopers, and Shifting News Production. *Media and Communication*, *6*(4), 70–78.

Jaffe, A. (2009). The Production and Reproduction of Language Ideologies in Practice. In *The New Sociolinguistics Reader*, ed. C. Nikolas & J. Adam (pp. 390–404). Palgrave Macmillan.

Kitchin, R., & Dodge, M. (2011). *Code/space: Software and Everyday Life*. MIT Press.

Knuth, D. E. (1998). *The Art of Computer Programming: Sorting and Searching* (Vol. 3). Addison-Wesley.

Leong, L. (2020). Domesticating Algorithms: An Exploratory Study of Facebook Users in Myanmar. *The Information Society, 36*(2), 97–108.

Mabweazara, H. M., & Mare, A. (2021). *Participatory Journalism in Africa: Digital News Engagement and User Agency in the South Disruptions* (1st ed.). Routledge.

Maldonado-Torres, N. (2007). On the Coloniality of Being: Contributions to the Development of a Concept. *Cultural Studies, 21*, 2–3.

Maldonado-Torres, N. (2011). Thinking Through the Decolonial Turn: Post-Continental interventions in Theory, Philosophy, and Critique-an Introduction. *Transmodernity, 1*(2), 1–15.

Mano, W. (2007). Popular Music as Journalism in Zimbabwe. *Journalism Studies, 8*(1), 61–78.

Mathe, L. (2023). Women's Political Participation in Zimbabwe: Play and Content Creation on Twitter. *Information, Communication and Society, 26*(13), 2598–2613. https://doi.org/10.1080/1369118X.2023.2250442

Mathe, L. (2024). Analysing Discourse-Stylistics on Peripheral Journalism Platforms: A Context of Indigenous Language News Outlets on Facebook. *African Journalism Studies, 45*(2), 94–114. https://doi.org/10.1080/23743670.2024.2388640

Mathe, L., & Motsaathebe, G. (2023). African Multilingual Public Sphere: A Critical Analysis of Minority Indigenous Language(s) Representation on Breeze FM Talk Radio in Zimbabwe. *African Identities*. https://doi.org/10.1080/14725843.2023.2251700

Mathe, L., & Motsaathebe, G. (2024a). Community Radio Content in Print Facebook Posts: Limitations and Opportunities for Indigenous Languages. *Communicatio, 50*(1), 42–67. https://doi.org/10.1080/02500167.2024.2332181

Mathe, L., & Motsaathebe, G. (2024b). Public Health Communication and the Exclusion of Minority Languages in Zimbabwe: Analysis of Community Radio Awareness Campaigns in Facebook Posts. In K. Aiseng & I. Fadipe (Eds.), *Public Health Communication Challenges to Minority and Indigenous Communities* (pp. 108–129). IGI Global Scientific Publishing. https://doi.org/10.4018/979-8-3693-0624-6.ch008

McKelvey, F. (2014). Algorithmic Media Need Democratic Methods: Why Publics Matter. *Canadian Journal of Communication, 39*(4), 597–613.

Mignolo, W. D. (2007). Delinking. *Cultural Studies, 21*(2–3), 449–514.

Mohammed, W. F. (2021). Decolonizing African Media Studies. *Howard Journal of Communications, 32*(2), 123–138.

Moyo, L. (2020). *The Decolonial Turn in Media Studies in Africa and the Global South.* Springer International Publishing. https://doi.org/10.1007/978-3-030-52832-4

Mpofu, P. (2023). Code Mixing in Kwayedza: Language Subversion and the Existence of African Language Newspapers. *African Journalism Studies.* https://doi.org/10.1080/23743670.2023.2179091

Mpofu, P., & Salawu, A. (2020). African Language Use in the Digital Public Sphere: Functionality of the Localised Google Webpage in Zimbabwe. *South African Journal of African Languages, 40*(1), 76–84.

Mutsvairo, B., & Salgado, S. (2020). Is Citizen Journalism Dead? An Examination of Recent Developments in the Field. *Journalism, 23*(2), 354–371.

Mutsvairo, B., & Salgado, S. (2022). Is Citizen Journalism Dead? An Examination of Recent Developments in the Field. *Journalism, 23*(2), 354–371.

Novo, E. (2011). *Sociologie du journalism* [in Persian]. (B. Jabarouti, Trans.). Souroush.

Nyamnjoh, F. B. (2011). De-westernizing Media Theory To Make Room for African Experience. In H. Wasserman (Ed.), *Popular Media, Democracy and Development in Africa* (pp. 35–47). Routledge.

Obonyo, L. (2011). Towards a Theory of Communication for Africa: The Challenges for Emerging Democracies. *Communication, 37*(1), 1–20.

Quijano, A. (2000). Coloniality of Power and Eurocentrism in Latin America. *International Sociology, 15*(2), 215–232.

Roberts, J. (2019). The Erosion of Ethics: From Citizen Journalism to Social Media. *Journal of Information, Communication and Ethics in Society, 17*(4), 409–421.

Siegel, L. (2008). *Against the Machine: Being Human in the Age of the Electronic Mob.* Spiegel & Grau.

Thrift, N. (2005). *Knowing Capitalism.* Sage.

van Dijck, J. (2013). *The Culture of Connectivity: A Critical History of Social Media.* Oxford University Press.

Vos, T. P., & Thomas, R. J. (2023). "They're Making It More Democratic": The Normative Construction of Participatory Journalism. *Digital Journalism, 1–25.*

Waisbord, S., & Mellado, C. (2014). De-westernizing Communication Studies: A Reassessment. *Communication Theory, 24*(4), 361–372.

Willems, W., & Mano, W. (2016). Decolonizing and Provincializing Audience and Internet Studies: Contextual Approaches from African Vantage Points. In W. Willems & W. Mano (Eds.), *Everyday Media Culture in Africa* (pp. 15–40). Routledge.

174   L. MATHE

Woolard, K. A. (1998). Introduction: Language Ideology as a Field of Inquiry. In B. B. Schieffelin, K. A. Woolard, & P. V. Kroskrity (Eds.), *Language Ideologies: Practice and Theory* (pp. 3–47). Oxford University Press.

Yarmohammadi, L. (2010). *Communication within Critical. Discourse Perspectives.* Hermes [Persian].

Zelizer, B. (1993). Journalists as Interpretive Communities. *Critical Studies in Mass Communication, 10,* 219–237.

Zelizer, B. (2012). Journalists as Interpretive Communities Revisited. In A. Stuart (Ed.), *The Routledge Companion to News and Journalism* (pp. 181–190). Routledge.

CHAPTER 9

"Negotiating Liquidity": South African Journalists' Perceptions of Their Identities on Social Media

Xolo Luthando Tyhalibongo, Blessing Makwambeni, and Trust Matsilele

INTRODUCTION

Journalism has gone through iterations in the past century and a half and has seen some acceleration since the turn of the millennium that came with new media affordances. Social media has been one of the major revolutionary tools that came into the mainstream, reconfiguring practices at

---

X. L. Tyhalibongo • B. Makwambeni
Department of Media and Communication, Cape Peninsula University of Technology, Cape Town, South Africa
e-mail: makwambenib@cput.ac.za

T. Matsilele (✉)
Department of English and Media, University of South Africa, Pretoria, South Africa

Research Fellow, Communication Department, University of South Africa, South Africa

© The Author(s), under exclusive license to Springer Nature Switzerland AG 2025
A. Sharra, U. Akpojivi (eds.), *Technologies and Media Production Cultures*, Palgrave Studies in Journalism and the Global South, https://doi.org/10.1007/978-3-031-78582-5_9

175

three levels—production, processing and distribution of news media products. However, these changes brought by the new media technologies have been accompanied by existential threats to the profession, from the political-economy aspects to negotiating identities. Supporting this view, Cochrane et al. (2013, p. 165) observed that "the Internet has transformed the news industry: its ability to make money, the means it uses to distribute its product and the way news workers practice their trade". In South Africa, for example, the Big Tech companies (Meta and Alphabet) now enjoy the lion share of the advertisement revenue which historically went to mainly the mainstream media platforms (Matsilele & Tshuma, 2023). The surge of social media has also upended professional journalism, reshaping its practices and self-conception. Social media has upended journalistic practice as well as how journalists perceive themselves. Writing on this, Hermida (2012, p. 312) intimates that "social media offers news organisations new ways to promote content, increase audience reach, and potentially build brand loyalty". It is this instrumentalisation of social media applications by journalists for professional purposes that is occupying attention in our present study. In a study, Moyo et al. (2020) centred the role of editorial metrics and analytics within the journalism ecosystem. The adoption of social media has added a layer of complexity to the identity of journalists and, by extension, journalism. In the past, journalists could neatly define their identities through established media institutions. However, the emergence of social media has blurred the distinction between professional journalism and citizens engaged in civic roles (Lu & Zhou, 2016). This transformation raises queries about whether journalists express their opinions as private individuals or as representatives of media entities, causing uncertainty among audiences (Lewis et al., 2014; Djerf-Pierre et al., 2016; Bossio & Sacco, 2016; Duffy & Knight, 2019). South Africa notably exemplifies this phenomenon, with journalists' identities becoming increasingly enigmatic, prompting investigations into their understanding and management of their online personas.

In South Africa, professional journalists navigate a complex landscape. On the one hand, Constitution Section 16(1) empowers all citizens, including journalists, to freely voice opinions. Conversely, working for media institutions subjects journalists to editorial directives limiting their expression. This contrast engenders conflicts between journalists' social media viewpoints—often on platforms like Facebook and Twitter (X)—and their roles within media outlets characterised by entrenched ideologies. This dynamic is reflected globally and in South Africa, where media organisations have introduced policies and press codes to guide journalists as brand representatives (Holton, 2015). The evolving digital realm introduces novel dynamics, blurring the lines between journalists' professional and personal online identities (Adornato & Lysak, 2017). Defining professional journalism parameters has grown challenging amidst fluid information sharing, as highlighted by de Zúñiga et al. (2016). Consequently, the criteria for effective journalism are transforming due to shifting media dynamics (de Zúñiga et al., 2016, p. 4). Many journalists have assumed the role of social media influencers, impacting public opinions on platforms like Laor and Galily (2020). However, there's a risk of misattributing these opinions to the journalist's affiliated media outlet. Research by Lee (2015) underscores how news organisations urge journalists to engage actively on social media to enhance readership and brand recognition.

Scholars like McBride in Podger (2009, p. 34) advocate for transparent online presence, bridging the gap between professional and personal personas. This transparency involves identifying as a journalist and exercising caution in social media posts to safeguard the newsroom's image. Podger (2009, p. 32) concurs, stressing the importance of transparency while enabling individual expression within boundaries that uphold the newsroom's reputation. In South Africa, numerous journalists disclose affiliations on social media, often using disclaimers to differentiate personal opinions from professional positions. Retweets also face scrutiny due to potential bias. The journalism profession adheres to a press code emphasising impartiality, fairness, objectivity, and accuracy (Bruns, 2019).

Social media's role as a journalistic tool is evident, with significant news often breaking there (Lee, 2016; Matsilele et al., 2023a). Previous studies examine social media's influence on news agendas (Jordaan, 2012; Thomas, 2013; Daniels, 2014; Trengrove, 2018; Moyo, 2019; Makwambeni et al., 2023), though few probe the effectiveness of newsroom policies or journalists' online identity perceptions. Social media empowers journalists to directly engage with audiences, reshaping journalism into a participatory endeavour (Hermida & Thurman, 2008; Makwambeni et al., 2023). Recent findings suggest that journalists revealing their personal lives on social media are perceived as more credible (Johnson, 2020). The debate on journalistic neutrality has evolved, with transparency about personal beliefs enhancing credibility (Sullivan, 2013). In South Africa, scant literature addresses journalists' online professional identities or media outlets' identity management mechanisms. Moyo (2015) contends that postmodern journalism diverges from traditional models. As journalism evolves, conventional ideas of objectivity are challenged and expanded (Johnson, 2020). To recap, digital media's ascent has transformed journalism, notably reshaping journalists' roles online. The impact of social media muddles identities, inciting investigations into how South African journalists navigate and comprehend these identities. Balancing personal views with institutional responsibilities presents a challenge, requiring transparency and adaptation to evolving journalistic norms. Despite limited local research, South Africa's media sphere grapples with these transformative dynamics.

1. How do South African journalists perceive their identities on social media?
2. How do editors and media institutions perceive journalists' identities on social media?
3. What mechanisms do media institutions employ to assist journalists to negotiate their identities on social media?

Review of Literature

In this section, we discuss the evolving tapestry of reconfigurations of journalism aided by social media applications. In this changing landscape, we borrow from the works of Broersma and Eldridge II (2019) who postulated that social media and journalism have come to be featured more and more in the same academic conversations as scholars have sought to join up their understanding of a familiar communicative practice in journalism. It is within this ambit of trying to understand the role of social media in the reconstruction of journalism practice that we explore the timeless conversation on the role of media in democracy and how the appropriation of social media by journalists is impacting their roles. Journalists shape society's narrative, constructing a shared reality (Carey, 1989). News fosters social cohesion, uniting readers in an imagined community (Anderson, 1983). It defines our local, national, and global roles via reading and debating. News unveils the ongoing tension between dominant ideologies and dissent (Hall et al., 1978; Cottle, 2006).

Janowitz (1975) underscores journalistic roles as gatekeepers and advocates. Weaver and Wilhoit (1986, 1996) expand with four tasks: disseminator, interpreter, adversary, and "populist mobiliser". Empowered by technology, democracy thrives with unprecedented citizen participation (Wahl-Jorgensen & Thomas Hanitzsch, 2009). Journalism and democracy are symbiotic, vital for informed governance (Wahl-Jorgensen &

Thomas Hanitzsch, 2009). It scrutinises power, fostering a transparent society (ibid.). In Western democracies, journalists guard against abuse of power, voicing public concerns (ibid.). Journalism is democracy's synonym, coexisting intrinsically. Under Eastern models, Arab journalists drive transformation (Pintak, 2014, p. 494). Indonesian and Pakistani journalists champion unity and societal progress (Pintak & Nazir, 2013; Romano, 2003). These ideals, prevalent in the global South, mirror development journalism (Xiaoge, 2005).

Vos (2018) lists journalist roles: information gathering, opinion shaping, agenda setting, watchdogging, messaging, and social engagement. Normative roles include monitoring, facilitating, collaborating, and radicalism (Vos, 2018). While rooted in Western ideas, these roles hold value beyond, except perhaps for joint functions. Web 2.0 tech like blogs, Google tools, microblogs, and social networks foster interactive discourse, content exchange, and social interaction. They transform passive consumption into active information creation and collaboration. Web 2.0 reshapes communication, fostering participatory media where journalists and audiences co-share news control. This shift challenges traditional news ownership, sparking debates (Hermida, 2012).

Impact of New Technologies on Journalism

Mass media has gone through some seismic shifts over the past two decades and half, in part, due to the introduction of social media affordances. Web 2.0 tools like blogs, Google apps, microblogs, artificial intelligence and social networks foster dynamic discussions, social interaction, and user-generated content exchange (Makwambeni et al., 2023). However, they also reconfigure the political-economy of news production with far-reaching implications for the media's normative role in democratic societies. This is because, as Fanta and Bachwitz (2020, p. 6) rightly observe, noting that "the role of news media in liberal democracies is sometimes referred to as the "fourth estate", acting as a corrective "that assumes a public watchdog role over the integrity and appropriateness of the three branches of government, the executive, the judicial, and the legislative". Writing on user-generated content, Pearce and Rodgers (2020, p. 1) argued that the shared "content via social media potentially *was* known to supplant traditional journalism in protest situations due to advantages such as first-hand access". Social media applications shift users from passive consumers to active contributors, transforming information creation. This shift significantly impacts journalism, reshaping industry dynamics and journalists' social media practices. The Web promotes interactive engagement, making information sharing and networking paramount (Gulyas, 2013).

These tools provoke debate about journalism's evolution in the Web 2.0 era. Deuze and Paulissen (2002, p. 216) note their influence on newsroom culture and the journalistic profession's roles and responsibilities. This is why, increasingly, small start-up news media entities consider social media savviness when it comes to hiring journalists (Mabweazara & Matsilele, 2023). Writing on the same but much earlier, Lewis and Molyneux (2018, p. 11), reflecting on newsrooms practices noted that "to be active on Twitter and Facebook, as well as Snapchat, Instagram, and the rest, was seen by many news managers as an obvious and necessary step in journalism's digital-first transformation". Beyond appropriations for news gathering and dissemination purposes, Web 2.0 technologies are redefining journalists' interaction with audiences, crucial for comprehending social media's impact (Kaplan & Haenlein, 2010). Web 2.0's participatory architecture transforms communication paradigms, granting journalists and audiences shared news access and control. This shift accelerates news cycles and alters information dissemination during critical events, reshaping the news landscape (Hermida, 2012).

Digital skills are essential for South African newsrooms to thrive, with both journalists and leaders embracing this transformation (McAdams, 2014). Establishing social media standards and policies in newsrooms is crucial for effective communication, especially as platforms like Twitter (X) become integral (Wits University, 2014). While Twitter is widely used, there's no unified approach to its professional utilisation in South Africa (State of the Newsroom South Africa, 2014).

Journalists Appropriating Social Media as a Journalism Tool

A few studies (Makwambeni et al., 2023; Matsilele et al., 2023b) have explored the instrumentalisation of social media by professional journalists. Also instrumental is the work of Weaver and Willnat (2016, p. 844) whose study found that "journalists use social media predominantly as information-gathering tools and much less to interview sources or to validate information". Social media significantly impacts and alters the pace of breaking news and information dissemination during crucial moments. Prioritising speed has long been a hallmark of news production (Hermida,

2012). As traditional news cycles fade, swift news creation gains prominence. Commentators note a shift from a 24-hour TV-based news cycle to a 1440-minute social media-based one (Bruno, 2011). This highlights the need for continuous news flow. However, this shift raises concerns about journalists' ability to manage multiple media channels and multimedia tasks, potentially jeopardising their effectiveness (Mitchelstein & Boczkowski, 2009).

This transformation also reshapes news definitions, values, and criteria as news construction evolves (Guylas, 2013). Gulyas (2013) underscores the rise of opinion journalism in the social media era, although many journalists remain ambivalent about its impact. One motivation for adopting social media is its transformative effect on news dissemination (Gulyas, 2013). Twitter's (X's) simplicity and real-time updates make it a prime tool for news researchers (Bruns & Burgess, 2012). Journalists, traditionally agenda-setters, now leverage social media to identify topics of interest for traditional media (Lee & Ma, 2012). Twitter (X) has evolved into a platform for reporting and sharing concise news (Hermida, 2010), forming an "ambient media system" of accessible information (Hermida, 2010).

The Influence of Social Media on the Professional Identities of Journalists

Traditional news outlets increasingly rely on social media for news distribution, as evidenced by Alzyoud's (2021) journalist survey. Some view traditional and social media as complementary, where traditional media feeds news to public-interest social networks, and social media becomes a communication platform for journalism. Yet, some respondents see a negative shift. They feel social media now leads public opinion, diminishing journalism's influence, and eroding trust due to its lack of oversight (Alzyoud, 2021). Participants in Alzyoud's study also debate personal and professional identities on social media. While some believe a professional journalistic ethic can coexist with personal expression, regular social media usage inadvertently blurs these lines. Conversely, others advocate for a clear separation between journalistic and personal personas, identifying as journalists while publishing articles and as citizens when expressing opinions.

182   X. L. TYHALIBONGO ET AL.

Findings reveal social media's benefits for journalism: broader news distribution, real-time public feedback, and improved user engagement (Baruah, 2012; Pathak, 2018). Social media aids content marketing, and branding, and enhances journalistic efficiency (Pathak, 2018). Journalists tap into social media to gather story ideas and share articles (Pradhan and Kumari, 2018). Simons (2016) highlights social networks as sources of content production and accessible education. Yet, most journalists find their professional and personal identities poorly mesh on social media, wary of reputational damage (Simons, 2016). Identity conflicts could hinder sharing personal information or ideas, impacting reputations on these platforms.

The Effect of Social Media on Conventional Journalism Norms

Mobile devices hold the potential to transform participatory journalism, eroding traditional media's monopoly on news and disrupting news cycle dynamics (Perreault & Stanfield, 2019). In a study by Lasorsa et al. (2012), analysing over 22,000 tweets, journalists exhibited a willingness to express ideas, challenging the journalistic standard of neutrality. Their blogs, however, often conformed to traditional norms, indicating a desire for gatekeeping even in dynamic participatory settings. Bentivegna and Marchetti (2018) found that Italian journalists adapt their rules for social media's co-creation culture by aiming to expand their follower base and news reach. To thrive in this evolving landscape, businesses should adjust newsroom policies, offer social media training, and foster media ethics understanding in Twitter (X) reporting (Herrera & Requejo, 2012; Boers et al., 2012; Scott, 2014). The concept of journalists as sense-makers aligns with established professional norms but faces challenges in the Twitter (X) era. Journalists strive to maintain standards while navigating the platform's complexities, especially in upholding neutrality (Degen and Olgemöller, 2021).

Self-Branding and Navigating Through Personal and Professional Postings/Tweets

Traditionally, a journalist's legitimacy was intertwined with the media agency they represented. However, the rise of platforms like Twitter has led to journalists gaining individual recognition, detached from their media outlets. This shift has elevated the role of individual journalists in public discourse, making their trustworthiness pivotal for open and independent discussions. Celebrities in journalism break down barriers between themselves and their followers by offering glimpses of their private lives, shaping a branded self that encompasses both public persona and everyday existence (Olausson, 2017). The transition from old to new media has fuelled journalist personalisation, altering the focus from media outlets to individual profiles (Verweij and Van Noort, 2014).

Olausson (2017, p. 3) examines the convergence of new brand marketing and journalists' fame in the concept of the "celebrated journalist". This phenomenon aligns with the ongoing individualisation of journalism (Deuze, 2008), with journalists investing more effort in building personal brands on platforms like Twitter than in promoting the news organisations they belong to (Holton & Molyneux, 2015). Active journalists, particularly on social media, emphasise personal branding over their affiliation with specific news outlets (Bruns, 2012; Hedman & Djerf-Pierre, 2013; Olausson, 2017). This practice is further enhanced by retweeting messages about themselves, which challenges conventional journalistic norms (Olausson, 2017).

While digital platforms offer opportunities for greater engagement, they also challenge traditional journalistic standards. Journalists, once confined to impartiality, are now more willing to express opinions in daily tweets, a shift not as evident in traditional media (Lasorsa et al., 2012). Even retweets, a rapid mode of communication for political journalists, reflect this trend. Concerns arise about how digitisation has impacted journalistic practices, prompting a standardisation of blogs to adhere to established norms (Lasorsa et al., 2012). Despite changes, many journalists maintain a gatekeeping role on platforms like Twitter (X), using them to engage with audiences, stay updated on news, and promote their work (Lasorsa et al., 2012).

Conceptual Framework

This study makes use of the concept of liquid journalism and social self to examine how professional journalists perceive their identities on social media. Deuze's concept of liquid journalism (2007) provides useful insights into the evolving landscape of contemporary journalism where the line between professional and personal identities have become increasingly blurred. On the other hand, the social self-concept complements the liquid journalism concept by providing a framework for comprehending and problematising how South African journalists perceive their identities on social media. The concept assists us to reflect on the intricate interplay that exists between journalists' online identities, audience interactions, and journalists' professional perceptions in the evolving ecology of contemporary journalism.

The concept of liquid journalism captures the transformative shifts that have taken place in journalism that have resulted in the development of liquid identities among journalists (Lu and Zhou (2016). Liquid identities among contemporary journalists emerge from a modern liquid culture that emanates from technological shifts that have transformed both journalism practice and journalists' role (Lu and Zhou, 2016). At its very core, the concept of liquid journalism undermines and erodes traditional journalistic routines, norms, and conventions. It is characterised by a shift of conventional news cycles with bureaucratic structures to an individualised action of online content sharing and curation that has resulted in the blurring of the lines between professional and non-professional news production. Other than blurring journalists' identities, liquid journalism erodes and undermines the core values of traditional journalism such as truth, objectivity, balance, and accuracy (Moyo, 2015). It deems traditional journalism sources of moral authority such as ethics as irrelevant and repose them more on personal impulses, subjectiveness, and individual discretion (Moyo, 2015). Thus, the advent of liquid journalism has led to the reconfiguration of individual journalists who now possess their own social media pages to share news and build their individual brands which are usually separate from those of the media institutions they work for (Lee, 2015). As a result, this re-configuration of journalists has seen the erosion of the traditional role of journalists as the conveyor of objective and undistorted information (Lee, 2015). Rather, as observed by Lee (2015), the emergent liquid journalists tend to deviate from traditional norms on social media by readily offering opinions like any other social media users resulting in audiences questioning their professionalism.

The social self-concept provides a useful framework for assessing how journalists perceive their identities on social media. It departs from the position that individuals possess unique social selves that are shaped by their interactions within various social groups and settings. The social self-concept views identity construction as a collaborative process influenced by the interplay between individuals and their audience (Goffman, 1959; Cooley, 2017). While the social self-concept underscores the significance of public perception in shaping one's identity, it views professional identity as contextual (Fredriksson and Johansson, 2014; Lewis, 2012). Professional identity encompasses how individuals perceive themselves professionally both in private and public realms. In the context of journalism, the social self-concept contends that there is an intricate interplay between journalists' online identities, audience interaction, and professional perceptions in the evolving landscape of contemporary journalism.

Extant studies have shown that although journalists may decide to change, shape, or modify their online identities, conflicts always arise when they negotiate these identities in their professional environment. As Boyd (2008) argues, when different audiences view journalists' online profiles for various purposes, the necessity to portray a unique identity, for example, as a professional, may make it difficult to use alternative self-presentation tactics, leading to conflicts (Boyd, 2008). Thus, for journalists seeking to negotiate the representation of a professional identity online, the apparent "contextless" environment creates tensions and becomes even more challenging given that maintaining a particular professional character is an essential aspect of professional journalism practice. Bossio and Sacco (2016) posit that the portrayal of journalists' professional identities online faces the challenge of conflicting demands of evolving organisational standards and professional, institutional norms in the newsroom.

METHODS

The study made use of a two-stage qualitative research design to collect data to understand, first, how South African Journalists perceive their identities on social media and, second, to unpack the mechanisms employed by media institutions and professional bodies to assist journalists to negotiate their identities on social media. In the first stage of the study, the researchers conducted semi-structured interviews with journalists and editors from mainstream media institutions in South Africa; 12 participants were interviewed. They were drawn from print, online, and broadcast media institutions in South Africa: the South African Broadcasting Corporation (SABC), Eye Witness News, Newzroom Afrika, Weekend Argus, Sunday Times, Daily Dispatch, News 24, and Daily Maverick, as well as the Press Council. Semi-structured interviews assisted us to understand the following. First, how South African journalists perceive their identities on social media. Second, how editors perceive journalists' identities on social media. Finally, third, to understand whether media institutions and professional bodies in South Africa have developed mechanisms to assist journalists to negotiate their identities on social media. Semi-structured interviews were used due to their propensity to allow the researchers to gather extensive data on the research questions. They are also a very flexible data gathering method that allows researchers to rephrase questions to gather relevant data while also observing non-verbal cues (Bruns, 2019).

The second stage of the research design consisted of virtual ethnography and document analysis. Virtual ethnography was employed to understand the news and information that South African journalists share on social media. In this light, the study analysed social media posts made by selected journalists between September and October 2022. The data gathered using virtual ethnography was triangulated with findings gleaned from semi-structured interviews. Document analysis was used as a tool to gather data on the social media policies and guidelines employed by media institutions in South Africa. Social media policies and guidelines of the SABC, Media24, Independent Media, Tiso Black Star/Arena Holdings, and the Press Council were used to corroborate findings from semi-structured interviews on the mechanisms used by South African media institutions to assist journalists to negotiate their identities on social media. The data gathered from the first and second stages of the study were analysed using qualitative content analysis. The focus of the analysis was to identify and develop themes and derive meaning in relation to the research questions of the study, as advised by Du Plooy (2009).

FINDINGS AND DISCUSSION

The findings of the study reflect the diverse representations of personal and professional identities that professional journalists occupy and negotiate on social media. These identities correspond with the evolving conflicts that arise from institutional, organisational, and professional dynamics that characterise the new media ecology characterised by liquidity (Moyo, 2015). In the emergent digital landscape, characterised by liquidity, professional journalists tend to exhibit varying combinations of personal and professional identities. In the South African context, professional journalists manifest different and at times intersecting identities on social media due to a complex interplay of factors that are largely institutional, organisational, and professional.

South African Journalists Perception of Their Identities on Social Media

The data analysed in the study reflects a wide spectrum of self-perceptions on social media among professional journalists in South Africa. Consonant with Bassio and Sacco's (2016) observation that there are predominantly three social media identities (transitional, branded, and social), the South African media context manifests three major identities: journalists who self-identify as ordinary citizens on social media, journalists who self-identify as professional journalists on social media, and a small group of journalists who reflect a hybrid identity where they view themselves both as professional journalists and private citizens on social media. These three emergent identities occupied and negotiated by South African journalists on social media underscore the nuanced and complex nature of the new journalism ecology in which journalists need to negotiate their identities (Deuze 2007; Moyo, 2015).

Identifying as Ordinary Citizens on Social Media

A sizable number of professional South African journalists who participated in the study self-identify as ordinary citizens as opposed to professional journalists on social media. Consequently, journalists who fall under this category view themselves as having the freedom to express their opinions and share content without being constrained by their professional obligations and their media institution's editorial policies and stance. However, the professional journalists who self-identify as ordinary citizens stated the challenges associated with balancing their professional and personal personas online. This tension between the journalistic and personal personas that confronts journalists in the digital age invites challenges such as apprehensions about diverting from core journalistic tasks, and fears of compromising credibility through individualised or brand-oriented content. An example of this tension is captured in the tweet below where a journalist comments on political developments in South Africa in their personal capacity as opposed to the editorial line of their media institution.

Direct interaction and criticism of a politician by an Arena Holdings journalist

Our findings show that the new media ecology in which journalists are practising is largely responsible for the liquid identities that journalists occupy. The drive towards audience engagement, branding, and self-promotion among other factors journalists in the evolving landscape of journalism is contributing to the existential conflict where journalistic identities become blurred. This tension becomes increasingly pronounced in media institutions that have not developed mechanisms to assist journalists to negotiate these emergent tensions (Deuze, 2007).

An analysis of the social media platforms of professional journalists in South Africa shows that a number of journalists view themselves as private citizens on social media. One of the subtle ways through which they circumvent limitations and air views that are not aligned with that of their media institutions is through meta voicing. According to Majchrzak et al. (2013), meta voicing usually occurs through retweeting, liking, and commenting on someone's post or through voting. A case in point is that of a senior journalist at the South African Broadcasting Corporation (SABC) who through retweeting employs meta voicing to express their opinions and support positions of selected political parties on contemporary issues. The journalist's partiality for the radical EFF party appears to come to the fore through the post below where they chose to retweet the EFF's post ahead of other organisations such as the South African Communist Party and the ANC which also wished the Communist Party of China well on the occasion of their 20th congress.

It is important to note that the Press Council of South Africa's Social Media Policy (2020, p. 7) discourages meta voicing that seeks to endorse certain content as described below:

> Do not share content posted by another person or another publisher in a manner that creates the impression that you are endorsing the content unless you are sure that by doing so, you are not breaching any aspect of this policy.

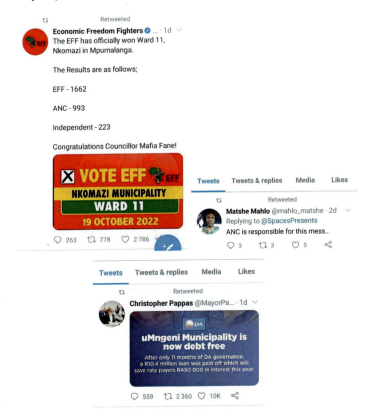

SABC employed journalists retweeting political messages

Journalists Self-Identifying as Professionals on Social Media

Despite the onset of liquid identities in the digital age that disrupts journalists' professional identities online as observed by Bossio and Sacco (2016), our findings show that a significant number of journalists in South Africa perceive their social media identities as an extension of their professional roles. For journalists who self-identify as professionals on social media, their online presence is seen as inextricably linked to their work and identities as professional journalists. Consequently, journalists who self-identify as professionals view themselves as extensions of their news organisation on social media with an obligation to safeguard the organisation's brand, reputation, and credibility both online and offline. This widely shared view is illuminated in the sentiments of two journalists (Newzroom Afrika Journalist, personal interview, October 13, 2022) (eNCA Journalist, personal interview, October 17, 2022).

> I tend to steer away from sharing my personal opinion about current affairs, because that's the space that I operate within the news.
> As a public figure and as someone representing a brand, you're clear of posting anything that could bring you into disrepute and the company to the city. And when it comes to editorial decisions, we believe in ethical and fair journalism that doesn't favour anyone. And isn't that where I try not to post anything that shows I'm politically inclined one way or because that will damage my credibility.

Thus, senior journalists in the newsrooms in South Africa view their social media identities as a continuum of their offline identities as professional journalists. Unlike their younger colleagues who are more outspoken on social media and largely viewed as blurring the lines between their roles as journalists and private citizens, they view themselves as representatives of their news organisations. Although senior journalists are conscious of the freedoms associated with the liquid media ecology in which they operate (Moyo, 2015), they view the new affordances as also entailing the responsibility to ensure that social media engagements do not directly impact the organisation's image or their journalistic work and identity. The data analysed in the study indicates that some journalists who self-identify as professional journalists on social media are influenced by the South African Press Council's Social Media Policy (2020, p. 2). The guidance provided by the press council inadvertently compels journalists to align their social media identities with their offline identities as inferred in the policy, "the statements that you make and content that you share on social media, whether publicly or privately, could impact your credibility as a journalist and, by extension, the company's credibility. Any content that damages the company's reputation regarding neutrality, fairness and credibility is unacceptable".

Emergence of Liquid Identities on Social Media

According to Fredriksson and Johansson (2014), journalists' identities have increasingly become contextual in the evolving landscape of contemporary journalism. The intricate nature of journalists' online identities is reflected in our findings where a significant number of journalists see themselves as both professional journalists and private citizens on social media depending on the social media application in use and the context. This duality is attributable to the complexities of the digital media landscape which affords journalists an opportunity to perform both their professional identities as journalists and their private identities as ordinary citizens. The tension between the two identities is captured by an SABC journalist (personal interview, October 12, 2022): "I've made particular distinctions to different platforms. I say that I'm a citizen when it comes to Facebook. I don't even want to be seen as a journalist because I would like to know that platform as a platform where I express and post pictures about my personal life".

The hybrid identities that are implied in the above quotation can also be linked to new pressures from news outlets themselves for journalists to maintain an active presence on social media as a way of enhancing readership and brand awareness (Lee, 2015). Consequently, it becomes extremely difficult to delineate between journalists' identities as professional journalists or as private individuals in the new digital landscape where attempts to balance the individual brand and the organisation's brand are increasingly becoming complex. As observed by Daniels (2014), the decentralisation of social media in the journalism context does not only pose challenges in brand control and the expansion of journalists' personal brands but also potentially exposes media institutions by exposing them to potential harm when online controversies arise (Brems et al., 2016). For instance, McBride in Podger (2009, p. 34) asserts that journalists on social networks should disclose their professional role. The adoption of social media has added a layer of complexity to the identity of journalists and, by extension, journalism. In the past, journalists could neatly define their identities through established media institutions. However, the emergence of social media has blurred the distinction between professional journalism and citizens engaged in civic roles (Lu & Zhou, 2016).

Arguably, the hybrid identities identified in the findings also reflect the tensions that arise from journalists' attempts to express their personal opinions in their private capacity while also remaining faithful to the demands of their media institutions and press codes. Liquid journalists must continually adapt as digital media transforms the journalism-reader relationship (Lu and Zhou, 2016). Deuze (2004) and Lu and Zhou (2016) argue that this new liquid digital landscape demands shifts and adjustment in journalists' online media's influence, storytelling methods, as well as producer-audience relationships (Lu and Zhou, 2016) if the credibility and reputations of the journalists and their affiliated organisations is to be sustained.

Media Institutions and Editors Perceptions of Journalists Identities on Social Media

Despite the transformative shifts that have taken place in journalism that have resulted in the development of liquid identities among journalists (see Lu and Zhou, 2016), South African media institutions still rigidly perceive professional journalists through their professional identities on social media. This perception contrasts significantly with most professional journalists who participated in the study who perceive their identities as fluid on social media. Unlike most individual journalists interviewed, editors who participated in this study argued that professional journalists' identities should be consistent in their professional and personal capacities. This view is captured below by two editors drawn from News24 Editor (personal interview, October 18, 2022) and Eyewitness News Editor (personal interview, October 17, 2022):

> You can't (as a journalist) rid yourself of your identity. I know that we have taken away that protection where you say I'm tweeting in my capacity. So, tweeting your capacity is not a protection from your company's policies.
>
> People identify and associate your name (as a journalist) with a certain media organisation. So, the perception is that what you do, and even if you might say this is in your personal capacity, it blurs the lines.

South African editors' perceptions of journalists' identities on social media resonate with the findings of an Independent Panel Report by the South African Editors Forum (SANEF) on Media Ethics and Credibility. The findings show that editors are contemptuous of journalists who have assumed new identities as brands and celebrities rather than professional journalists on social media. The mutation of journalists into celebrities is broadly seen by South African editors and SANEF as a threat to public interest and the integrity of the press (SANEF, personal interview, October 13, 2022). The above views are reflected in the extracts below:

> The Tweets and other social media utterances of journalists who have become "personalities" attract considerable public attention. The writers may regard their Twitter output as a personal activity unrelated to the media outlets with which they are associated. However, Johnny Copelyn told the Panel this was a "sensitive area" because such Tweets become associated with that media outlet. It may be particularly problematic because of the compressed format of Twitter.
>
> Journalists who have assumed celebrity through such activities have ceased to be journalists. Their work loses credibility as the public loses trust in them as authoritative reporters of fact who are capable of furnishing truth and dealing fairly with opposing opinions.

As noted above, the evolving digital landscape has introduced new dynamics that blur the lines between journalists' professional and personal online identities (Adornato & Lysak, 2017). The appropriation of social media journalists has added a layer of complexity to the identity of journalists and by extension, journalism. While in the past, journalists' identities could be neatly defined through established media institutions, the emergence of social media has blurred the distinction between professional journalism and citizens engaged in civic roles (Lu & Zhou, 2016). As evidenced in the SANEF report, the new celebrity identities that journalists have assumed have raised serious concerns about the credibility of journalists in the new digital ecology. It has also raised serious concerns about conflict of interest, particularly where there is dissonance between what they say in their private capacity and the editorial decisions they contribute to in their professional capacity as journalists.

Mechanisms Introduced to Assist Journalists to Negotiate Their Identities on Social Media

Although the digital age has disrupted journalists' professional identities, as observed by Bossio and Sacco (2016), our findings show that media institutions in South Africa have not developed comprehensive and coherent mechanisms to assist professional journalists to negotiate the resultant liquid identities. Different media institutions in South Africa have introduced strategies that include social media policies, the press code guidelines on the use of social media, and strict utilisation of privacy settings to assist journalists to negotiate their identities on social media (Lewis, 2012; Newman et al., 2013). The introduction of social media policies in this regard contributes to the construction of professionalism in alignment with professional and organisational norms (Lewis, 2012). As argued by Newman et al. (2013), news organisations are employing social media guidelines to uphold their established values and brands.

SOCIAL MEDIA POLICIES AND GUIDELINES

A number of media institutions in South Africa such as Media 24 have developed social media policies to assist journalists to negotiate their identities on social media and other digital platforms. Media 24, for example, has developed clear guidelines on how to deal with social media. The essence of the social media policy and guidelines is articulated by a journalist from News24 (News24 journalist, personal interview, October 6, 2022): "So, we do have a social media policy, and we are guided against issues of libel or defamation and criminal jury. We shouldn't be posting anything that's going to bring the company into disrepute because you will then face a sanction of dismissal".

The social media policies developed by media institutions in South Africa corroborate the guidelines provided by the South African Press Council's Social Media Policy (2020). The press code underlines the criticality of journalists to safeguard their professional identities and news values on social media. These guidelines resonate with McQuail's position that the guiding principles of journalism should transcend traditional media and also apply in the social media space (2010), "The statements that you make and content that you share on social media, whether publicly or privately, could impact your credibility as a journalist and, by extension, the company's credibility. Any content that damages the company's reputation regarding neutrality, fairness and credibility is unacceptable".

As demonstrated above, a number of South African media organisations have implemented strategies to assist journalists to negotiate their identities online. However, some media institutions lag behind in this regard. However, our findings show that media institutions in countries such as the USA and the UK have been more advanced in developing and implementing social media policies although resistance has been experienced in some European countries (Opgenhaffen & Scheerlinck, 2014). According to Opgenhaffen and Scheerlinck's (2014), some journalists perceive social media guidelines and policies as restrictive to their freedom of expression. Media institutions and journalists occasionally differ regarding the criteria for acceptable personal messages on social media platforms like X (Twitter).

Similarly, in the South African context, despite the prevalence of a press code that assists journalists to navigate their social media identities and also define what is acceptable or otherwise in the new media ecology, as observed by Opgenhaffen and Scheerlinck (2014) in a European context, our findings captured below indicate that several journalists still undermine the press council's social media policy by retweeting information from political pages without providing any accompanying explanation:

> As shown in the tweets above from timelines two journalists working for the SABC. South African media institutions still have to develop acceptable and comprehensive strategies to assist journalists to navigate their identities on social media in a new media ecology where fixed notions about journalists' professional identities are being challenged and expanded. (Johnson, 2020)

Conclusion

This study sought to understand how South African journalists perceive their identities on social media. It was also within the purview of the chapter to examine whether media institutions in South Africa have introduced mechanisms to assist journalists to negotiate their identities on social media. The findings of this study show that South African journalists have varied understandings of their identities on social media. While some journalists perceive themselves as private individuals with the freedom to engage on any issue autonomously like any other citizens, other journalists perceive themselves as professional journalists on social media whose engagement on social media is still guided by journalism ethics and the editorial stance of the media institutions they identify with. Thus, our findings reflect a divergence between journalists who regard social media as a personal space that allows for freedom of expression distinct from their professional identity and roles and those who view social media as an extension of their professional role and obligations as journalists.

Conversely, the data analysed in the study indicates that most editors and media institutions in South Africa perceive professional journalists as professionals on social media who are not exempt from following journalistic ethics and values even when they engage on social media in their personal capacities. Thus, although most editors and media institutions view professional journalists as extensions of their media institutions' brand on social media in South Africa, few entities have developed comprehensive and coherent policies and guidelines to assist journalists to negotiate their identities in the new journalism ecology characterised by fluidity and liquidity. Although some media institutions have developed mechanisms such as social media policies and guidelines to guide journalists to negotiate their identities on social media, there are still massive disparities across the media landscape with a significant number of media institutions yet to provide such measures. The vacuum created by the absence of these mechanisms does not only create tension among individual journalists but also creates confusion among audiences.

REFERENCES

Adornato, A. C., & Lysak, S. (2017). You Can't Post That! Social Media Policies in U.S. Television Newsrooms. *Electronic News, 11*(2), 80–99.

Alzyoud, S. (2021). The Concept of "New Media" Among News Producers. https://doi.org/10.20944/preprints202111.0193.v1

Anderson, B. (1983). *Imagined Communities: Reflections on the Origin and Spread of Nationalism* (Revised ed.). Verso.

Boyd, D. M. (2008). *Taken Out of Context: American Teen Sociality in Networked Publics.* University of California, Berkeley.

Bruns, A. (2012). Journalists and Twitter: How Australian News Organisations Adapt to a New Medium. *Media International Australia, 144*(1), 97–107.

Bruns, N. (2019). *South African Journalism Graduates' Preparedness for Newsroom Ethics: Views of Early-career Journalists at News24, Eyewitness News and Independent Online.* Unpublished Master's thesis, Stellenbosch University.

Bruns, A., & Burgess, J. (2012). Researching News Discussion on Twitter: New Methodologies. *Journalism Studies, 13*(5–6), 801–814.

Bossio, D., & Sacco, V. (2016). From "Selfies" to Breaking Tweets. *Journalism Practice, 11*(5), 527–543.

Brems, C. et al. (2016). Personal Branding on Twitter. *Digital Journalism, 5*(4), 443–459. https://doi.org/10.1080/21670811.2016.1176534

Broersma, M., & Eldridge, S. A., II. (2019). Journalism and Social Media: Redistribution of Power? *Media and Communication, 7*(1), 193–197.

Cochrane, T., Sissons, H., Mulrennan, D., & Pamatatau, R. (2013). Journalism 2.0: Exploring the Impact of Mobile and Social Media on Journalism Education. *International Journal of Mobile and Blended Learning (IJMBL), 5*(2), 22–38.

Cooley, C. H. (2017). *Human Nature and the Social Order.* Scribner's.

Cottle, S. (2006). *Mediatised Conflicts.* McGraw-Hill Education.

Daniels, G. (2014). How Far Does Twitter Deepen Democracy through Public Engagement?: An Analysis of Journalists' Use of Twitter in the Johannesburg Newsroom. *Journal of African Media Studies, 6*(3), 299–311.

De Zúñiga, H. G., Diehl, T., & Ardèvol-Abreu, A. (2016). When Citizens and Journalists Interact on Twitter. *Journalism Studies, 19*(2), 227–246.

Deuze, M. (2004). What is Multimedia Journalism1? *Journalism Studies, 5*(2), 139–152. https://doi.org/10.1080/1461670042000211131

Deuze, M. (2007). Journalism in Liquid Modern Times: An Interview with Zygmunt Bauman. *Journalism Studies, 8*(4), 671–679.

Deuze, M. (2008). The Professional Identity of Journalists in the Context of Convergence Culture. *Observatorio (OBS*), 2*(4), 103–117. https://doi.org/10.15847/obsobs242008216.

Djerf-Pierre, M., Ghersetti, M., & Hedman, U. (2016). Appropriating Social Media. *Digital Journalism, 4*(7), 849–860. https://doi.org/10.1080/21670811.2016.1152557

Du Plooy, G. M. (2009). *Communication Research: Techniques, Methods and Applications* (2nd ed.). Juta & Co, Ltd.

Duffy, A., & Knight, M. (2019). Don't Be Stupid: The Role of Social Media Policies in Journalistic Boundary-setting. *Journalism Studies, 20*(7), 932–951.

Fredriksson, M., & Johansson, B. (2014). The Dynamics of Professional Identity. *Journalism Practice, 8*(5), 585–595.

Goffman, E. (1959). *The Presentation of Self in Everyday Life.* Anchor.

Hedman, U., & Djerf-Pierre, M. (2013). The Social Journalist. *Digital Journalism, 1*(3), 368–385. https://doi.org/10.1080/21670811.2013.776804

Hermida, A. (2012). Social Journalism: Exploring How Social Media is Shaping Journalism. *The Handbook of Global Online Journalism, 12,* 309–328.

Hermida, A., & Thurman, N. (2008). A Clash of Cultures: Integrating User-generated Content Within Professional Journalistic Frameworks at British Newspaper Websites. *Journalism Practice, 2*(3), 343–356.

Holton, A. E., & Molyneux, L. (2015). Identity Lost? The Personal Impact of Brand Journalism. *Journalism, 18*(2), 195–210.

Holton, A. E., Coddington, M., Lewis, S. C., & De Zuniga, H. G. (2015). *Reciprocity and the news: The role of personal and social media reciprocity in news creation and consumption. International journal of communication, 9*, 22.

Janowitz, M. (1975). Professional Models in Journalism: The Gatekeeper and the Advocate. *Journalism Quarterly, 52*(4), 618–626.

Johnson, K. A. (2020). I Got a New Puppy! The Impact of Personal, Opinion, and Objective Tweets on a Journalist's and a News Organisation's Perceived Credibility. *Journalism Practice, 14*(1), 48–66.

Jordaan, M. (2012). *Social Media in the Newspaper Newsroom: The Professional Use of Facebook and Twitter at Rapport and the Mail & Guardian.* Unpublished Master's thesis, Stellenbosch University, Stellenbosch.

Laor, T., & Galily, Y. (2020). Offline VS Online: Attitude and Behaviour of Journalists in Social Media era. *Technology in Society, 61*, 101239.

Lasorsa, D. L., Lewis, S. C., & Holton, A. E. (2012). Normalising Twitter: Journalism Practice in an Emerging Communication Space. *Journalism Studies, 13*(1), 19–36.

Lee, J. (2015). The Double-edged Sword: The Effects of Journalists' Social Media Activities on Audience Perceptions of Journalists and Their News Products. *Journal of Computer-Mediated Communication, 20*(3), 312–329.

Lee, J. (2016). Opportunity or Risk? How News Organisations Frame Social Media in Their Guidelines for Journalists. *The Communication Review, 19*(3), 106–112.

Lewis, S. C. (2012). The Tension between Professional Control and Open Participation: Journalism and Its Boundaries. *Information, Communication & Society, 15*(6), 836–866.

Lee, C. S., & Ma, L. (2012). News Sharing in Social Media: The Effect of Gratifications and Prior Experience. *Computers in Human Behaviour, 28*(2), 331–339.

Lewis, S. C., Holton, A. E., & Coddington, M. (2014). Reciprocal Journalism: A Concept of Mutual Exchange between Journalists and Audiences. *Journalism Practice, 8*(2), 229–241.

Lewis, S. C., & Molyneux, L. (2018). A Decade of Research on Social Media and Journalism: Assumptions, Blind Spots, and a Way Forward. *Media and Communication, 6*(4), 11–23.

Lu, Y., & Zhou, R. (2016). Liquid Journalism and Journalistic Professionalism in the Era of Social Media: A Case Study of an Online Outlet's Coverage of the Oriental Star Accident. *Communication and the Public, 1*(4), 471–485.

Mabweazara, H. M., & Matsilele, T. (2023). Recruitment and Retention Practices in a Changing African News Media Ecosystem. In *Happiness in Journalism* (pp. 59–68). Routledge.

Majchrzak, A., Faraj, S., Kane, G. C., & Azad, B. (2013). The Contradictory Influence of Social Media Affordances on Online Communal Knowledge Sharing. *Journal of Computer-Mediated Communication, 19*(1), 38–55.

Makwambeni, B., Matsilele, T., & Bulani, J. G. (2023). Between Utopia and Dystopia: Investigating Journalistic Perceptions of AI Deployment in Community Media Newsrooms in South Africa. In *Digitisation, AI and Algorithms in African Journalism and Media Contexts: Practice, Policy and Critical Literacies* (pp. 17–32). Emerald Publishing Limited.

Makwambeni, B., Matsilele, T., & Msimanga, M. J. (2023). Through the Lenses of the Sociology of News Production: An Assessment of Social Media Applications and Changing Newsroom Cultures in Lesotho. *Journal of Asian and African Studies*, 00219096231179661.

Matsilele, T., Makwambeni, B., & Mugari, S. (2023a). Social Media Applications and the Changing Newsroom Cultures in Africa: A Case Study of Lesotho. In *New Journalism Ecologies in East and Southern Africa: Innovations, Participatory and Newsmaking Cultures* (pp. 59–76). Springer International Publishing.

Matsilele, T., Makwambeni, B., Nkoala, S., & Bulani, G. J. (2023b). Youth Audiences and Social Media Integration in Community Radio Stations in South Africa: A Case Study of Zibonele FM and Bush Radio. In *Converged Radio, Youth and Urbanity in Africa: Emerging Trends and Perspectives* (pp. 123–153). Springer International Publishing.

Matsilele, T., & Tshuma, L. (2023). Through the Media Looking Glass: Journalists' Perceptions on South Africa's Funded Environmental Journalism. *African Journalism Studies, 44*(1), 58–72.

McQuail, D. (2010). *McQuail's Mass Communications Theory*. Sage.

Moyo, D., Mare, A., & Matsilele, T. (2020). Analytics-Driven Journalism: Editorial Metrics and the Reconfiguration of Online News Production Practices in African Newsrooms. In *Measurable Journalism* (pp. 104–120). Routledge.

Moyo, L. (2015). Digital Age as Ethical Maze: Citizen Journalism Ethics during Crises in Zimbabwe and South Africa. *African Journalism Studies, 36*(4), 125–144.

Moyo, N. (2019). *The Effects of Social Media on Setting the Agenda of Traditional Media*. Unpublished Master's thesis, University of South Africa, Pretoria.

Newman, N., Dutton, W., & Blank, G. (2013). Social Media in the Changing Ecology of News: The Fourth and Fifth Estates in Britain. *International Journal of Internet Science, 7*(1).

Opgenhaffen, M., & Scheerlinck, H. (2014, January). Social Media Guidelines for Journalists. *Journalism Practice, 8*(6), 726–741.

Olausson, U. (2017). The Celebrified Journalist. *Journalism Studies, 19*(16), 1–21.

Pearce, S. C., & Rodgers, J. (2020). Social Media as Public Journalism? Protest Reporting in the Digital Era. *Sociology Compass, 14*(12), 1–14.

Perreault, G., & Stanfield, K. (2019). Mobile Journalism as Lifestyle Journalism? Field Theory in Integrating Mobile in the Newsroom and Mobile Journalist Role Conception. *Journalism Practice, 13*(3), 331–348.

Podger, P. J. (2009). The Limits of Control: With Journalists and Their Employers Increasingly Active on Social Media Sites like Facebook and Twitter, News Organisations Are Struggling to Respond to Various New Ethical Challenges. *American Journalism Review, 31*(4), 32–38.

Sullivan, M. (2013). When Reporters Get Personal. *The New York Times.*

Thomas, C. (2013). *The Development of Journalism in the Face of Social Media.* Unpublished Master's thesis, University of Gothenburg, Sweden.

Trengrove, I. (2018). *Investigating Whether Twitter Plays Any Role in SABC's Television News Production and, If So, How.* Unpublished Master's thesis, WITS University, Johannesburg.

Verweij, P., & Van Noort, E. (2014). Journalists' Twitter Networks, Public Debates and Relationships in South Africa. *Digital Journalism, 2*(1), 98–114.

Wahl-Jorgensen, K., & Hanitzsch, T. (Eds.). (2009). The Handbook of Journalism Studies. Routledge.

Weaver, D. H., & Willnat, L. (2016). Changes in US Journalism: How Do Journalists Think about Social Media? *Journalism Practice, 10*(7), 844–855.

CHAPTER 10

The Attention Economy of Micro-Influencers in Malawi: The Case of Stanford Sinyangwe

Nick Mdika Tembo

INTRODUCTION

Stanford Sinyangwe—a.k.a. Prophet Habakkuk—is one person every Malawian needs to know. That may seem odd, considering that the self-proclaimed Prophet does not possess any talent that would normally make him worthy of note. However, the Pentecostal Assemblies of Malawi faithful and founder of Prophetic Foundation Ministry Upon Malawi has become a social media sensation in Malawi and an emblem of a new era in digital media shaping societal discourse. His rise to fame began with a simple comedic video antic that went viral on TikTok in mid-2023. In that video, Stanford Sinyangwe—probably irked by insinuations being made about him that he had finally found love and would soon be getting married—decides to set the record straight by explaining himself in the following categorical terms: *Sindinapeze! Uyu ndi sister timapanga naye*

N. M. Tembo (✉)
Department of Literary Studies, University of Malawi, Zomba, Malawi

University of Free State, Bloemfontein, South Africa
e-mail: ntembo@unima.ac.mw

© The Author(s), under exclusive license to Springer Nature
Switzerland AG 2025
A. Sharra, U. Akpojivi (eds.), *Technologies and Media Production Cultures*, Palgrave Studies in Journalism and the Global South,
https://doi.org/10.1007/978-3-031-78582-5_10

201

202   N. M. TEMBO

[kwaya] ku [GOPIM] ministry kwa a Prophet athu a Brave ku Mzuzu [...].
Ine ndimatsogolera Pentecostal Ministry. Uyuyu ndi sister [...] ("I have not
really found love. This lady is just a sister in the GOPIM[1] ministry that is
led by Prophet Brave who is based in Mzuzu [...]. I am the pastor in this
ministry, while she is a chorister"). Interest in the video quickly grew,
given the fact that the self-styled Prophet had, in an earlier TikTok video,
called on members of his ministry to pray for him as he was suffering from
unrequited love: *Ndikudutsa mu Zowawa. Muzindipempherera ndithu.*
Ndinali ndi mkazi Medayi Mulenga. Tinapangana kuti tikwatirana.
Mkazi ameneyu tinamvana. Ndinampatsa ndalama zokwana MK8,000 pa
katundu amene ndimamugulira. Anabwera ku nyumba. A chibale ama-
muuza kuti ukhazikike [koma] wakana kuti sindingakwatiwe ndi mwana
wanu[2] ("I'm passing through tough times. Pray for me. I had a fiancée by
the name of Medayi Mulenga. We agreed to get married. I spent MK8,000
on her. She used to come to my house often. My relations even told her to
settle down with me, but she told them she cannot get married to their
son"). This was followed by more shareable locally made content on
Instagram, WhatsApp and Facebook, some of which were picked up by
several traditional and online media channels, including Zodiak Malawi
Online, Times360, Malawi24 and Mijedo Corner. I discuss the centrality
of these mainstream media outlets later in this chapter. My point for now
is to highlight how Malawi's television and online media platforms succeeded in drawing the public's attention to the plight of an otherwise
little-known Stanford Sinyangwe who was mostly captured begging for
alms. This is a key value within the attention economy discourse, as I also
discuss in this chapter.

I bring up Stanford Sinyangwe not to talk about his private life and/or
ministry, but to signal the central preoccupations of this chapter. It is a
study about the discourse surrounding the attention economy, with a
focus on establishing whether or not content created by micro-influencers
and shared on social media creates enough interest and intrigue to not
only find its way into the mainstream media but also influence consumers
to make purchase decisions. The assumption the study makes is that
micro-influencers are the new attention holders, and that they successfully

---

[1] GOPIM is an acronym for God Open the Way International Prophetic Ministry. Source:
Joab Frank Chakhaza, "Cruise5 with Prophet Habakkuk Stanford Sinyangwe."
[2] "Tchutchutchu featuring Prophet Habakkuk Sinyangwe."

create innovative content formats and audience consumption habits at little or no cost, thereby creating deeper engagement metrics with a more loyal and attentive audience that traditional journalists are at pains to seek out.

The study is premised two related strands of thought. The first has to do with the concept of micro-influencers, understood by Gupta and Mahajan (2019, p. 189) as a class of individuals who "aren't celebrities in the real sense but can be termed as micro-celebrities." They are, for the most part, social media users who are famous and appreciated by their followers. Emily Hund's understanding of micro-influencers is that they are "people with a few thousand followers, not big names" (2023, p. 145) while Terri Senft considers micro-influencers or micro-celebrities as "a new style of online performance that involves people 'amping up' their popularity over the Web using technologies like video, blogs and social networking sites" (2008, p. 25). The operative words in this construction are *celebrities*—which entails someone has clout through their digital channels or social currency that enables them to be followed or listened to—and *amping up*—which is synonymous with augmenting something. What this means is that micro-influencers perform their identities. They gain their fame by using social media networks to reach out to their niche audience.

The second idea develops from the understanding that micro-influencers often draw the attention of their followers. The chapter thus works with the concept of attention economy, which simply refers to competition for people's attention or the commodification of human attention, where time and focus become valuable resources that digital media and social platforms compete for. The term was first popularized by Michael Goldhaber (2006) in the mid-1980s, who construed it as "a system that revolves primarily around paying, receiving, and seeking what is most intrinsically limited and not replaceable by anything else, namely the attention of other human beings." In the attention economy, Goldhaber (2006) adds, "one is never not on, at least when one is awake, since one is nearly always paying, getting or seeking attention, in ways and modes that are increasingly organized and tend to involve ever–large and more dispersed audiences." Goldhaber (2006) is careful in his delineation of the term, pointing out that attention economy should not just be seen as a resource, mostly of interest to advertisers. In his view, attention economy is not "the economy based on money, markets and standardized industry, where almost the essence of life is business." The term has since then become a central theme in discussions about media, technology and society. Indeed, various social media platforms have capitalized on the attention economy discourse by designing algorithms that prioritize content that grabs and holds user attention. I likewise highlight the centrality of Stanford Sinyangwe's utterances in the attention economy discourse in this study. In "From Fake to Junk News: The Data Politics of Online Virality," Venturini makes a similar case, stating that the micro-celebrity culture is an integral part of the attention economy or the "economy of virality" (2019, p. 128).

As I also discuss in this study the attention economy plays a pivotal role in how mainstream media sets its agenda, with significant implications for the types of news stories covered and how they are presented to the public. Reading Sinyangwe's TikTok video antics through the notion of attention economy thus enables me to unpick his utterances in terms of the sensation they provoke in his followers, regardless of their accuracy or depth. It also allows me to establish the enduring connection between micro-influencers, on the one hand, and the attention economy, on the other. Micro-influencers are vital players in the attention economy in the sense that they excel at capturing and sustaining audience attention. In the world of business, this makes them valuable assets for business owners and brand executives looking to navigate, negotiate and thrive in the complex landscape of the attention competition.

To fully flesh out the micro-influencer and attention economy discourse in this study, I proceed in three key stages. I begin with a discussion of the theoretical and methodological insights that inform the study. Next, I demonstrate how Stanford Sinyangwe has risen from a state of insignificance to gain the micro-influencer label among the Malawian public. The section also segues into how social media is fast becoming an alternative source for news consumption and discourse creation. My intention is to show the various and nuanced ways through which social media competes with some traditional media—broadcast television, broadcast radio and cable distribution firms—in shaping public opinion and facilitating dialogue on various issues. I then work with the selected TikTok, Facebook and online news posts relating to the self-styled Prophet to exemplify how the attention economy discourse works.

Theoretical Insights

With regard to the theoretical framework, I combine agenda-setting theory with insights from the political economy of communication. Conventional models of agenda-setting hold that mainstream media, through its ability to identify and publicize issues, plays a pivotal role in shaping the public agenda by leading audience attention, and perceived importance, to certain issues (Feezell, 2017, p. 1). The proponent of agenda-setting theory, Maxwell McCombs, notes that the media does not tell people what to think but rather what to think about. He further avers that the mass media have the ability to transfer the salience (i.e. most prominent and perceived important) of items on their news agendas to the public agenda (2015, p. 285). Thus, when someone shares a news story through social media, they simultaneously convey issue salience and relevance; this combination makes it likely that the issues encountered through social media, especially from trusted sources, may convey even more salience than if they were encountered through mass media alone (Feezell, 2017, p. 4). These statements highlight the interesting ways in which human beings are attracted to and comment on the media's perception of what it considers topical and therefore demands our interest. I use agenda-setting in this study to draw out and critically analyse Mr Sinyangwe's utterances in terms of whether they influenced public discourse about what is saleable or worth paying attention to.

To show how economic and political forces shape the production, distribution and consumption of communication and media content, I use the political economy of communication as my interpretive framework. Vincent Mosco (1996, p. 2) defines political economy as "the study of the social relations, particularly the power relations, that mutually constitute the production, distribution, and consumption of resources, including communication resources." The political economy of communication is, therefore, a theoretical approach within media and communication studies whose focus is attenuated towards providing critical insights into the complex interactions between media, economics and power. In "On the Political Economy of Communications," Dallas Smythe (1960, p. 564) states that the "central purpose of the study of the political economy of communications is to evaluate the effects of communication agencies in terms of the policies by which they are organized and operated" as well as "the structure and policies of these communication agencies in their social settings." The theory thus emphasizes the importance of understanding media not just as a cultural or technological phenomenon, but as a site of economic and political struggle that shapes society in profound ways. In the context of this study, the political economy of communication enables me to explain how light cultural elements such as what Prophet Habakkuk utters find their way into mainstream media because of social media metrics.

The relationship between agenda-setting and the political economy of communication is complementary, influenced by the two theories' shared focus on how media influences public perception and societal power structures. Agenda-setting theory explains the *how* of media influence—how the media shapes public perceptions by highlighting certain issues. The political economy of communication explains the *why*—why certain issues are given prominence, based on underlying power structures and economic interests. Together, they offer a comprehensive understanding of the role of media in society, especially in relation to political power and public opinion formation.

Methodology

Data for this study were collected from TikTok, Facebook, Twitter and Malawi News RSS Feeds using a netnographic approach, which is "a technique for the cultural analysis of social media and online community data" (Kozinets et al. 2014, p. 262). This chapter focuses on eight texts, all of which appeared between June 2023 and June 2024. This study purposively focuses on Prophet Habakkuk and what was either written or reported on him during the stated period. I used a qualitative approach based on an interpretivist research design to study purposively selected TikTok videos, Facebook and online news feeds surrounding Stanford Sinyangwe from agenda-setting theory and the political economy of communication perspectives. Saunders et al. (2019) assert that the interpretivist research design is based on the belief that as human beings, we experience reality differently because we do not interpret it in the same way. As a result, the meanings that can be generated from a given event or data set can be different depending on who the social actor is. In this regard, I acknowledge *in toto* that the interpretations others might have about Stanford Sinyangwe's TikTok utterances might be different from mine.

From Insignificance to Social Media Fame: Wearing the Micro-Influencer Label

The traditional understanding of micro-influencers is that they are people who wield some considerable reach and command a sizeable group of followers. On the face of it, Stanford Sinyangwe (a.k.a. Prophet Habakkuk) does not necessarily fit these attributes. Yet, as we shall see later in this study, he holds considerable sway over the people who have come to know him through his fun video and audio clips on social media—the kind of sway that has prompted commercial banks, business enterprises and mobile network companies to draw on his characteristic utterances for business purposes.

Stanford Sinyangwe's knowability, therefore, has to be fetched from a different niche audience—one that may not necessarily be an online family. I am persuaded to think that since Mr Sinyangwe is leader of a religious grouping, he commands some significant trust and credibility within this group of followers. He also relates well with them, and they, in turn, look up to him for guidance not only on spiritual matters but also in ethical and sometimes practical aspects of life. What this means, then, is that his position in the Church allows him to leverage a fair degree of influence over his followers' beliefs, behaviours, moral values and even the choices and life decisions they make.

There is also another way through which Stanford Sinyangwe cultivated his micro-influencer label from a state of insignificance to social spotlight: an interview he granted to Times Television, where he was captured pleading to the general public for financial and material help. As word of the television interview spread, Mr Sinyangwe became a target of incessant meanness and cruelty by complete strangers on social media, some of whom thought he had some mental health issues and therefore he should not be taken seriously. But then, his appearance on Times Television also meant that he gained some positive attention from his sympathizers. In wake of the television interview, his plight was scaled up by other media houses and social media celebrities, including comedian Felistas Ngwira and Prophet Shepherd Bushiri. Ngwira specifically launched a fundraising campaign on her Facebook page towards supporting the self-styled prophet. Her plea for support also appeared in *Malawi24*, an online newspaper (Nzangaya, "Onetsa Love"). On his part, Prophet Shepherd Bushiri made a cash donation of MK6 million to Prophet Habakkuk (Nyasatimes, "After Begging"). The donation in question came after the latter had

208   N. M. TEMBO

made a distress call, specifically "asking Prophet Bushiri for one Million [Malawi] Kwacha to pay rent and also to buy food" (Kalumbi, "Bushiri"). Underpinning the efforts made by Stanford Sinyangwe, on the one hand, and Ngwira and Bushiri, on the other, is the fact that both sides used the media to ensure that the self-styled man of God was ably assisted. This is consistent with what Rainie and Wellman (2012, p. 14) say about the power of social media: it "allow[s] people to tell their stories, draw an audience, and often gain social assistance when they are in need."

This is not to go down the road of people circulating, textualizing and commodifying the Other's pain or accounts of extreme situation, even though the lines feeding into that sort of narrative seem clear in Ngwira's publicization of Prophet Habakkuk's plight and Bushiri's "timely" intervention to save the fellow Man of God. As well as letting the outside world know about the self-styled prophet's plight, the actions of the media houses and social media celebrities speak to what psychologists call *pain empathy*, where one enters the pain of the Other not necessarily to poke fun but to humanize them while also sharing a sense of solidarity that they are not alone. In that sense, shared pain can be taken as a social glue that has the potential to promote both awareness and solidarity. The fact that aid started pouring in soon after Stanford Sinyangwe's plight went viral is testament enough that the media houses and local celebrities meant well for him. Against this background, it is worth exploring the influence of social networking sites on traditional journalism. Mr Sinyangwe may have been a social nonentity, struggling to make ends meet and begging for alms. The moment his plight was made known to online and social media users, however, his name took on a life of its own. It was amplified by consumers to the extent that it found favour among virtual avatars and in celebrity circles.

Two essential issues emerge in the scenario being presented here, both relating to how micro-influencers are made or build their portfolios. One is the difficulty of determining whether or not Prophet Habakkuk's meteoric surge to social fame automatically gained him the micro-influencer label considering that he was earlier seen begging for alms. Lisa Harrison's finding is that it is possible for people without pre-existing celebrity status to become micro-influencers (2022, p. 3). The other is the centrality of social media in amplifying Mr Sinyangwe's image from the nadir of his existence to what is arguably the crest of his fame. The media, especially social media, contributed a lot to reinforcing and heightening certain forms of his sociability through what was circulated. This is consistent with what danah boyd (2009) says about the might of social media: it "scales things in new ways" to the extent that "conversations that were intended for just a friend or two might spiral out of control and scale to the [...] whole world."

These assertions reflect how the rise of social media has changed the character of the overall media environment. Compared to traditional journalism, social media has successfully created new formats and audience consumption habits at little or no cost, in the process creating deeper engagement metrics with a more loyal and attentive audience to the extent that traditional journalists often founder in its wake. In his book *Twitter Power* Joel Comm makes a similar case, stating that social media allows anyone to create content and make it available for other people to enjoy at literally no cost. The fundamental question we probably need to ask ourselves, therefore, is: does this mean social media has replaced traditional journalism? Indeed, some observers have viewed the rise of various social media outlets and the new opportunities they have brought to consumers as adequate countervailing forces to the declines in traditional journalism. The reality, as Philip Napoli (2019, p. 91) also observes, "is that these developments have not been able to fully replace the loss of news workers and news reporting that has resulted from the economic declines affecting traditional media" even though "the increase in the number of media outlets and channels has contributed to the decrease in the production of genuine journalism." Similar views are echoed by Nicholas Carr (2010) who notes that the hype that is associated with social media does not in the least mean traditional forms of media have disappeared. Thus, while social media has become a significant force in shaping public discourse and news consumption thereby offering opportunities for diverse voices and increased civic engagement, it also presents challenges related to misinformation, polarization, and the quality of public discourse.

Here then is the extent to which social media's charge that it is a creative writer, cobbling together seemingly true and fake news and then, in a master stroke, packaging all this into a believable narrative comes into play. Given the empirical connection between amplification and falsity, to the extent that most social media posts are tinged with traces of misinformation, disinformation and general garbage largely because the brains behind what is shared are mostly not on scene to *actually* capture events as they unfolded, the likelihood of fake news making it through social media posts and (re)tweets increases, and the likelihood of consuming legitimate news that has passed through the able hands of a genuine editor decreases. This assertion is reinforced by Siva Vaidhyanathan's (2018, p. 19) finding that if you wanted to build a machine that would distribute propaganda to millions of people, distract them from important issues, energize hatred and bigotry, erode social trust, undermine journalism, foster doubts about science, and engage in massive surveillance all at once, you need to look no further than social media sites or social networking sites. Ryan Holiday (2012) thinks this is the case because most social media platforms and devices immediately publish the content their subscribers and participants post, often without filters or checks on accuracy of the content posted.

The Work of Attention Economy

To further understand my claim that Prophet Habakkuk is a micro-influencer, we must first step back to understand the attention economy discourse in which his newfound status now operates. In its original, undiluted form, the term *attention economy* refers to "the economic market where consumers give media developers their attention in exchange for a service (e.g., a news feed), and where developers sell consumer attention to advertisers" (Aylsworth & Castro, 2024, p. 69). Tim Wu traces the beginning of the term *attention economy* to 1833 America, when Benjamin Henry Day founded the *New York Sun*, the first penny press newspaper. During the early days of newspaper's circulation, Day is on record to have posited huge losses until he devised a strategy of including lots of classified adverts in his newspaper because he discovered that they attracted a lot of attention from the readership. The *New York Sun* was also notorious for publishing sensational stories. Wu claims that Day was able to do all this because he "discovered the public's weakness for death and violence, incessant trolling, and, finally, fake news" (2016, p. 14). Soon, his newspaper sales picked up until he found himself among "the first attention merchants worthy of the title" (2016, p. 14); literally speaking, Day had gained his place among people that sought the general public's attention for the purposes of getting it to do something, especially buying their products.

Before delving into an analysis of Prophet Habakkuk's utterances in relation to the work of the attention economy, it is useful to consider why his love words are at the centre of the attention economy discourse in Malawi. His unrequited love messages highlighted at the beginning of this study, which followed hard on the heels of yet another TikTok comedic

10 THE ATTENTION ECONOMY OF MICRO-INFLUENCERS IN MALAWI... 211

video antic called "Ndiwe wakuti Mamie," provide a sense of the imbrication between discourse creation and their circulation on social media networks. In the "Ndiwe wakuti Mamie" video, Mr Sinyangwe is heard speaking to his would-be sweetheart in the following endearing terms:

Tsono ndiwe wakuti, ameneku ukufuna kuti ukhale sweetie wa ine? Ndikukwatire tizitumikira ntchito yamulungu. Ndiwe wakuti Mamie? [...]. Ndikudziwe ndiwe wakuti. Udzabwera liti? Ine ndimakhala ku Rumphi Boma [...]. Ngati umandikondadi, ubwere ku Rumphi ku Boma udzaone pamene ndimakhala. Ndidzakuonetsa kwa azibusa anga kuti uyuyu akufuna ndimukwatire [...]. Utumize ndalama MK10,000 pa Airtel money pa ndalama yangapo kuti uyuyu akufuna kuti ndimukwatiredi [...]. Uonetse lavu! Utumize mawa. Ndizavomereza kuti uyu ali serious.

[So where are you from, you that would like to be my sweetheart? I want to marry you so we can work in the Lord's vineyard. But where are you from, Mamie? (...). I want to know where you come from. When will you come and visit me? I stay at Rumphi Boma (...). If you really love me, come and see where I stay. I will introduce you to my fellow pastors and tell them that you want me to marry you (...). Show some love by sending me money tomorrow. This will prove to me that you are indeed committed and serious.]

These words, spoken after Mr Sinyangwe had released the "Ndikudutsa mu Zowawa" TikTok video, form the core of this section of the study. The man, in troubadour fashion, courts his woman and asks her to create time for him—time during which she must come and visit and be introduced to the man's immediate associates. Soon after the "Ndikudutsa mu Zowawa" TikTok video was released, the Malawian social network was inundated with laughing emojis considering that the MK8000 (an equivalent of 4 dollars) that Mr Sinyangwe allegedly spent on Medayi Mulenga is not an amount worth complaining about in love circles where men spend huge amounts of money on their lovers. His endearing words in this passage thus engage the Malawian public space as a site that produces and reproduces narratives of love in the force-field of courtship, whether in jest or to genuinely appreciate what someone has done for his lover. Of specific interest here is the manner in which the "Ndiwe wakuti Mamie" video was circulated by Malawians on their e-gadgets and social media platforms, where consumers invoked the titular phrase either to challenge their loved ones to go the extra mile or to compliment and appreciate them for whatever they had done.

In his book titled *Hooked*, Nir Eyal (2014) makes a very important observation about what he calls "habit-forming products" in the world of business. Eyal's aim in his book is to provide insights on how business entities can create user habits that capture wide attention, as well as provide actionable steps for building products that would appeal to users. For him,

> forming habits is imperative for the survival of many products. As infinite distractions compete for our attention, companies are learning to master novel tactics to stay relevant in users' minds. Amassing millions of users is no longer good enough. Companies increasingly find that their economic value is a function of the strength of the habits they create. In order to win the loyalty of their users and create a product that's regularly used, companies must learn not only what compels users to click but also what makes them tick.

The "Ndiwe wakuti Mamie" thread is arguably one of the "novel tactics" or new strategies Malawian individuals and business entities have adopted to get the users' attention and prompt them to act. For example, the National Bank of Malawi (NBM) included the following expression in one of the adverts it posted on its Twitter and Facebook accounts of 22 June 2023: "*Ndili pa Mo Mammie. Tumiza uonetse lavu!*" (loosely translated, "I'm on Mo Mamie. Send [money] to show your love"), which echoes Stanford Sinyangwe's *uonetse lavu* (or show some love). These words are followed by the picture of a man making a phone call to his supposed "Mammie" or lover. The "Mo" in question is Mo626, a National Bank of Malawi virtual transaction initiative aimed at assisting its customers to easily transact business online or do e-purchases within the comfort of their homes. Information posted on the Bank's website describes Mo626 as a "self-service, do it yourself banking solution that enables customers to perform banking transactions from their mobile phone anywhere in the world anytime 24/7" (NBM, "Mo626 Digital +"). The website lists a number of product attributes or features, which include; funds transfer within NBM and to other local banks; transfer funds to mobile wallets (TNM & Airtel); utility bill payment; DSTV subscription; MASM contribution; airtime purchases; airtime purchases; balance enquiry; MRA tax payment; mini and full statements; balance enquiry; plus many more (NBM, "Mo626 Digital +"). Also included are the benefits of using Mo626 to the user. These include application-based solution accessible from anywhere in the world; customer access to account 24 hours a day 7 days a week; an efficient self-service channel for all basic account transactions; safe and secure through the use of two factor authentication, and ability to allow customer self on-boarding (NBM, "Mo626 Digital +").

What the National Bank of Malawi does here is an example of how the attention economy works in that Mr Sinyangwe's utterances are appropriated to get the attention of the Bank's retail customers to take interest in its products. The Bank is probably aware that it is operating in an environment where there are "infinite distractions that compete for [the user's] attention"; therefore, it is almost impossible for its products to stand out and maintain user engagement without the Bank itself thinking outside the box. To achieve its goals, then, the Bank decides to tap into smaller, more targeted social networks of Mr Sinyangwe to reach out to its clientele. By doing this, it cultivates a social media presence that is authentic and fun, while also ensuring that its products are easily accessible to an audience that can relate with him. Megaji and Danbury (2017, p. 7) call this a form of advertising appeal, which has the power to provide "the basis for attracting the attention or interest of consumers and/or influencing their feelings towards a product or service." In that sense, the National Bank of Malawi fits the description of an attention economy institution.

To show that Stanford Sinyangwe's words were not appropriated by the National Bank of Malawi alone, I turn to a fortuitous Chichewa (i.e. Malawi's national language) news story that appeared on the *Malawi24* webpage of 17 June 2023. The story in question draws attention to Mr Sinyangwe as a social influencer and *Mneneri* (i.e. the Prophet). The story's headline, "*Ponya Kaye K10,000 Mami, Onetsa Lavu*"—*Mneneri Habakkuk Watekesa pa Intaneti* (First Send Me K10,000 Mami, Show Some Love—Prophet Habakkuk Takes the Internet by Storm), captures the author's central concerns: to establish how exactly Prophet Habakkuk had shaken the internet by storm. The author further qualifies Prophet Habakkuk as the man of the moment in the following terms: "*sizochitaso kukambirana kuti mneneri Habakkuk watenga mitima ya mazana mazana ya aMalawi. Timutche mneneri wa pa intaneti?*" (Nzangaya, "Ponya Kaye") [it is indisputable that Prophet Habakkuk has stolen the hearts of thousands of Malawians. Should we call him the internet Prophet perhaps?]. The author, Archangel Nzangaya, then proceeds to say that Prophet Habakkuk "has a very sharp tongue. His words act like a magnet when he speaks such that he will leave you speechless and awestruck" [*ali ndililime lakuthwa lomwe likayankhula chinthu, mawu ake akumakhala achikoka ndipo akumatha kukusiya munthu kukamwa kuli yasaa, osavetsa*]. Here, Nzangaya appears to suggest that rather than just call him *mneneri* (or Prophet), Malawians should also focus on the social functions that this *mneneri* performs amaong his people. While Nzangaya's pronouncements may purely be words of praise for Stanford Sinyangwe, I borrow his construction of the self-styled prophet as being gifted with a sharp tongue (*ali ndi lilime lakuthwa*) and that his words act like a magnet (*mawu ake akumakhala a chikoka*) to read Stanford Sinyangwe as an emerging micro-influencer and someone who words draw a lot of attention from the masses.

To embrace Stanford Sinyangwe as a micro-influencer is thus to re-signify the meaning of this category of people and to adopt an understanding of it that is diverse and more accommodating of the various identities that choose to adopt it. Contrary to the commonly held perception that micro-influencers are supposed to have a sizeable number of followers behind them; or, that they are supposed to be active promoters of a given brand, I read Mr Sinyangwe as the silent-yet-effective type of micro-influencers; one that is not directly involved in promoting a given brand or product, but whose image and utterances are nevertheless appropriated as useful advertising gimmicks to make consumers and potential clients patronize brands and products. Partially owing to this perception, an unnamed retail shop owner (in Fig. 10.1) uses Prophet Habakkuk's image to promote what looks like a phone accessories business.

Fig. 10.1 Prophet Habakkuk's image to promote what looks like a phone accessories business. (Source: Author)

10 THE ATTENTION ECONOMY OF MICRO-INFLUENCERS IN MALAWI... 215

This micro-influencer strategy works because it draws potential consumers to Prophet Habakkuk's image. The shop owner is probably aware that it is not about the number of people that follow Stanford Sinyangwe that is the most important factor. Instead, it is the level and quality of engagement that the self-styled man of God can achieve with his followers that has the potential of making the shop owner's products sell. This implies that companies and brands can use micro-influencers as agents to announce and commercialize their products as well as promote their brand.

The final example for this content analysis involves a Facebook post by Floodgate Tours and Tyre Express. The post in question begins with a bit of a disclaimer that all the company is doing is "promoting Zomba tourism, Malawi tourism and Zomba City." The post does not directly refer to Mr Sinyangwe as is the case with the previous two examples discussed above, but the tagline is clear in its subtle reference to words authored by Stanford Sinyangwe. In choosing to appropriate his words to promote its brand, Floodgate Tours and Tyre Express must be tapping into what has been said above, that the self-styled prophet is an internet sensation and a crowd-puller; that, therefore, using his name is enough to draw the attention of consumers to the brand and/or product:

> *Nditenge ku Zomba Mamie uonetse lavu! Anthu okonda family yawo pano azipita ku Zomba weekend iliyonse for leisure. Ife a Floodgate Tours and Tyre Express takukonzerani activities oti azikupasani busy every weekend for free bola mugule one of our services.* (Floodgate Tours and Tyre Express)
> [Take me to Zomba Mamie, show some love. People that love their families should be going to Zomba every weekend for leisure. At Floodgate Tours and Tyre Express, we have planned for you activities that will keep you busy every weekend for free, provided you buy one of our services.]

The passage above demonstrates how clever and innovative people can become. The person behind the advert begins by talking about the "activities" the transport company has lined up for its patrons at the event. He also promises them fun before entreating them that all they need to do is buy one of the company's products for them to enjoy the rest of the activities. The Floodgate Tours and Tyre Express owner thus taps into the

216 N. M. TEMBO

supposed power that Prophet Habakkuk's image has to promote their events and tourist destinations so users will be interested in travelling to check them out. The owner is most likely riding on the hope that by turning up at the event and being exposed to the company's many products, the patrons might "buy one of the services" and possibly do a business transaction with the company. It is not surprising that we see the company opening the "floodgates" of advertisement even wider in its reference to other products and services it has in store for its potential consumers:

> You can also choose to go for a morning Zomba plateau hike from 7am to 10am at K10,000 per person without transport (optional). Later join others for the activities that will make your day memorable. Pa Tyre Express Complex pali barbershop, kugula new tyres, tyre alignment, 3D alignment and wheel balancing. Ife a Floodgates Tours tili ndi hospitality service menu yomwe mutha kugula tea,coffee, chips, Hungarian sausage, soft drinks, juices, ice cream, breakfast service komanso pali art gallery and chitenje souvenirs. Uku mukuonera magule kwinaku mukumwa ndi kudya or kumetetsa tsitsi lanu. (Floodgate Tours and Tyre Express)
> [You can also choose to go for a morning Zomba plateau hike from 7am to 10am at K10,000 per person without transport (optional). Later join others for the activities that will make your day memorable. We have a barbershop at the Tyre Express Complex, where you can also buy new tyres, do tyre alignment, 3D alignment and wheel balancing. As Floodgates Tours, we have a hospitality service menu where you can order tea, coffee, chips, Hungarian sausage, soft drinks, juices, ice cream, [and] breakfast service. We also have an art gallery and chitenje souvenirs. You will be watching traditional dances while you are also drinking and eating or having a haircut.]

Floodgate Tours and Tyre Express is here using the carnival promise of pleasure to capture the attention of its users and prompt action in them. What the company is also hoping is that by posting the message on Facebook, other people will take it up and share with those in their social networks. In doing so, the company will have succeeded in using the consumers themselves to help advertise its products and services.

Conclusion

We live in the world of attention; an age that sparks an addiction to consumption of content that brings strange forms of passion. In this convergence of media and society, we are quick to circulate content whose authenticity or source we hardly question. This view, that human beings are addicted to the production and consumption of stories that tickle their fancy and literally make them sell themselves to themselves has been the central focus of this study. It delved into the otherwise mundane utterances made by Stanford Sinyangwe (a.k.a. Prophet Habakkuk) in his TikTok fun video posts for the effect and currency they draw in individuals and business entities. The reason why the Malawian public got excited with Prophet Habakkuk's utterances is because he carefully selected content for his TikTok posts to feed the passions of his audience. This is consistent with what Tim Wu has said elsewhere, that "with ably managed utterances, one could grow one's following, and with it one's general sense of influence and currency in the new sector of the attention economy" (2016, p. 313). My focus in this study was not on the advertising angle that the attention economy discourse mostly lays emphasize on, but on how individuals and groups in Malawi capitalized on Stanford Sinyangwe's TikTok utterances to garner public attention and entice users to consider doing business with them.

This study contributes to an ongoing trend in research on understanding the enduring connection between micro-influencers and the attention economy. The fact that the study inserts little known Stanford Sinyangwe into mainstream news discourse can be considered as one of its strengths. Nonetheless, several limitations must be addressed. The research is descriptive and qualitative in nature and intended to suggest more research into a quantitative analysis of how people like Stanford Sinyangwe have provided algorithmic support, community building, and monetization opportunities to shape the attention economy discourse. The limitations and potential bias in the three self-selected case studies are also acknowledged. The fact that Stanford Sinyangwe is being touted as a micro-influencer when there is no clear data to go along with the grand claims made in the study is also considered to be a limitation of this study.

References

Aylsworth, P., & Castro, C. (2024). *Kantian Ethics and the Attention Economy: Duty and Distraction.* Palgrave Macmillan.

boyd, d. (2009). Social Media is Here to Stay… Now What? *Microsoft Research Tech Fest,* Redmond, Washington, February 26. https://www.danah.org/papers/talks/MSRTechFest2009.html

Carr, N. (2010). *The Shallows: What the Internet is Doing to our Brain.* W.W. Norton & Company.

218   N. M. TEMBO

Chakhaza, J. F. (2023). Cruise5 with Prophet Habakkuk Stanford Sinyangwe. https://www.youtube.com/watch?v=4PXBo7Z8c1M&ab_channel=JoabF rankChakhaza

Comm, J. (2010). *Twitter Power 2.0: How to Dominate Your Market One Tweet at a Time*. John Wiley & Sons, Inc.

Eyal, N. (2014). *Hooked: How to Build Habit-Forming Products*. Penguin.

Feezell, J. T. (2017). Agenda Setting Through Social Media: The Importance of Incidental News Exposure and Social Filtering in the Digital Era. *Political Research Quarterly, 1–13*. https://doi.org/10.1177/1065912917744895

Floodgate Tours and Tyre Express. (2023). Nditenge ku Zomba mamie uonetse lavu! https://m.facebook.com/floodgatestours/posts/753586383438338

Goldhaber, M. H. (2006). The Value of Openness in an Attention Economy. *First Monday*. 11(6). https://doi.org/10.5210/fm.v11i6.1334

Gupta, S., & Mahajan, R. (2019). Role of micro-influencers in affecting behavioural intentions. *International Journal of Recent Technology and Engineering 8*(4S5), 189–92. Accessed July 11, 2024. https://doi.org/10.35940/ijrte.d1045.1284s519.

Harrison, L. M. (2022). What Makes a Micro-influencer? Converting the Personal Branding Strategies of Successful Social Media Users into a Professional Development Program. PhD thesis. Queensland University of Technology. https://eprints.qut.edu.au/233168/1/Lisa_Harrison_Thesis.pdf

Holiday, R. (2012). *Trust Me I'm Lying: Confessions of a Media Manipulator*. Penguin.

Hund, E. (2023). *The Influencer Industry: The Quest for Authenticity on Social Media*. Princeton University Press.

Kalumbi, M. (2024. May 6). Bushiri Turns Habakkuk into a Millionaire. *Malawi24*. https://malawi24.com/2024/05/06/bushiri-turns-habakkuk-into-a-millionaire/

Kozinets, R. V., Dolbec, P.-Y., & Earley, A. (2014). Netnographic Analysis: Understanding Culture Through Social Media data. In K. U. Flick (Ed.), *The SAGE Handbook of Qualitative Data Analysis* (pp. 262–275). SAGE.

McCombs, M. (2015). Agenda-setting. In J. D. Wright (Ed.), *International Encyclopedia of the Social & Behavioral Sciences* (2nd ed., pp. 285–288). Elsevier.

Megaji, E., & Danbury, A. (2017). Making the Brand Appealing: Advertising Strategies and Consumers' Attitude Towards UK Retail Bank Brands. *Journal of Product & Brand Management, 26*(4), 1–44.

Mosco, V. (1996). *The Political Economy of Communication*. Sage.

Napoli, P. M. (2019). *Social Media and the Public Interest: Media Regulation in the Disinformation Age*. Columbia University Press.

National Bank of Malawi. (n.d.). Mo626 digital +. https://www.natbank.co.mw/retail/electronic-banking/mo626-digital

Nyasatimes. (2024). After Begging K500 000, Prophet Habakkuk gets K6 million from Bushiri. https://www.nyasatimes.com/after-begging-k500-000-prophet-habakkuk-gets-k6million-from-bushiri/

Nzangaya, A. (2023a, July 5). Onetsa Love Malawi: Nya-uyu Raising Funds for Prophet Habakkuk. *Malawi24*. https://malawi24.com/2023/07/05/onetsa-love-malawi-nya-uyu-raising-funds-for-prophet-habakkuk/

Nzangaya, A. (2023b, June 17). 'Ponya kaye K10,000 mami, onetsa lavu' – mneneri Habakkuk watekesa pa intaneti. *Malawi24*. https://malawi24.com/2023/06/17/ponya-kaye-k10000-mami-onetsa-lavu-mneneri-habakkuk-watekesa-pa-intaneti/

Rainie, L., & Wellman, B. (2012). *Networked: The New Social Operating System*. The MIT Press.

Saunders, M., Lewis, P., & Thornhill, A. (2019). *Research Methods for Business Students*. Prentice Hall.

Senft, T. M. (2008). *Camgirls: Celebrity & Community in the Age of Social Networks*. Peter Lang.

Smythe, D. W. (1960). On the political economy of communications. *Journalism & Mass Communication Quarterly, 37*(4), 563–572.

Tchutchutchu featuring Prophet Habakkuk Sinyangwe. https://www.youtube.com/watch?v=vxGP2fsXD3c&ab_channel=Times360Malawi

Vaidhyanathan, S. (2018). *Antisocial Media: How Facebook Disconnects Us and Undermines Democracy*. Oxford University Press.

Venturini, T. (2019). From Fake to Junk News. The Data Politics of Online Virality. In D. Bigo, E. Isin, & E. Ruppert (Eds.), *Data Politics. Worlds, Subjects, Rights* (pp. 123–144). Routledge.

Wu, T. (2016). *The Attention Merchants: The Epic Scramble to Get inside Our Heads*. Atlantic Books.

CHAPTER 11

Conclusion: Technologies and Journalism in African Newsrooms

Albert Sharra and Ufuoma Akpojivi

This book has demonstrated that recent advancements in technologies have caused unprecedented changes to the journalism profession. Unlike early analyses, this book comes at a time when it is becoming clearer as to how newsrooms and journalists are engaging with technologies, which has simplified our understanding of the ways technologies are affecting the journalism profession. We have argued in the introduction that journalism, since its founding, has thrived on new technologies. The only difference is the level of advancements in technologies and their impact on traditional systems. Although Africa plays a catchup role in technology adoption, the last decade has seen the newsrooms in the continent not

A. Sharra (✉)
Department of Political Studies, University of Witwatersrand, Johannesburg, South Africa

Centre of African Studies, University of Edinburgh, Edinburgh, UK

U. Akpojivi
Advocates for International Development, London, UK

Communication Science, University of South Africa, Johannesburg, South Africa
e-mail: Ufuoma.Akpojivi@a4id.org

© The Author(s), under exclusive license to Springer Nature Switzerland AG 2025
A. Sharra, U. Akpojivi (eds.), *Technologies and Media Production Cultures*, Palgrave Studies in Journalism and the Global South, https://doi.org/10.1007/978-3-031-78582-5_11

221

only adopting new technologies to sustain traditional newsrooms but also closing down traditional newsrooms for new media (Roper, 2021). This is well documented in countries like South Africa, Nigeria, Ghana, Kenya and Zimbabwe and the reasons for each country vary.

Nonetheless, the political economy of the media sits in front of all these factors. Advanced media systems, developed economies and high literacy level, among others, have led to quick adoption of new technologies in some countries than in others in the continent. For instance, in countries like Zimbabwe, it was easy for an individual to establish an online news media like +263Chat and create a big audience of online news consumers unlike in Malawi where, until 2024, internet users and online news consumers were below 20 per cent (Kainja, 2019; Times Reporter, 2022) making online media not a very profitable business. The growing number of promotional posts by different media houses in the continent celebrating achieving one million followers on social media is evidence of this. As Sharra (2023) argues, low internet penetration and access in developing countries affect both the number of people accessing news media online and the media organisations' interest to adopt new technologies for journalism, especially in developing economies. Currently, most traditional media organisations are adopting new technologies to complement the traditional newsroom. Several scholars describe this as digital first (Hendrickx & Picone, 2020; Robotham & Pignard-Cheynel, 2024; Sharra, 2023; Prenger & Deuze, 2017). Traditional news organisations have also developed e-papers and e-payments which are helping them maintain and create new customers.

As of 2024, the debate on the future of traditional media was shifting and pointing towards a direction many avoid talking about. Traditional media is expected to dominate and monopolise the new media industry through digital-first mechanism characterised by dual-management system or shifting completely to digital journalism, as witnessed with top publications like *Kick-Off Magazine* which moved completely online after decades of being a leading print magazine in South Africa and beyond (Lambley, 2022). There is also an ongoing campaign to convince the Global North companies like Facebook to create systems that should ensure that traditional media organisation benefit from online content. Recent developments like paying online content producers on platforms like YouTube and TikTok promise a better future as there is a potential for such arrangements to benefit news content producers like journalists and media organisations in the Global South.

We have argued in this book that technology adoption in African newsrooms happens at two levels: individual journalists and newsrooms. Although journalists can adopt technologies to aid their journalism work, the impact is more visible when the technologies are adopted by the media organisations. There is no comprehensive study that demonstrates how many journalists are using technologies like AI to aid their journalism except for a few studies including the recent global report on journalists and AI which shows that there is growing understanding and use of AI among journalists and newsrooms globally (Beckett & Yaseen, 2023).

However, adopting technologies in the newsroom has been a challenge in some African countries due to the cost. Nonetheless, as some of the chapters in this book show, a growing number of newsrooms have attempted to invest heavily in technology adaptation. An example is Nation Publications Limited (NPL) in Malawi which endeavoured to automate its whole newsroom processes, including other departments like marketing. Although the system failed due to costs and other issues, the attempt speaks volumes about the future of traditional newsrooms in developing nations. Several other chapters in the book support this observation. Therefore, when analysing technology use in African newsrooms, it is important to avoid broad generalisations and instead focus on country-specific case studies. We need more country-based case studies.

As chapters in this book demonstrate, new media is a product of traditional media and there is a thin line that distinguishes the two. However, as we have argued in the introduction, including some chapters in the book, media culture and practice have been affected by three key aspects of journalism: agency, production and engagement (Hobart, 2010; Couldry, 2004). For the media to serve their audiences well, technologies have been vital to meet these aspects. This happens at both newsroom and journalists levels. The +263Chat stands out as one of Africa's most innovative online news outlets, and over the last few years, new media ventures targeting online news consumers have been emerging. What is so unique with these ventures is that they follow traditional format but take a digital approach. Examples include *The Continent* in South Africa which is one of the most unique publications in the region which produces African news in a summary format and distributes it in pdf format. Malawi's *Platform for Investigative Journalism* (*PiJ*) has proven to be a force to reckon with, particularly with its investigative pieces that have turned it into the most favoured online newspaper. The uniqueness of *PiJ* and *The Continent* is that they were founded and run by individual journalists who quit the industry to try a different kind of journalism that targets online audiences. They help us appreciate journalists' efforts to innovate with technologies. The rise of PiJ to become a top investigative journalism platform in Malawi also tells us how limiting traditional journalism can be in doing successful investigative journalism and the opportunities that come with the new media. Also the like of NPL and its attempt to adopt News-Wrap software represent the growing interest in technology adoption at the traditional newsroom level.

Conclusively, these examples demonstrate what is really changing in journalism, and through case studies from different countries in the continent, this book presents stories that help to understand the ways technologies are shaping African journalism. Culture is naturally dynamic and, as more technologies continue to enter the newsrooms, we expect to see major changes to doing journalism.

This book focused on media culture and practice, and we believe more studies focusing on particular newsrooms in the continent will help us to further understand how technologies are affecting media culture and practice.

References

Beckett, C., & Yaseen, M. (2023). *Generating Change: A Global Survey of What News Organisations Are Doing with AI*. London School of Economics. chrome extension://efaidnbmnnnibpcajpcglclefindmkaj/https://static1.square-space.com/static/64d60527c01ae7106f2646e9/t/656e400a1c23e22d a0681e46/1701724190867/Generating+Change+_+The+Journalism+AI+re port+_+English.pdf

Couldry, N. (2004). Theorising Media as Practice. *Social Semiotics, 14*(2), 115–132. https://doi.org/10.1080/1035033042000238295

Hendrickx, J., & Picone, I. (2020). Innovation beyond the Buzzwords: The Rocky Road Towards a Digital First-Based Newsroom. *Journalism Studies, 21*(14), 2025–2041.

Hobart, M. (2010). *What Do We Mean by "Media Practices"?* Theorising Media and Practice; Berghahn Books.

Kainja, J. (2019). Digital Rights: How Accessible Is the Internet in Malawi? *Misa Malawi* (blog). https://malawi.misa.org/2019/02/15/digital-rights-how-accessible-is-the-internet-in-malawi/

Lambley, G. (2022). Top South African Football Magazine Prints Its Final Copy. *The Southern Africa.* https://www.thesouthafrican.com/sport/soccer/psl-south-africa/top-south-african-football-magazine-kick-off-prints-final-copy-iconic-breaking-trending-sunday-21-august-2022/

Prenger, M., & Deuze, M. (2017). 12 A History of Innovation and Entrepreneurialism in Journalism. In *Remaking the News: Essays on the Future of Journalism Scholarship in the Digital Age* (pp. 235–250). MIT Press.

Robotham, A. T., & Pignard-Cheynel, N. (2024). You Said Digital First! A Five-Dimensional Definition According to Journalists from Three Swiss Newspapers. *Journalism Practice, 18*(7), 1702–1721. https://doi.org/10.1080/17512786.2022.2104745

Roper, C. (2021). South Africa. *Reuters Institute* (blog). https://reutersinstitute.politics.ox.ac.uk/digital-news-report/2021/south-africa

Sharra, A. (2023). "Digital First" as a Coping Measure for Malawi's Print Newspapers. In *New Journalism Ecologies in East and Southern Africa: Innovations, Participatory and Newsmaking Cultures* (pp. 113–132). Springer.

Times Reporter. (2022, August 14). What Are Malawians Doing on the Internet? *Times Group*. https://times.mw/what-are-malawians-doing-on-the-internet/

Index[1]

A
Africa, vii, ix, 4, 5, 7, 9, 10, 13, 16, 20, 23, 33, 63–65, 68, 81, 87, 104, 131, 133, 152–154, 166–169, 221, 223
African language, viii, 151–170
Analogue, 20, 64, 131, 138
Artificial Intelligence (AI), vii, viii, 6–10, 13, 14, 19–38, 44, 47, 55–56, 90, 92, 93, 98, 223
Attention economy, vii–viii, 8, 9, 15, 201–217
Audience, viii, ix, 7–12, 15, 21–23, 25, 29, 65, 68, 70, 72, 73, 75, 110, 111, 114, 115, 123, 124, 131–136, 138–146, 153–155, 161, 162, 165–170, 176, 177, 179, 180, 183–185, 188, 196, 203–205, 207–209, 213, 217, 222, 223
Automation, 9, 10, 14, 85–105

C
Case study, viii, 9, 10, 12, 14, 44, 65, 67, 70, 71, 80, 87, 89, 139, 217, 223, 224
Contextual factors, viii, 14, 44
Convergent media, 43, 45

D
Developing, 3, 14, 22–24, 57, 59, 64, 67, 73, 75, 99, 104, 105, 133, 134, 195, 222, 223
Digital audio, 78
Digital first, 7, 14, 63–81, 88, 180, 222
Digital journalism, 47, 48, 57, 112–113, 115–117, 119, 122, 151, 155, 167, 222
Digital media in Zimbabwe, 110, 113
Digital news production, 67, 90
Digitisation, 47, 48, 64–66, 183

---

[1] Note: Page numbers followed by 'n' refer to notes.

© The Author(s), under exclusive license to Springer Nature Switzerland AG 2025
A. Sharra, U. Akpojivi (eds.), *Technologies and Media Production Cultures*, Palgrave Studies in Journalism and the Global South, https://doi.org/10.1007/978-3-031-78582-5

228 INDEX

E
Effective journalism, 19–38, 177
Emerging technologies, viii, 5, 14, 44, 47
Environmental factors, 20

F
Facebook algorithm, 156, 169

G
Global South, vii–ix, 5, 7, 9, 10, 87–89, 152, 179, 222

H
Hatirare263, 15, 153, 155, 159–163, 165–167, 169
Hybridity, viii, 135
Hyperlinks, 43, 45, 46, 55, 59, 66, 143
Hypermediality, 45, 46
Hypertextuality, 45, 46

I
Identities, 5, 15, 155, 157, 160, 175–196, 203, 214
iHarare.com, 15, 152, 153, 155, 159–166, 169
Instantaneity, 45
Institutional factors, 53, 59
Interactivity, 7, 45, 46, 132, 136, 169

J
Journalism practice, vii, 11, 14, 44, 45, 47–49, 54–57, 59, 87, 88, 110, 111, 113, 151, 153, 178, 184, 185

Journalism transformation, 53
Journalistic roles, 155, 178

L
Liquid journalism, 183, 184

M
Machine Learning, 14, 44, 47, 55–56
Malawi, viii, ix, 14, 15, 44, 53, 55, 64–73, 75, 77, 79–81, 85–105, 201–217, 222, 223
Media culture, vii, 3–16, 223, 224
Media practice, viii, ix, 10–14, 44, 124, 180
Media scholarship, 47, 55
Micro-influencers, 15, 201–217
Multimedia, ix, 7, 15, 43–46, 55–57, 59, 64, 67, 119, 120, 132, 138, 140, 143–146, 181

N
Networked news, 47
News consumption, 9, 21, 75, 110, 112, 114, 121–124, 204, 209
News media, 12, 48, 67, 72, 111, 114, 176, 179, 180, 222
News Wrap, 14, 85–105, 224
Non-mainstream, 152–156, 161, 167, 168

O
Online news sites, 74
Organisational structure, 90, 91, 102

INDEX 229

P

Peripheral journalism, 153–155
Platforms, vii–ix, 6–8, 12, 14, 15,
  20–22, 36, 43, 45–47, 54, 57,
  58, 64, 65, 67, 68, 70–73, 75,
  76, 78–81, 89, 92, 94, 109–115,
  118, 120, 122–124, 132,
  134–136, 138–145, 153–155,
  157, 162, 163, 167–169, 176,
  177, 180–183, 188, 191, 194,
  195, 202–204, 210, 211, 222
Professional ethics, 25, 26
Professional journalists, 55, 176, 180,
  183, 186–188, 190–194, 196

S

Social media, vii–ix, 7, 8, 15, 20–22, 27,
  47, 66–68, 75, 78, 80, 89, 113,
  114, 131–139, 142, 144–146, 152,
  153, 156, 159–162, 167–170,
  175–196, 201–211, 213, 222
Social networking sites (SNSs), 89,
  151, 154, 168, 169, 203,
  208, 210
South Africa, 5, 12, 66, 176–178, 180,
  185–188, 190, 194–196, 222, 223
Stanford Sinyangwe, 15, 201–217

T

Technological innovations, ix, 6
Technology, vii, 3, 19–38,
  44, 63, 87, 109,
  131–146, 151, 176,
  203, 221–224
Technology adoption, 14, 43–59, 79,
  221, 223, 224
Traditional journalism, 15, 151, 179,
  184, 208, 209
Traditional media, viii, 11–14,
  21, 58, 64–66, 73, 75, 81,
  92, 112, 114, 117, 118,
  121, 122, 124, 125,
  131–146, 181–183, 194,
  204, 209, 222, 223
Tradition radio
  programming, 145–146

U

Uganda, viii, 15, 131–146
User experience, 105

Z

Zimpapers Hub, 112, 117,
  121–123, 125

Printed in the United States
by Baker & Taylor Publisher Services